June 16th, '63

Happy Father's Day Barney,

Love
Jill
Bill
and
aaron

Jane
&
al

They Sailed Into Oblivion

Other Books by A. A. Hoehling

The Last Voyage of the *Lusitania*
Lonely Command
A Whisper of Eternity
Last Train from Atlanta

THEY SAILED INTO OBLIVION

by
A. A. Hoehling

NEW YORK · Thomas Yoseloff · LONDON

© 1959 by A. A. Hoehling
Library of Congress Catalog Card Number: 59–10904

Thomas Yoseloff, *Publisher*
11 East 36th Street
New York 16, N.Y.

Thomas Yoseloff Ltd.
123 New Bond Street
London W. 1, England

First printing August 1959
Second printing August 1962

Printed in the United States of America

"Hold me up in mighty waters,
Keep my eyes on things above,
Righteousness, divine atonement,
Peace, and everlasting love."

(From the Episcopal Church hymn
"Autumn," played by the ship's
band as the *Titanic* sank)

Foreword

SOME POETS HAVE LYRICIZED ABOUT THE SEA WITH TENDER AFfection. Others have excoriated it as a malevolent force, ever poised to strike.

Few writers in the history of literature have been able to ignore the sea entirely. For that matter, few people can say that they have lived their lives totally unaffected by the world's oceans. Even if one does not inhabit their shores or earn his living upon their waters, his economic existence is indirectly conditioned by goods shipped across them.

The seas also contribute to the weather complexity, far inland, make an area temperate or cold and damp. In wartime they assume a Jekyll-Hyde duality of bulwark as well as highway for invasion.

What happens upon them also has had much to do in hastening national decisions as to war or peace. The British-built Confederate raider *Alabama* all but sparked a rupture between the Federal government and Great Britain. The sinking of the *U.S.S. Maine* was the single factor in launching America into a war against Spain. The sinking of the Cunard liner *Lusitania* in 1915, with the loss of American lives, followed by the torpedoing of a succession of United States vessels unquestionably inspired Congress to declare "a state of war" against the Kaiser's Germany.

Destinies of nations, already at war, have been decided at least as much upon the open waters as they have on the field of battle. This was as true in the days of Troy as in such decisive World War II engagements as Midway and Leyte Gulf.

On a canvas of far less magnitude, the destinies of people can be altered by the sea and its whims or, possibly, the whimsical judgment of those in whose hands they have temporarily entrusted their lives. Often, there is seemingly a wilful caprice on the part of nature to upset man's all-consuming plans and desires.

This is acutely etched in the cases of passengers who have made herculean efforts to arrive on board before the gangplank is pulled away. Such breathless and "lucky" ocean voyagers were the Grahams, in 1848, as they dashed onto the *Ocean Monarch* at Liverpool, and a number of somewhat more contemporary voyagers who barely secured passage that Saturday morning in May for the *Lusitania's* once-a-month express service to England.

Whether personal or national tragedy may be involved, fate has a way of making itself heard through the great, restless seas, reminding man in his overwhelming conceit of his minuscule qualities and inability to do more than rail ineffectually at the elements.

This book is composed of many accounts of ships and people and the hapless, if enigmatical, events that brought them together.

Contents

Illustrations

They Sailed Into Oblivion

The Immigrants

GOLD RUSH IN AMERICA, POTATO FAMINE IN IRELAND, CROWDED cities in Europe—they all contributed to the surging tide of immigration in the eighteen-forties.

The New World beckoned with the glitter of a torchlight parade, and so many responded that a hitherto little desired commodity—transatlantic accommodations—suddenly enjoyed premium status. Vessels hitherto sailing to the Indies, to Africa, India, or Australia were diverted to the immigrant trade. From the United States, ships that had once made the long voyage to the Orient were hastily refitted for fast Atlantic Ocean turn-arounds and a different cargo: human.

One such was the 1,300-ton packet *Ocean Monarch*, out of Boston, owned by Train's Line. In addition to passengers, she could carry several times her own tonnage in her deep cargo holds.

When she was towed into the Mersey River, Liverpool, early Thursday morning, August 24, 1848, she was in every respect a pack horse of the seas: beneath her tarpaulined hatches were 200 bales and cases of "fine goods," 220 crates of earthen ware, 96 tons of salt, and 600 tons of iron. Including the crew, there were at least 380 on board, almost all immigrants. There were so many children in arms and afoot that Captain James Murdoch himself was frustrated in arriving at an accurate count.

In the first class cabin accommodations, the Yankee master's problem was simple: there were only seven passengers. They

1

included Mr. Southwell, the artist, and Mr. Gregg, Salem, Massachusetts, businessman. A second class cabin, nearly as desirable as first class, was solidly booked: nineteen adults and children.

Among them were Mr. and Mrs. Graham, from Manchester, whose train had been delayed. They arrived at the Mersey docks only minutes before the last hawsers were pulled aboard the departing packet.

They considered themselves lucky.

Steerage was an odorous, brawling cubicle of confinement, an area echoing with the crying of babies. Here there were names —just names—which commenced with Anderson, Thomas and Mary Anne, and ended with Wynne, Mary. The largest families were those of the Cashmans and Sullivans, who counted five children each.

At 8 A.M., six hours after a steam tug had pulled her out past Liverpool Bar, the *Ocean Monarch* dropped the pilot and spread her canvas to the winds of the Irish Sea. The telegraph station on the sand flats at the entrance of the Mersey logged her departure. It was a bright, breezy morning and, as the master himself logged, there was "nothing worthy of note."

Life settled into its routine of tedium. Stewards opened the food and liquor stores. The cooks kindled galley fires as the big ship headed for St. George's Channel and the Atlantic. Cabin passengers were soon seated at breakfast, while the immigrants were lined up at the galley door, awaiting their turns.

This morning, the narrow, choppy Irish Sea was crisscrossed with traffic: ships of commerce, as well as ocean-going yachts. Among the latter was the handsome *Queen of the Ocean*, belonging to Thomas Littledale, Liverpool millionaire merchant and commodore of the Royal Mersey Yacht Club. He was returning from a regatta.

Late in the morning, abreast of an outjut of land, Great

Ormes Head, Littledale spotted the *Ocean Monarch*. She appeared to be about six miles offshore. He was, as he put it, "admiring the beauty of the splendid ship as she was pursuing her course to the Atlantic."

Also bent on pleasure was the Brazilian frigate *Affonso*, commanded by the Marquis d'Lisboa. Her forty guns were muzzled lest their martial sight disquiet ladies on board, all guests of the Brazilian taxpayers, all bluebloods. There was the Prince de Joinville, his lady "and suite"; the Duke and Duchess d'Aumale, the Brazilian minister, the Chevalier d'Lisboa, Admiral Grenfell "and daughters"; also "other distinguished individuals."

The *Affonso*, a trim steamer, was on trial runs, just having been built in England for the Brazilian Navy. The Marquis d'Lisboa, however, was not in an undue hurry to complete the testing period.

There were less pedigreed vessels coursing the Irish Sea that morning. They included the coastal steamer, *Prince of Wales* and the New York-bound packet, *New World*.

The *Queen of the Ocean* was the first to observe that something had happened aboard the immigrant ship. Littledale saw that she had "put up her helm as if returning to Liverpool." Next he watched a flag of distress being hoisted up her forward yards.

On the *Ocean Monarch* no one knew quite what had happened, other than that smoke had commenced to pour from inside the vessel. Captain Murdoch, while supervising the hauling of the main yard, was advised that a steerage passenger had lit a fire—presumably to cook his own lunch—under an aft ventilator.

"I immediately sent the steward and another man to extinguish the fire," reported Murdoch, "and bring up the delinquent who had made it.

"Immediately after this, one of the cabin passengers came on deck and stated that the cabin was full of smoke, which was coming from below. On hearing this I ran down to ascertain the position of affairs, and found that the ship was actually on fire. I then hurried back to the deck and gave orders to have water poured upon it, and directed that the ship should be kept before the wind in order to lessen the draft; but the flames with a rush, almost as instantaneous as lightning, burst forth, and in less than five minutes the whole stern of the ship was completely enveloped in the fiery element. I then gave orders to have the ship brought to the wind. All was now a scene of the utmost confusion, noise, and disorder. My orders could not be heard. Despair had seized almost every soul on board. The scene which presented itself was awful to contemplate, much more to look upon."

Gregg, the Salem businessman, was lying on a sofa in the cabin when he became aware of "a strong smell of smoke and fire." He recounted:

"On more minute examination, found that it proceeded from the scuttle, down which the stores had been conveyed, and which is under a part of the first class passengers' cabin. The steward and captain were instantly informed, and an alarm given. The smoke increased most rapidly, and soon filled the cabin with its density.

"The scuttle was pulled off, and some buckets of water were thrown down, but without effect. In twenty minutes from its being first perceived, the fire in that part of the ship had gained so much head that it was impossible to remain below; and the narrator, who went to his stateroom to procure a valuable part of his luggage, was almost overpowered in the attempt, and was only saved from suffocation by being drawn on deck through the skylight."

Others thought a lighted candle had been dropped among

the spirits. Whatever the cause, the conflagration had gained a headway that could not be retarded. The cry rang through the ship—"Fire, fire!" The thin wooden bulkheads that had been hastily constructed to convert the *Ocean Monarch* into an immigrant vessel ignited like dry birch bark.

Captain Murdoch continued:

"The flames were bursting with immense fury from the stern and center of the vessel. So great was the heat in these parts that the passengers, male and female, adults and children, crowded to the forepart of the vessel. Their piercing, heart-rending shrieks for aid were carried by the breeze across the dark blue waves. In their maddened despair women jumped overboard with their offspring in their arms, and sank to rise no more.

"Men followed their wives in frenzy and were lost. Groups of men, women, and children also precipitated themselves into the water in the vain hope of self-preservation, but the waters closed over many of them forever, and fearfully realized the inspired declaration, that 'in the midst of life we are in death.' In vain did I entreat and beg of the passengers to be composed. I pointed out to them that there were several vessels around us, and that, if they preserved order, they would all be saved; that although the case was desperate, it was not hopeless. It was of no avail. Howls of lamentations and cries for help were the only answers which I could obtain to my entreaties.

"Finding that every effort which I made was unavailing, and that nothing could be done to avoid the total destruction of the ship, in consequence of my orders not being heard, I directed that the anchors should be let go, so as to allow the ship to get her head to the wind, and thus, if possible, confine the flames to the stern. In a few minutes, the mizzenmast, went overboard—a few minutes more, and the mainmast shared the same fate. There yet remained the foremast. As the fire was making its way to the fore part of the vessel, the passengers and crew, of course, crowded still further forward. To the jib boom they clung in clusters as thick as they could pack— even one lying over another. At length the foremast went overboard, snapping the fastenings of the jib boom, which, with its load of human beings, dropped into the water amidst the most heart-rending screams, both of those on board and those who were falling into the water. Some of the poor creatures were enabled again to reach the vessel, others floated away on spars, but many met with a watery grave.

"Meantime, I gave orders to get the ship's boats afloat. Two were got overboard, and while in the act of getting the others ready, and cutting away the lashings, the fire reached them and they were immediately enveloped in flames. On seeing this the passengers became more unmanageable than ever. It was a painful moment. The shrieks of terror and alarm baffled all description. Maddened by despair, and in the vain hope of being rescued they knew not how, numbers again jumped overboard. Seeing their sad plight and the awful sacrifice of life which was going on, despite of every effort which I made, I gave direction to throw every moveable article overboard, that those who had left the ship might cling to them until help arrived."

Gregg found the scene as terrifying as Murdoch. He was at the same time dismayed at the sailors' behavior.

"The crew appeared early," he noted, "to have been influenced by the desire of self-preservation rather than that of assisting their commander in preserving order and rendering the best assistance they could to their fellow sufferers; the masts were suffered to fall as they consumed—nothing was cut away; and the only seamanlike operation performed by them, after the extent of the calamity was ascertained, was to bring her to anchor. Many of the passengers rendered praiseworthy assistance to their fellow sufferers. . . .

"The stewardess lost her life in courageously attempting to get the powder out of the cabin. There were about twenty-five pounds weight on board, and when she went below to get it, it is supposed she was suffocated. The powder exploded with a report like that of a cannon, but not being confined, and there being no person at that part of the vessel, no damage it is supposed was done by the explosion. At the time orders were given to let go the anchors, a number of women and children were seated in some way near the cable and were drawn by it into the water."

Commodore Littledale, aboard his *Queen of the Ocean,* after seeing the flames from the stricken packet, started toward her as quickly as his yacht would sail. One of his party, Sir Thomas Hesbeth, described the scene:

"On nearing her, although there was a still breeze blowing, with a heavy swell, the boat of the yacht was lowered, and proceeded to the ship for the purpose of rendering what assistance she could. Of course, with the swell on, it would have been next to certain destruction to the yacht had she been run alongside the ship, but the exertions of Mr. Littledale were of the noblest description, and he has the satisfaction of knowing that he has been the means of rescuing thirty-two persons from a watery grave.

"The scene which presented itself to Mr. Littledale, on nearing the vessel, was one of the most appalling and harrowing description. That gentleman truly describes it as awful and such as he hopes never to witness again. . . .

"In about an hour and a half after the yacht reached the vessel, the Brazilian steam frigate *Affonso,* which was out, we believe, on a trial trip, came up. She anchored immediately to windward and close to the burning vessel. She got a rope made fast to the *Ocean Monarch*, and by its use, her boats were enabled to go backward and forward to the burning vessel with great facility, and by this means a large number of persons were saved. *The Prince of Wales* steamer, which was on her passage hence to Bangor, came up shortly afterward, and, with the *New World* packet-ship, bound for New York, sent boats to the rescue of the passengers, which were the means of saving a large number. . . .

"When the *Affonso* discovered the *Ocean Monarch*, no time was lost in bearing down on her, and it was intended to anchor right under her bow, but the wind changed a little and prevented this from being accomplished. Four boats were, however, at once lowered, and were soon followed by the large paddle-box boat. The Marquis d'Lisboa jumped into one and Admiral Grenfell into the other, and they were untiring in their exertions to save the poor people. The Prince de Joinville stripped his coat, and was particularly assiduous in assisting the passengers on board the frigate. The heat was very intense and, even to those on board the boats alongside, was very oppressive. What it must have been to those who were crowding on the poop and bowspit of the vessel none can tell but those who experienced it. It was sufficient, however, to make them jump into the water, seeking succor from one element by taking shelter in another equally as destructive but far less agonizing in its effect. Because of the crowd of human beings in the water clinging to the spars, etc., the boats were unable to get as close to the vessel as they otherwise would have done, and, of course, considerable time was unavoidably consumed in rescuing the poor unfortunates.

"We understand that as soon as the alarm was given, the two boats belonging to the ship were lowered. The mate, with some of the crew and passengers, got into one. A portion of the crew and passengers got into the other, and they set off for

Liverpool. They were, however, picked up by a smack. Had they made to Mr. Littledale's yacht, placing their living freight on board of her, and returned again to the vessel, the loss of life would probably have been much less.

"A noble fellow, a seaman belonging to the New World, went to the wreck when there was little hope of saving any more, and stuck to the hull of the vessel till every soul had left her. It is said this praiseworthy individual, by his own hand, lowered a hundred persons to the boats below, of whom a great portion were women and children."

Captain Murdoch recalled that his last act was the throwing over of the topgallant yard, "made fast with a rope to keep it alongside." He was assisted by the carpenter and two seamen.

"I then told those who could hear me to jump overboard," he said, "and cling to the spar. A good many obeyed my directions. At this time I was surrounded on all sides, both fore and aft, by the flames, and seeing no possible chance of escaping if I remained for a moment longer, I followed the spar I had sent overboard. I entreated some of them to let go or they would perish, and showed them the example by swimming to a plank, by which I was enabled to sustain myself for about half an hour in the water, when I was picked up by the Queen of the Ocean.

"The Queen of the Ocean remained alongside till three o'clock. At that time the vessel was burnt to the water's edge, and there were only a few of the passengers on board, several boats being alongside endeavoring to take them off.

"Finding that the yacht could do no more, Mr. Littledale ordered her to start for Liverpool, where we arrived about seven o'clock in the evening.

"Although I did not see the part taken by the officers and distinguished party on board the Brazilian frigate, yet I am bound to return them my thanks for the very laudable and successful efforts in rescuing the lives of so many human beings from a watery grave or the still more fearful death by fire. Of Mr. Littledale and his company and crew, I know not how to speak; their conduct is beyond all praise. May He in whose hands are the issues of life and death, grant them in another and a better world the full reward which such philanthropy and benevolent conduct eminently deserves."

A reporter from Wilmer and Smith's *Times* was at the Liverpool docks to record the landing of the survivors:

"Sixteen persons arrived on Thursday at Seacombe, having been picked up by a fishing boat. Messrs. Parry, of the hotel, treated them in a very hospitable manner. They crossed to Liverpool by the eight o'clock boat. Mr. Baker, the celebrated comedian, was on board, and a collection was made amongst the passengers for the relief of the poor sufferers, who had lost their all, and 21.4s . . . for each of the sixteen, were collected and divided amongst them. Amongst these were six seamen. One poor Irishman and his sister were also amongst the number. The sister was rescued by the brother seizing her by the hair of the head just as she was sinking.

"When they landed at the pierhead, some of the messmates who had arrived in the yacht greeted the newcomers in the most tender terms, and the meeting of these hardy sons of Neptune, after their 'hair-breadth,' is described as one of the most affecting. The men actually hugged each other in a rough but honest embrace, and tears were drawn from many of the spectators who witnessed the touching scene. The men inquired eagerly after others of their comrades, and tears, both of joy and sorrow, ran down their cheeks.

"Several pounds were collected on board the yacht for the relief of the sufferers; and on arrival here it was distributed to the poor people by Mr. J. A. Tobin, who was on board the yacht.

"The *Affonso* rescued in all about 160 persons, including thirteen seamen. Of these about 140 landed, and the remainder preferred staying on board the frigate all night, the Marquis d'Lisboa having given directions that all who were desirous of remaining should be accommodated in the best way possible. The dead body of a child is on board the frigate.

"One poor woman was on the landing stage bemoaning the loss of her two children, and we have heard that a boy and girl, unclaimed, are still on board the frigate.

"The following persons are in the Northern Hospital: Anna Roper, (beside other injuries,) contused leg, very badly bruised, and child. This woman took her child in her arms, seized hold of a rope, and jumped overboard from the vessel. She held on by the rope, till the boat came to her rescue. Michael Gleason, in addition to other injuries, very severe laceration on the hand. His brother, uninjured, is also in the hospital. Margaret Kershaw with her child. She was nearly drowned, and is suffering from immersion in the water. Several persons were taken to the Birkenhead Hospital.

"Michael Gleason states that there were several persons on board the *Affonso* with their arms and legs fractured, besides being otherwise injured.

"When the *Affonso* arrived in the river she anchored in the Sloyne, and the distinguished company landed at the new stage, in one of the ferry steamers. The passengers who were saved were transferred to the *President* steamer, and landed at the north end of the Prince's Pierhead, doubtless with the view of being near to the Northern Hospital, whither those who were burned and otherwise injured were conveyed. Mr. Dowling, with the district superintendent and a body of the police, attended, with the view of providing lodgings for some for the night. On landing they presented a sad and pitiable spectacle.

Many of the men and women were almost in a state of nudity. Some of them had their heads bandaged; and some their arms, legs, and other parts of their bodies bound up, having been injured by their contact with spars in the water, by knocking against the boats, and in other ways.

"The greatest sympathy was expressed for the poor people and every exertion was made to mitigate their sufferings as much as possible. The exertions of Mr. Littledale and those on board the yacht are spoken of in the highest terms, and those of the distinguished party on board the Affonso, especially those of Captain Grenfell, the Marquis d'Lisboa, and the Prince de Joinville, are beyond all praise. The reward of all those who exerted themselves in so praiseworthy a manner must be in the inward satisfaction of having done the best they could to save the lives of their fellow creatures under the most distressing circumstances."

Among the lost were all of the Sullivans except the mother, Abbey, and one child Geoffrey. Mary Cashman faced life that night an orphan; her mother, father, brothers, and sisters all were gone. The Grahams, who had barely made the sailing, died.

There remained nothing more to do than take the final count of the dead and missing. Of the 380 or more who had sailed that Thursday morning, 176 perished.

The agents, however, remembered one more detail. They offered "a free passage" to the survivors who wished to try a second time to reach America. Otherwise, they would refund the fares.

Murdoch sailed for Boston. The months passed. He remained "on the beach." A captain who had lost a ship—and many passengers' lives—was not considered lucky. Finally, he booked out of New Bedford as pilot on a whaler.

His fortunes continued indifferent. During his long spells ashore he decided to write a book about the subject which haunted his subconscious. He put into words the fiery destruction of his last, and best, command. A deliberate man, he took time over the project.

Six years later, Murdoch had a title for his book. It was not succinct, but it covered the subject: *A True Account of That Terrible Catastrophe, The Burning of the Ocean Monarch, of Train's Line, in Which 150 Lives were lost.*

It was now August, 1854. On the 18th of that month, another ship master, Captain M'Leary, of the bark *Mary Morris*, out of Glasgow, was inching through heavy seas and fog about six hundred miles due west of Scotland when he "fell in" with the hull of a large iron vessel.

To his experienced eye, the vessel was apparently Clyde-built. It was painted black with a bright red bottom. Captain M'Leary hove to and set a boarding party onto the derelict to obtain a more detailed description. The party discovered the craft was compartmented, and contained "machinery," indicating it was of the latest steam-sail design. Every bit of woodwork, however, had been burned out.

The *Mary Morris* sailed on.

The next day, she encountered a seven-foot female figurehead floating in the water. Her hands were extended, a wreath had been carved about her dress. To Captain M'Leary it added up. No "iron vessel" had been reported lost in three years—not until the *City of Glasgow* failed to arrive at her destination, Philadelphia, in April.

On March 1st, as on most other days this busy 1854, *The Times* of London carried an advertisement: "STEAM TO AMERICA: The Liverpool and Philadelphia Steamship Co. intend to dispatch their favourite Iron screw steamships from Liverpool to Philadelphia every four weeks:

City of Manchester
City of Glasgow

The rates were reasonable: $100 for sharing a two-berth cabin; $85 for a three-berth; $40 for bunking with "a number of passengers."

The *City of Glasgow* grossed 1,087 tons. The 399 persons —including a number of infants—who had booked passage on her could be accommodated easily. In addition, there were seventy-four officers and crewmen.

She was amply provisioned: one pound per person per day of fresh and salted meats for forty-six days; one pound of bread and flour for fifty-four days; six tons, total, of potatoes and vegetables; and three and one-half tons of coffee, sugar, and smaller items; also forty days' supply of water, regulation "government allowance."

The ship was also equipped with distilling apparatus.

If necessary, the food and water could be rationed to sustain life of all on board for more than two months. The coal had been bunkered for a twenty-six-day voyage. However, the *City of Glasgow* could make equally fast time under sail, given fair winds.

Her compasses had been adjusted within five days of sailing. Altogether, she was ready, provisioned, and in "a perfect efficiency at starting," according to Richardson Brothers and Company, her agents.

Wednesday, March 1st, her date of sailing, was one of the busiest which the port of Liverpool had witnessed in many months. A total of thirty-five ships cast off their hawsers and poked into the Mersey, bound for world ports. Of that number, thirteen were headed for America.

In England itself that day eyes were turned on the mounting crisis in the Crimea, which had already pitted Turkey and

Russia against one another. But there were lesser punctuations in the chronicle of existence, as well:

St. Peter's, Cornhill, arranged a Lenten series of lectures. The London Orchestra announced four concerts in Dublin, commencing March 11th.

"A young lady 22 years of age," read an advertisement in *The Times*, "is desirous of obtaining a comfortable home in a respectable school." For $120 a year, a suburban house with seven rooms, "fine spring water and a good garden" could be rented.

At Paddington Bridge a "young Newfoundland dog" was found by one Mr. Keen, of Chigwell. Mr. G. Hodson, "the celebrated Irish comedian," was rehearsing for his "new entertainment, 'Paddy's Portfolio,' " at the Strand Theater.

At Freemason's Hall there would be a lecture: "Shall Slavery Continue?"

In Liverpool, the thoughts of voyagers were not of events in London or elsewhere in England, but of the new life they would start across the Atlantic. Today, there was a light breeze. Skies were clear. It was propitious weather for all ships.

The *City of Glasgow* sailed past Birkenhead and into the Irish Sea. Several hours ahead of her was a vessel bound for Rio de Janeiro: the *Lusitania*, long considered a lucky name for a ship.

On April 8th, the *City of Glasgow* should be steaming up the Delaware River, headed for the crowded Philadelphia waterfront.

April came and went: The *City of Glasgow*, overdue, was unreported in Philadelphia, at any other ports, or by vessels at sea. The first week in May, Richardson Brothers and Company made a statement:

"We believe the vessel to be detained in the ice on the banks of Newfoundland and unable to make her way out of it, in corroboration of which view the *Baltic* steamer was three days in it, the *Charity* screw steamer was nine days in it, and a sailing vessel, some years ago, in the same place was thirty days in it without being able to move."

On May 10th, the agents were in receipt of a dispatch from Queenstown. The captain of the vessel *Baldaur* had sighted in mid-Atlantic on April 21st, about two miles distant a "large steamer with great beam, hull and funnel black, inside painted drab, with yellow paddle-boxes." Her fore and foretop sails were set, though she carried nothing on the mainmast.

The officers of the *Baldaur* noted the vessel to be listing "strongly" to port. There was no evidence of any persons on board, no smoke from her funnel. When the unidentified "large steamer" altered course, which had been northerly, and started toward the *Baldaur*, a small bark, hidden in the other vessel's lee, came into view. The latter packed on all her sail and headed south.

A fog swept in, and the *Baldaur* never saw either ship again. On the water "large quantities of biscuit boxes" bobbed past the *Baldaur's* bows. Was this piracy, Richardson Brothers asked?

Aside from the paddle-boxes, which the *City of Glasgow* did not have, since she was a propeller vessel, the owners and agents were inclined to accept the *Baldaur's* sighting as the *City of Glasgow*.

Now Britain and France were themselves at war with Russia in the Crimea. One missing ship, even though laden with immigrants, assumed less importance in the midst of greater preoccupations.

However, reports continued to drift back. A gentleman in Londonderry claimed to have received a letter from a "Mr. Smilio," one of the missing ship's passengers. He purportedly had written from Africa, where all passengers and crewmen were said to have been landed after the steamer had "foundered."

On May 22nd, the agents who had checked into the matter satisfied themselves there was "no truth in the report." May turned into June and June into early July. A newspaper in the United States, the *Jersey Blue*, carried a tale concerning "an intelligent, happy-looking Englishman about forty-five years of age . . . a man of pleasing manners" who kept coming to the Liverpool and Philadelphia Steamship Company's offices in Philadelphia to inquire for mail. With him each time was his twelve-year-old son.

The pair awaited news of the remainder of their family, who were following them to America on the *City of Glasgow*. One letter from the man's wife had advised that she and her other children would sail on the sister ship, *City of Manchester*, but she had canceled passage when she could not pack in time.

In the meanwhile, the gentleman had acquired and furnished a house in the city. The newspaper continued that where at first the man was "plump, happy-seeming of face," now he was "haggard" as his visits to the booking office were met day after day with the same gloomy word: "No news."

When he learned of a rumor that placed the *City of Glasgow* safely in the Bahamas, the article noted, "Oh how false hope brightened his countenance."

Now in early July, the paper concluded, the man was discovered "in a lunatic asylum, 'a raving maniac.'"

Richardson Brothers, in Liverpool, confirming that there was such a family aboard, conceded that the Philadelphia gentleman was "much distressed" but "perfectly sane."

What had happened to the *City of Glasgow*? The sighting by Captain M'Leary the following month of the burned-out hull seemed, to some shipping officials, to confirm the fate of the hapless immigrant ship. When added to the *Baldaur's* report, the ever-present possibility of piracy and murder was all the more strengthened.

The weather in April had not been unduly severe. If the *City of Glasgow* had burned accidentally, some survivors—as with the *Ocean Monarch*—would have made land.

But at Lloyd's and other establishments where the comings and goings of ships were noted, only a question mark could be put against the name of the *City of Glasgow*. And no more evidence was ever found to remove or alter the question mark.

In Lowell, Massachusetts, however, the disaster which had befallen the *Ocean Monarch* finally had a happy ending of sorts. Captain Murdoch found a publisher, the H. P. Huntoon Company, to print his book with the long title.

There was but one hitch. He would have to pay for it himself.

Expedition to Nowhere

Capt. McClintock landed yesterday at Portsmouth from the *Alarm* pilot boat, which vessel had brought him ashore from the *Fox*, screw delivery vessel, arrived at the Isle of Wight from the Arctic regions.

On landing, Capt. McClintock at once proceeded by train to London, taking with him two cases containing relics of the long-missing expedition of Sir John Franklin.

Capt. McClintock stated he was in possession of papers that would fully elucidate the mystery which has so long hung over the fate of these brave men.

The Times, London, Sept. 22, 1859

CAPTAIN FRANCIS LEOPOLD MCCLINTOCK, R.N., STOOD UPON THE shore of King William Island on a snowy morning, May 31, 1859. Beside him was a broken, weathered ship's boat and, next to it, two double-barreled shotguns, with one chamber of each loaded, the hammers cocked.

On the floor boards of the boat rested two piles of bones, obviously human. One pile, fragmentary and splintered, appeared to have been gnawed by wolves. The other heap was larger and in generally better shape. There were other telltale remnants—faded, tattered bits of clothing, food containers, parts of boxes—which in their sum wrote *omega* to a story which had begun fourteen years earlier at the English port Greenhithe, on the Thames.

It was another May, in 1845, far removed from the northern

19

reaches of Hudson Bay, when townspeople and well-wishers, including lords of the Admiralty, watched Sir John Franklin and an expedition of two Royal Navy ships, the *Erebus* and *Terror*, and nearly 150 men sail toward the Northwest Passage. It was a quest which already had frustrated men such as Sir James Ross and Sir Edward Parry.

Franklin, who had led two parties through northern Canada by way of training, was the object of optimistic talk at men's meeting places of the Explorers Club character. Sir John, it was generally conceded, would make it.

For that matter, a feeling of confidence had infused Franklin's entire expedition. Commander James Fitzjames, captain of the *Erebus*, flagship and larger of the two, had no doubts as to success.

"I say," he wrote an old school friend, "we shall get through the Northwest Passage this year."

His companion skipper, Captain F. R. M. Crozier, of the *Terror*, a previous voyager to the Polar Sea, shared Fitzjames' opinion.

Their two sloops, each with the unique equipment of 25-horsepower auxiliary engines, were indicative of the preparations of this most ambitious Arctic expedition ever outfitted. Piping, another refinement, carried hot water from the boilers to fo'csles and cabins. And, to be sure there would be ample food, the supply ship *Barreto* would trail the *Erebus* and *Terror*, like a native bearer on safari, to the Arctic Circle. Ten live oxen bellowed in the *Barreto's* heavily-loaded hold.

At sixty, Franklin was not a physically commanding figure to head so massive and spectacular a venture. He was bald, stocky, moon-faced—the antithesis of a Nelson or Drake, or others of the dashing, salty tradition. He had, however, served under Lord Nelson at Trafalgar.

More sensitive about his age than his appearance, he recently had rejoined when Lord Haddington, First Lord of the Admiralty, had questioned his qualifications on the basis of his age: "My Lord, I'm only fifty-nine."

Franklin, if he were in short supply of good looks, amply possessed qualities of seamanship as well as benevolence.

"His conversation is delightful and most instructive," Fitzjames wrote home as the ships wallowed across the North Atlantic towards Greenland. "He is in much better health than when we left England. He takes an active part in everything that goes on. Of all men he is most fitted for the command of an enterprise requiring sound sense and perseverence."

Franklin, born in Lincolnshire in 1786, had been of a persevering nature ever since boyhood. The youngest of eleven children, John persevered his way out of a fashionable school at the age of fourteen and a possible career in the ministry to sign on the 64-gun frigate *Polyphemus*.

At fifteen, John Franklin, with rating of First Class Volunteer, was with Nelson at the Battle of Copenhagen, when Danish shore batteries and most of the tiny country's fleet were wiped out.

Later, on duty in the Pacific, he was among the crew of a small boat which sailed across fifty miles of open ocean to Sydney, Australia. His ship had been wrecked on an uncharted reef.

At Trafalgar, October 21, 1805, Franklin was a signal midshipman aboard the 74-gun ship of the line *Bellerophon*. He stood on the high poop dck, under cannon and small-arms fire, through the battle which ended in the defeat of the French and Spanish fleets (and inspired a statue as well as a name for London's most famous square).

Among the few on the *Bellerophon* to escape death or serious injury, young Franklin received his first wound seven years later at the Battle of New Orleans in the War of 1812. There he commanded a division of small vessels against superior American gunboats.

Six years later he tasted the Arctic with a small, unsuccessful expedition. Its avowed object was the North Pole. The next year, 1819, Franklin, a Naval lieutenant resolved to seek the Northwest Passage, which supposedly extended across the top of the world from the Atlantic to the Pacific.

He would strike overland from an outpost, York Factory on Hudson Bay, more than fifteen hundred miles to Great Slave Lake, then follow a river known as the Coppermine up to the Arctic Ocean and parallel the coastline eastward.

Lieutenant Franklin, Dr. John Richardson, a naturalist, and Midshipmen George Back and Robert Hood, along with John Hepburn, a petty officer, established their base camp, "Fort Enterprise," late in 1820, close to the headwaters of the Coppermine. With French-Canadian woodsmen and Indian guides they waited out the winter there and in June, 1821, set forth on their journey.

The group reached the ocean then forged east along the shore for six hundred fifty miles. Winter, however, overtook the men, and they turned back for Fort Enterprise. Food ran out, game was scarce, and the explorers were reduced to eating a type of lichen the natives called "tripe de roche." A month later, after the party had split into separate groups, Franklin arrived at Fort Enterprise—to find it deserted and the food stored there stolen.

His associates, Dr. Richardson and John Hepburn, arrived a few days later with a tale of murder. A French-Canadian guide, apparently mad from hunger, had shot and killed Midshipman Hood before the guide himself could be slain by the doctor. Other guides had gone for help. Two had died of starvation on the way.

Franklin came home to England early the next year, where he

found his commander's stripes awaiting him. He also found a wife. Pretty Eleanor Anne Porden had written a sonnet inspired by John Franklin's exploits in the Arctic, and mailed it to him, though the two were strangers at the time. The correspondence and the poetry led to matrimony, in 1823.

The next year a daughter, Eleanor, was born, and with John about to embark on another voyage, Eleanor Anne had hand-sewn a silk Union Jack, which she gave to him with the request: "Don't unfurl it until you get to the ocean."

On his arrival in Canada, he learned that his wife had died six days after he sailed. Sorrowfully, he continued on to the tidal waters of the Arctic—or Polar—Sea, where he planted the flag in obedience to Eleanor Anne's last wish.

What John lacked, perhaps, in husbandly responsibility, he more than compensated for in exploring prowess. On this trip, he mapped twelve hundred miles of coastline in the regions above Hudson Bay.

When he returned in 1828, Franklin was completing a decade of nearly continuous Arctic duty. And this time a new reward awaited him: a knighthood, by edict of His Majesty, King George IV.

The newly-titled Sir John was married again, to Jane Griffith, a young lady with strong will and an ample inheritance. Even so, it took more than a wife and his daughter Eleanor to moor him to home. He was off to the Mediterranean, with the marriage vows ringing in his ears. Sir John was the new commander of the formidable frigate *Rainbow*.

His man-o'-war soon became dubbed "Franklin's Paradise," attesting to his efficient, compassionate leadership—qualities previously evident in the Canadian wilderness where Indian guides had their own sobriquet, "Big Chief Who Wouldn't Hurt A Mosquito."

By the mid-thirties, Sir John was appointed governor of Tasmania. He had visited there in his early map-making cruises of waters "down under." At last, he was on a duty where his family could accompany him. Franklin, however, was growing older and increasingly independent. Even good Queen Victoria, who had recently succeeded to the throne, knew that a Royal Governor could not side with the natives of any British possession against the Colonial Office.

In 1843, he was summoned home.

When he arrived at Westminster, he repeated outspoken contentions uttered in his governor's palace: the Empire was "haughty and imperious" in its administration of the Tasmanians."

During his nearly ten years in Tasmania he had met Sir James Ross, who was sparring with the Antarctic in two vessels, the *Erebus* and *Terror*. Talking with Ross had rekindled Franklin's own fires.

In London, his former associate, George Back, reviewed his own accomplishments during the years when Sir John had been at the other extremity of the earth. Back had mapped the coastline along the "roof" of North America, from the Bering Sea to the Boothia Peninsula, which fingered northward from Hudson Bay. He had transited much of the Northwest Passage.

An unknown waterway from Barrow Strait southward to King William Island remained to be traversed to prove a passage did, indeed, run the continental length and that a ship could enter the Hudson Strait and emerge at the Bering Strait, between Alaska and Siberia.

There were a mere three hundred uncharted miles which prevented the Northwest Passage from being a reality. For one, Sir John Barrow, known as the "father of Arctic exploration," believed this three hundred miles to be the last link. His prodding of the Admiralty was in large part responsible for Sir John Franklin's quest.

The *Erebus* and *Terror* were brought back from the Antarctic and made available by the government to Franklin.

Such was the genesis of Franklin and his Royal expedition.

Off Greenland, Sir John scribbled a dispatch to the Admiralty and sent it aboard the returning supply vessel *Barreto:* "The ships are now provisioned for three years."

The date was July 10, 1845. Two weeks later, the sloops overhauled a whaler, the *Prince of Wales*, then continued west toward Lancaster Sound, at the northern tip of Baffin Land, and at the mouth of Barrow Strait. Tauntingly near to Boothia Peninsula and King William Island, Franklin nonetheless decided to winter at little Beechey Island and to continue ferreting for the elusive, three hundred-mile gap in the spring when the ice thawed.

The men set up an ice colony. There was an observatory for the scientists, recreational areas for the men. A newspaper was published regularly on a small hand press. An otherwise snug winter was marred by the deaths of two seamen and a Royal Marine from causes unknown. Also, the carefully calculated food supply was thrown off balance by the spoiling of several hundred cans of meat.

The two ships moved southward again in August. In less than 150 miles, ice was encountered. By early September, the *Erebus* and *Terror* had inched their way to the tip of King William Island and an icy headland: Cape Felix.

Go east or west? Neither Frankin nor anyone else was entirely certain whether this northerly land parcel were a true island. He had to run the risk of encountering impenetrable pack ice or a rocky land bridge.

Sir John navigated his two sloops south along the western shore until he reached Point Victory. There, on September 12th, the fleet became icebound once more.

Morale remained surprisingly high this second year in the ice. So far as records were kept, there were no deaths.

Spring arrived again. On May 24th, a party set forth for Cape Herschel with Lieutenant Graham Gore in charge. This group primarily was seeking two cairns, which should contain vital navigational information. One had been erected by Thomas Simpson, a Hudson Bay Company official; the other by Sir James Ross, who fifteen years before had crossed to King William Island over the ice from the Boothia Peninsula.

Gore's quest was frustrating. He located neither cairn, though he left one of his own at Point Victory. Disheartened, he led his men back to the ships—only to find a worse tragedy had befallen the expedition. Sir John Franklin was dead.

The scanty chronicles which were later to be written did not record the cause of death. Illness attendant to his advanced years? Exhaustion, starvation (which was unlikely), or freezing? Suicide or murder?

There was no evidence by which any possibility could be arbitrarily ruled out. His body was presumably deposited in the ice off Point Victory, though Captain Crozier, who succeeded to command, left no record.

With the partial thaw in July, the ships continued their slow progress southward. However, the two vessels were not making headway on their own. Prisoners of the pack, they drifted only at the ice's whim. Progress, in total, was but a few miles.

Fall came. The long nights returned, with their dark, icy lullabies. Food was dwindling. Fuel for the engines was nearly exhausted. Morale ebbed in the stillness of the Arctic winter.

Before spring reluctantly returned, Gore, eight other officers, and fifteen men had died.

There was one chance left, Crozier knew. That was to attempt the trek over the ice to King William Island and around its shore to a point where a crossing could be made to the mainland. Then the men could move southwestward down the estuary of the Great Fish River, which George Back had discovered several years before, and go upriver, hoping to find food and shelter.

It would mean that the 105 survivors, most of them already weak, would have to carry enough supplies for a trip of several hundred miles. It was a scant hope, but it was the only hope, Crozier believed. On April 22, 1848, he gave the "abandon ship" order. The heavily-laden party began its icy hegira to the mainland.

By the time the men had covered the fifteen miles to Point Victory, it was evident they would have to jettison all but the barest essentials. It had required three days to make that short distance. With urging from the officers, the men abandoned such weighty and useless items as lightning and curtain rods, brass from a marine's shako, shovels, extra blankets, storage bottles.

Going was slow. The boats were lugged on the sledges across the ice. In leads of open water, the sledges were stowed inside the boats. Even so, the start of the homeward journey after so many months of imprisonment was heartening. The survivors possessed sufficient supplies. What they lacked was leadership, as neither Crozier nor Fitzjames knew the Arctic as Franklin had.

On April 25th, Gore's cairn of the previous year was discovered at Point Victory. The brief record he had left was supplemented with marginal notes, telling of Sir John's death and the commencement of the overland journey toward civilization. Captain Crozier himself signed the document, postscripting: "Start on tomorrow, 26th, for Back's Fish River."

In England, concern grew for the safety of the expedition. The Hudson Bay Company forwarded extra supplies to its outermost stations. Rewards were offered to the captains of whalers for any information about Franklin. Lady Franklin herself posted an additional reward.

As 1848 arrived, Sir James Ross was dispatched northward. The famous explorer crisscrossed Lancaster Sound, at one time coming within 160 miles of where the *Erebus* and *Terror* had been abandoned. Diminishing supplies, however, forced the prudent Ross to turn toward home.

The government, increasingly fearful that the expedition on which it pinned an Empire's hopes had met disaster, boosted its reward to 20,000 pounds. To this, Lady Franklin added 3,000 to her previous 2,000 pounds.

Shortly, fifteen ships were bucking the North Atlantic, eagerly on the hunt.

In the late fall of 1850, the first trace of Franklin was discovered by a fleet under the command of Captain Horatio Austin. His men came upon the remains of the Beechey Island camp. They also located the piles of meat tins which had been discarded. The condition of the camp and the indication of the depleted food supplies added fuel to doubts that any man engaged in the great endeavor could still be alive.

But no news was interpreted as better than bad news. The search was pushed. After Beechey Island, however, the trail seemed to vanish. No further trace of Franklin was found in the following years, although the quest added to knowledge of the Arctic.

Parties from the Austin expedition searched more than fifteen hundred miles of coastline, including eight hundred fifty miles hitherto unmapped. At times, searchers came close to the last known position of the abandoned vessels. In 1853, Richard Collinson arrived within twenty miles of the position, but no ships were spotted.

The next clue appeared in 1853, when Dr. John Rae was sent by the Hudson Bay Company to explore the Boothia Peninsula.

In April of 1854, he met Eskimos who had knives and forks engraved with the names or initials of certain members of the Franklin expedition. The Eskimos' stories varied as to how they came in possession of the articles. Further questioning failed to elicit any hint as to Franklin's disappearance.

The silverware and other trinkets were enough, however, to satisfy the English government that the long-missing explorers had met an unknown fate. On the basis of Dr. Rae's evidence, it was decided to pay him ten thousand pounds of the reward money and close the ledgers.

Lady Jane Franklin wasn't satisfied. Neither were various scientists and Navy Arctic experts. They sent urgent appeals for further investigation. More action was needed, "to satisfy the honor of our country and to clear up a mystery that has excited the sympathy of the civilized world."

Lady Franklin followed this up with a letter to the Admiralty. She pointed out that the area where her husband had disappeared had been narrowed down, that Dr. Rae's discovery provided more acute indication of the course Sir John had been pursuing, and therefore the search ought to be pressed harder.

The government, busy with other matters, ignored both pleas. Officials let it be known that, as far as they were concerned, England had more important fish to fry. This cooling of the Admiralty's ardor only kindled Lady Franklin's own determination. By herself, she would finance another band to seek the Erebus and Terror.

Captain McClintock, emerging as the Royal Navy's latest authority on the Far North after serving with Ross, was chosen to command the new expedition. Captain Allen Young, a hardbitten merchant marine officer and soldier of fortune, had put up a measure of his own money to back the voyage. He would go along to see that his pounds were expended to the best advantage.

The group would use the 177-ton, well constructed steam yacht, *Fox*, which Lady Franklin presented to McClintock as a gift. He could feel free to take the vessel anywhere he wanted.

Before the *Fox* sailed from Aberdeen on July 1, 1857, many Englishmen were so moved by Lady Jane's determination that they raised enough money by public subscription to pay more than half of the expedition's expenses.

The *Fox* reached Melville Bay toward the end of the Arctic summer and plowed into trouble in the form of ice. The tiny vessel, ensnared, was carried southward more than a thousand miles by the ice floes, which continually threatened to crush the ship. After one particularly harrowing experience, McClintock returned to his cabin to write in his diary: "After yesterday's experience, I can understand how a man's hair can turn gray in a few hours."

The little yacht, in April, 1858, shook herself free. As soon as he was in water again, McClintock set a course northward. This time he made in through Melville Bay and into Lancaster Sound.

By August, McClintock reached Beechey Island and was ready to start his search in earnest. Skipping in and out of ice floes, his *Fox* fought her way to Bellot Strait, separating the island from the peninsula. After three attempts to push westward through the strait were frustrated by the ice, McClintock gave up and put into a small cove at the eastern end of the strait to wait out the winter.

As winds sent the temperature past sixty below zero, Captains McClintock and Young set out to explore the surrounding territory. Despite the viciousness of the Arctic winter, they pushed farther and farther from their base each trip. Finally their efforts were rewarded.

On March 1, 1859, McClintock came across Eskimos who had relics of the Franklin expedition. One easily identifiable

item was a silver medal marked with the name of Dr. Mac-
Donald, assistant surgeon on the Terror.

They hadn't personally seen any white men, the Eskimos insisted, but had been told that a ship with three masts had been
crushed to the west of King William Island. They had received
the medal and other trinkets by barter.

With that information, McClintock decided to head southwest to cross the peninsula and the frozen water separating it
from King William Island and conduct a thorough search there.

Meanwhile, Young would hasten directly west to Prince of
Wales Island to check reports that a ship had gone aground
there. With the temperature still daily averaging far below
zero, the two groups set out. McClintock split his party into two
sections, one headed by himself, and the other by Lieutenant
Hobson, the second-in-command to McClintock. They had provisions for nearly three months.

When they reached King William Island, Hobson headed
along the north shore and McClintock set course southward
down the west shore. When they met, halfway around the island, they would have covered the whole coastline. Their
planned meeting place was near Cape Herschel, where Simpson
had crossed over from the mainland and erected a cairn.

Hobson's party, moving across Cape Felix on April 28th, encountered the first sign of the Franklin expedition: a cairn containing a blanket, tent, and some old clothes.

A trench was dug around the cairn. Other objects, including
a boat's ensign and broken bottles which once might have contained messages, were found scattered about.

Moving on, Hobson a few days later came across the cairn on
Point Victory where Crozier had deposited his message. Nearby
were many of the articles abandoned by expedition members
before they started south. Hobson hastily tore rocks from the
cairn and there, undamaged by the years of Artcic weather, lay

the first definite indication of what happened to Franklin's men: the unsealed canister containing the Crozier message.

Reading it, Hobson became the first to know that Sir John Franklin was dead and that the remaining members of his expedition had decided to head south toward civilization.

Captain McClintock, who was making his way down the east coast of the island, on May 8th came across an Eskimo village with less than forty inhabitants. From them he purchased several silver plates with the initials of Sir John Franklin, Crozier, and other members of the party engraved on them.

These Eskimos revealed to McClintock that the wreckage of the vessels from which the plates came was "four or five" days' journey, on the west coast of King William Island. An old woman informed McClintock that when the ships were abandoned the explorers made their way southward.

"The white men dropped by the way as they went to the Great River," she said, "and some were buried and some were not."

The searchers continued southward. Just after midnight on May 25th, about ten miles east of Cape Herschel, the party arrived at the first indication of the tragedy that had overtaken Franklin.

A bleached skeleton, partly covered with snow, lay atop a ridge. Around the skeleton were fragments of European clothing. By digging away the snow, McClintock discovered a small pocketbook, containing hard-to-decipher letters.

Pushing on in search of more evidence, McClintock discovered a cairn that had been built by Hobson a few days previously near the place where they were supposed to meet. It told of the record, with its valuable information, at Point Victory. Hobson had gone back up the coast to continue the search, and McClintock intensified his efforts.

On May 30th, the captain viewed a strange sight: the old

boat with its two skeletons and the guns, cocked and ready for use. He opened a box, beside the guns, containing more than thirty pounds of chocolate.

It led him to doubt that starvation had been the final nemesis of the boat's occupants. There were, also, tea bags, tobacco, five pocket watches, two table knives with white handles, eleven spoons, eleven forks, ammunition, two brass pocket compasses, clay pipes, and a bar of scented soap.

The craft's bow, pointing northward, seemed testimony to the fact that the survivors were attempting a return to the *Erebus* and *Terror*. The two skeletons further indicated to McClintock that the other occupants of the boat had continue northward on foot after the death of their companions.

The first skeleton, on the ridge near Cape Herschel, and the boat with its other human bones seemed to McClintock mute if morbid evidence that Sir John Franklin's men had arrived at the missing gap in the Northwest Passage, even if they had neither traversed it nor lived to report their experience.

The book, apparently, had been closed on the record of the Franklin expedition. *The Illustrated London News* editorialized:

There is but one speck on the bright picture: the cold, stolid, selfish apathy of the government that would not stir a finger to determine their fate, but left the whole charge of the expedition to be defrayed by his noble widow.

That Lady Franklin may neither ask nor need the money is not a point in question. Her fame is high and pure and will last as long as our history. Poets will hereafter sing of her as the model of wifehood and her place will be assured in the affectionate regard of future ages.

But history did forget about Lady Franklin. Great Britain, perhaps less surprisingly, forgot about the Northwest Passage.

It was not until 1904 that the Lorelei-like waterway was traversed from start to finish. And then it was a Norwegian, Roald Amundsen, not an Englishman, who achieved the goal that had claimed the lives of so many in previous generations.

Yet, Franklin himself is as real today within the milieu of explorers as he was a hundred years ago. Land parties of Canadians and Americans, for example, who work north of Hudson Bay to service the DEW radar line, a keystone in North America's air defense system, still half expect to come across the actual remains of Sir John.

For that matter, his mapping expeditions helped open up northern Canada—and made the DEW Line possible.

Death on the Mississippi

AT MIDNIGHT, APRIL 26, 1865, THE ST. LOUIS AND NEW ORLEANS packet *Sultana* finished coaling from barges at Memphis and continued paddling its way up the Mississippi.

It was a particularly black night. A light drizzle was beginning to fall.

Captain Mason squinted ahead from his wheelhouse, blew a blast of the two-year-old side-wheeler's whistle, and hoped. With at least twenty-three hundred persons on board—twice her capacity—plus more than 150 horses, cows, and pigs, the *Sultana* provided ample cause for any skipper to worry. And Captain Mason was worried.

During the evening he had told one of the army men that he would sell his interest in the 1700-ton side-wheeler "if" he reached Cairo, Illinois, the destination. However, he hoped the mists and darkness would lift within the next two hours, when he would be safely past the shoaly islands known as the Old Hen and Chickens. They were so low in the river as to be practically invisible on such a night.

Down below, Second Engineer Clemmans had just relieved Chief Engineer Nate Wintringer. Clemmans, a veteran of side-wheelers, was also more dependable than most for the tedium of night watches. He was a total abstainer.

Wintringer had reason to want his most trusty assistant on duty tonight. In addition to the *Sultana's* overload, one of her boilers—a new "experimental" type—had sprung a serious leak

35

coming up from New Orleans. Repairs had been made only four days ago, in Vicksburg.

In the largest of the steamer's many cabins and saloons, Chester D. Berry, twenty-one, of South Creek, Pennsylvania, had finally finished singing "Sweet Hour of Prayer" with the other men.

"All went gay as a marriage bell for awhile," wrote Berry. "A happier lot of men I think I never saw than those poor fellows were. The most of them had been a long time in prison, some even for about two years, and the prospect of soon reaching home made them content to endure any amount of crowding. I know that on the lower deck we were just about as thick as we could possibly lie all over the deck, and I understood that all the other decks were the same. The main thought that occupied every mind was home, the dearest spot on earth."

Now he slept, oblivious to the heat and the stenches of the river packet and its swarming humanity—and animals.

At that Berry was lucky. He had a cot to lie on. He was in a passenger compartment. Others, such as Otto Barden, twenty-four, of Wooster, Ohio, dozed on gratings and in recesses of the greasy, steamy engine room. Barden was so tired that the smell of coal and the throb of pistons had been at once anesthetic and lullaby to him. He slept. Besides, as he had said earlier in the evening, he was on his way "to God's country."

P. L. Horn, twenty-one, also of Wooster, had different tastes from those of his Ohio neighbor. He had stretched his bedroll on an upper deck, and there he slept, in the night air and drizzle. He was, however, by no means alone. Boots of other sleepers ringed his body.

Back in the miasmic cabin heat, Lieutenant Joseph Taylor Elliott, of Indiana, was having "some very unpleasant words" with a Captain McCoy, of Ohio, over possession of a double-decker cot. Joe Elliott, who had been tramping around

Memphis during the evening in vain search of "amusement," was now footsore and tired and in no mood for opposition.

The epithets grew hotter, and the two men clenched their fists and faced one another.

Both youthful Civil War veterans were lean, hard, their impulses still dictated by the laws of survival. After almost a year in Andersonville prison, decorum or life itself held much less meaning for them.

President Lincoln had been dead for two weeks. The war had ended the ninth day of this fateful April.

Elliott and McCoy were but two of approximately twenty-one hundred officers and men released by victory from the pestilence of Confederate prison camps: Andersonville, Macon, and a lesser known purgatory, Cahaba, Alabama.

The *Sultana's* sailing from Vicksburg had been attended by confusion and uncertainty. Camp Fisk, nearby, was overflowing with Federal soldiers who were dominated by one desire: to get home. River packets were experiencing a boom business.

Almost as soon as the steamers tied up, the boisterous, dirty soldiers stamped aboard, along with cargo, horses, and livestock. It was a matter of coaling up, and the side-wheelers were off again, paddling up river.

While the *Sultana* was delayed for boiler repairs, the *Olive Branch* arrived and took a load. The *Pauline Carroll* then warped to the Vicksburg wharves. At that point, Captain Mason said the *Sultana* was ready.

It was a case of more passengers, more fares. It seemed to many on the crowded *Sultana* that the load should have been divided between her and the *Olive Branch*, another river "tramp."

Besides the freed prisoners of war, there were two companies of armed infantry, both to protect the steamer from guerrillas and to guard a group of Confederate prisoners. Twelve ladies of the Christian Commission also were aboard.

In addition to the animals on the *Sultana*, the cargo included one hundred hogsheads of sugar, for ballast.

In Helena, Arkansas, and later at Memphis, much of the cargo was unloaded. The passengers, who had turned to as stevedores to earn extra money, were glad to see the livestock off. But the smell remained.

Lieutenant Joe Elliott was impressed with the "careful" qualities of the *Sultana's* captain at Helena, where he cautioned the passengers not to crowd to one side of the boat.

After sailing from Memphis, Elliott never quite started his fight with McCoy. A friend appeared and separated the two, persuading Elliott to take another cot at the end of the same cabin. It was not long before he was in the land of dreams.

Except for the crew, almost the entire swarming boatload of humanity had joined Joe Elliott in his dreamworld by two A.M. Those without the blandishment of cots slept from exhaustion, wherever they had curled up and in whatever position.

At this hour, Mason was picking up the misty outlines of the Old Hen and Chickens Islands. The drizzle continued but visibility was somewhat improved.

The *Sultana* was opposite Tagleman's Landing. Mason had but to pass between the island scattering and the landing and he would be in the clear. In fact, the Mississippi was three miles wide here.

Anchored two miles south of Tagleman's was the ironclad *U.S.S. Essex*, battle-scarred veteran of river warfare. Her young executive officer, Ensign James H. Berry, had "hit the sack" for the night. On watch was Ensign Earnshaw. At two A.M, he logged the passage upriver of a "large side-wheeler," prominently illuminated. There was, however, no way of identifying it.

On shore, the sentries of Fort Pickering swung their arms in the gathering chill and dampness. The soldiers belonged to Company A. Third U.S. Colored Artillery (Heavy). Their officer, Lieutenant Wilson, had briefed them on the continuing danger of guerrillas, after he in turn had been briefed by Colonel I. G. Kappner, in command of the fort.

The men obtained the impression from Wilson that they should shoot at anything which moved on the river or along its banks. Indeed, every picket hoped that something, somewhere might move before dawn, and break the monotony of their long watch.

Chester Berry, the young man from South Creek, Pennsylvania, had also been concerned over the threat from die-hard Confederates. He noted:

"It would be a grand opportunity for guerrillas. If they only knew that there was such a boatload of prisoners coming up the river, how they could plant a battery on the shore, sink the boat, and destroy nearly if not all of the prisoners on board."

The *Sultana* was poking her blunt prow past the first of the Old Hen and Chickens group. From the bridge, the spring chorus of young frogs could be heard croaking in the marshy islands.

It was Thusday, April 27th.

Berry's abrupt realization that something had happened was impelled by a stick of cord wood striking him on the head. He was sure it had fractured his skull.

"The first thought I had was that while the boat lay at Memphis someone had gone up the river and prepared such a reception for us and that what had only been *talk* was now a realization. I lay low for a moment, when the hot water soaking through my blanket made me think I had better move. I sprang to the bow of the boat, and turning, looked back upon one of the most terrible scenes I ever beheld. The upper decks of the boat were a complete wreck and the dry casings of the cabins, falling in upon the hot bed of coal, were burning like tinder. A few pailsful of water would have put the fire out, but, alas, it was ten feet to the water and there was no rope to draw with; consequently the flames swept fiercely through the light wood of the upper decks.

"I had often read of burning vessels and nights of horror on the deep, and almost my first thought was, 'Now, take in the scene,' but self-preservation stood out strongest. I went back to where I had lain and found my bunkmate, Busley, scalded to death; I then secured a piece of cabin door casing, about three or four inches wide and about four feet long; then going back to the bow of the boat I came to the conclusion I did not want to take to the water just then, for it was literally black with human beings, many of whom were sinking and taking others with them. Being a good swimmer, and having board enough to save me, even if I were not, I concluded to wait till the rush was over."

Otto Barden, of Wooster, Ohio, who had been sleeping in the engine room, was spared, even though he was in the center of the blast—apparently caused by the patched-up boiler exploding. He wrote:

"Hot steam, smoke, pieces of brickbats and chunks of coal came thick and fast. I gasped for breath. A fire broke out that lighted up the whole river. I stood at this hatch-hole to keep comrades from falling in, for the top was blown off by the explosion. I stood here until the fire compelled me to leave. I helped several out of this place. I saw Jonas Huntsberger and John Baney go to the wheel house, then I started in the same direction. I tried to get a large plank, but this was too heavy, so I left it and got a small board and started to the wheel to jump into the water. Here a young man said to me, 'You jump first, I cannot swim.' This man had all of his clothes on. I had just my shirt and pants on. I said to him, 'You must paddle your own canoe, I can't help you.' Then I jumped and stuck to my board."

On deck, soldiers such as P. L. Horn, also of Wooster, Ohio, and William H. Norton, of Summit County, Ohio, prepared to abandon the burning packet. Norton listened in morbid fascination to "that awful wail of hundreds of human beings burning alive in the cabins and under the fallen timbers." Horn reacted with less mental detachment. He took off his coat and shoes, then plunged overboard, certain the Confederates had blown up the vessel.

Twenty-two-year-old J. P. Zaizer of Limaville, Ohio, had been asleep on the upper deck, close to the steamer's bronze bell. He wrote: "The smoke stack fell across it and split and one half of it fell over, thereby killing Sgt. Smith who laid by us. I jumped overboard."

Chief Engineer Nate Wintringer, sure his assistant Clemmans must have expired in the holocaust below, was of a similar frame of mind as Horn:

"I stood bewildered for a moment, and then saw the river perfectly alive with human beings struggling in the water, and the cry from all quarters was 'Put out the fire!' which was getting good headway by this time. But there was such a mass of confusion and such a complete wreck of the boat that nobody, apparently, could get out of the position they were in. I managed to get hold of a shutter and saw that the fire would soon force me off of the boat; I took my chances and jumped into the river."

Ensign Berry, on the Essex, was awakened by a pounding on his door. Earnshaw, his watch officer, had shocking news: a side-wheeler had blown up within sight of the ironclad's anchorage, and was burning furiously, showering sparks high into the dark night.

"I ordered all the boats manned," reported Berry, "which was done immediately, and I went in the cutter, which boat was the first ready, and we went out to the middle of the river. The morning was very dark, it being about one hour before daylight and the weather overcast, and the shrieks of the wounded and drowning men was the only guide we had. The first man we picked up was chilled and so benumbed that he couldn't help himself, and the second one died a short time after he was taken on board. We soon drifted down to Fort Pickering, when the sentry on the shore fired at us, and we were obliged to 'come to' while the poor fellows near us were crying out and imploring us for God's sake to save them; that they couldn't hold out much longer.

"We pulled a short distance toward the shore and hailed the sentry, who ordered me to come on shore, and who, it seems, had not hailed me before, or if he had his hail had been drowned by the groans of the men drowning in the water. I asked the sentry why he had fired at me, and he said that he had obeyed his orders. I told the sentry what had happened, and that I was picking up drowning men.

"The sentry did not give me any answer, and we went out again to the middle of the river, where we fell in with the gig laying near a lot of drift which was covered with men drowning, who were so benumbed that my boats' crews were obliged to handle them as if they were dead men."

P. L. Horn, of Wooster, went down twice before he managed to maintain his head above water by kicking and dog-paddling. There was no question in the Ohioan's mind now, though his first sleepy belief had been that this was another railroad wreck. Only weeks ago he had survived a prison train smashup near Athens, Georgia.

"When I collided with the water this impression was soon corrected. How far or how high I was blown into the air I do not know, but I remember that my feet first struck the water and with the exception of being slightly hurt on my left side I suffered but little from the shock. It was not a laughable matter when during the night we were clinging with a death grip to the wreck, and a mule—another floating waif of this disaster—swam along and dumped us all into the river, compelling us all to exert our strength to regain our hold on the wreck. The current at times would compel the men to relax their grip and with the greatest difficulty they would recover it again."

The "wreck," it turned out, was a part of the Sultana's deck stairs. Joseph McKelvey, who had been sleeping next to him, soon joined Horn on the half-awash place of refuge.

"Are you hurt?" Horn asked.

"Yes," McKelvey gasped. "Scalded from head to foot."

Soon, a skiff came along. Horn and the others helped McKelvey aboard:

"The boatman removed his coat and put it around McKelvey to prevent him from taking cold. We then started up the river toward Memphis and when crossing the river in the direction of the Tennessee side (we were then on the Arkansas side), we were fired upon by some Negro guards (Union men) who thought that we were Confederates and who were guarding the river some distance below Fort Pickering."

William Norton, of Summit County, Ohio, soon came out of his trance induced by the wail of the "hundreds of human beings." He, too, went into the dark, cold Mississippi:

"As I arose to the surface several men from the boat jumped upon me and we all went down together. Others leaping on us forced us down until I despaired of ever reaching the surface again; but, by a desperate struggle, I succeeded in getting out from under them and reached the surface. I tried to swim through the crowd of men but could not. One man caught hold of me but I managed to get away from him, and not knowing what to do or which way to go I instinctively turned toward the burning boat.

"Reaching that and swimming alongside, I found the ring which is used in tying up the boat. I had no sooner caught hold of it than a drowning man clasped his arms around me in a death grip.

"I told him he must let go, but it was of no use; he never said a word, but all the while I could feel his arms tightening around me. Hanging on to the ring, with one hand I tried to free myself from him with the other but could not. The situation was becoming terrible.

"To let go the ring was death to both of us. The strain on my arm was such that I could not hold out but a few minutes longer. Another man now got hold of the ring and still another grasped him by the throat and a desperate struggle was going on between them."

Meanwhile, Otto Barden, the Ohio boy, was having similar experiences. Altogether, it had been a bad war. Last fall, he had been captured by General Bedford Forrest's cavalry.

"I went down so far," he noted, "that I let go of my board and paddled to get on top of the water. I strangled twice before I reached the top; then the young man caught me and he strangled me twice. By this time I was about played out. I then reached the wheel, and clung to it until I tore off all of my clothes, with the intention of swimming with one hand. I looked around and recognized Fritz Saunders, of my regiment, by my side.

"I said: 'Saunders, here is a door under the wheel, let us get it out.' We got it out and found it had glass panels in it. I said: 'Let this go, here is a whole door.'

"The rest on the wheel took the first door and we started after them with the other. We had not more than started when a man swam up and laid across the center of our door. I looked back and saw the wheel house fall—it had burned off and fell over. If we had remained there one minute longer it would have buried us in the fire.

"I said to Saunders, 'Let's go to the right, it is nearer to shore.'

"He replied, 'No, there is a boat; I will paddle for it.'

"And when we were in the center of the river the steamer was about out of sight. We met three young men clinging to a large trunk; they grasped our door for us to steer them into the timber. We had not gone far until these bore too much weight on our door; that put us all under the water. I gave the trunk a kick and raised on the door and brought it to the surface of the water.

"Then I said: 'Boys if you don't keep your weight off of the door, then you must steer the trunk yourselves.' By this time I was cold and benumbed and was in a sinking condition, but having presence of mind, I reached and got my board and called aloud to God for help. I rubbed my arms and got the blood in circulation again."

Chester Berry, of South Creek, realized he was in poor shape to face the exigencies of such a night. He had been captured at Fredericksburg and had suffered from typhoid fever in addition to the usual hardships of prison camp. He recorded:

"Such swearing, praying, shouting and crying I had never heard; and much of it from the same throat—imprecations followed by petitions to the Almighty, denunciations, by bitter weeping. I stood still and watched for a while, then began wandering around to other parts of the boat, when I came across one man who was weeping bitterly and wringing his hands as if in terrible agony, continually crying: 'O dear, O dear.' I supposed the poor fellow was seriously hurt. My sympathies were aroused at once. Approaching him, I took him by the shoulder and asked where he was hurt.

" 'I'm not hurt at all,' he said, 'but I can't swim, I've got to drown. O dear.'

"I bade him be quiet, then showing him my little board I said to him: 'There, do you see that; now you go to that pile of broken deck and get you one like it, and when you jump into the water put it under your chin and you can't drown.'

" 'But I did get one,' said he, 'and someone snatched it away from me.'

" 'Well, then, get another,' said I.

" 'I did,' said he, 'and they took that away from me.'

" 'Well then,' said I, 'get another.'

" 'Why,' said he, 'what would be the use, they would take it from me. O dear, I tell you there is no use; I've got to drown, I can't swim.'

"By this time I was thoroughly disgusted, and giving him a shove, I said: 'Drown then, you fool.'

"After looking at the burning boat as long as I cared to, and as the waters were comparatively clear of men, I sprang overboard and struck out for some willows that I could see by the light of the burning boat, they appearing to be about one-half mile distant. I had gone but about twenty or thirty rods when, hearing a crash of breaking timbers, I looked back. The wheel house or covering for the wheel (it was a side-wheel steamer) had broken away partially from the hurricane deck, and a poor fellow had been in the act of stepping from the hurricane deck onto the wheel house. I presume it was then the hurricane deck fell in. When it reached an angle of about forty-five degrees it stopped, for some unaccountable reason, till it nearly burned up. He succeeded in reaching the wheel house but got no further, for it broke and let him part way through, then held him as in an iron vise till he burned to death."

Lieutenant Joe Elliott, who had been dreaming that he was

"in the regions of eternal torment," noticed with surprise that many men slept on after the explosion.

"The thought came to me," he recalled, "that I had the nightmare, and in that condition of mind I turned around and made for the stern of the boat, hardly knowing what I was doing. The ladies' cabin was shut off from the men's cabin only by curtains, and I pushed back a curtain and started through, when I was confronted by a lady, who I supposed was in charge of the cabin, with: 'What do you want in here, sir?' I paid no attention to her but went ahead, saying that there was something wrong with the boat.

"I went on through the cabin to the stern of the boat and climbed up to the hurricane deck. Throwing myself across the bulwark around the deck, I looked forward toward the jackstaff. The boat's bow was turned toward the Tennessee shore, one of the boat's chimneys was down, and all the men were in commotion. As I started back, realizing that it was not a dream, I heard the men calling: 'Don't jump; we are going ashore.'

"I answered, saying that I was going back to where I came from. On getting back and looking down into the river, I saw that the men were jumping from all parts of the boat into the river. Such screams I never heard—twenty or thirty men jumping off at a time—many lighting on those already in the water—until the river became black with men, their heads bobbing up like corks, and many disappearing never to appear again. We threw over everything that would float that we could get hold of, for their assistance; and then I, with several others, began tearing the sheeting off the sides of the cabin, and throwing it over. While doing this I became more calm and self-possessed.

"About this time one of the Tenth Indiana Cavalry boys came to me, asking: 'Have you seen my father?' I said, 'I have not; but I know the stateroom he occupied,' and started with him to go into the ladies' cabin. As we entered the door we met his father, who was coming out. They threw their arms around each other, and as they embraced I looked up to the ceiling and saw the fire jumping along from one cross-piece to another in a way that made me think of a lizard running along a fence.

"I now made up my mind to leave the boat, and walked around the right side of the cabin to the wheel house. I feared that it was too far to jump, and on looking over to see what the distance was, I saw one of the fenders hanging just behind the wheel house. I lost no time climbing over the side of the boat and 'cooning it' down to the lower deck. This feat was accomplished so easily that I could never tell just how it was done. Casting my eyes around, I could see nobody, and stepping to the edge of the boat and looking to see that the river was free from any poor struggling soldier, I dived off. I knew that I could do no more than save myself, and as I had the utmost confidence in my swimming ability, I had some hopes of gaining the shore.

"I had no sooner struck the water than I saw that I could not depend altogether on my own exertions, for as I went into the river it was colder than 'Greenland's icy mountains,' and I went down so far that I thought I would never come up. Then my drawers began to slip down around my feet, and it became necessary to get rid of them as soon as possible. I finally got them off and struck out for the shore. Having gone about fifty feet from the burning vessel, I came to a man who was supporting himself on the steps that had led up over the wheel house from the cabin deck to the hurricane deck. I asked him if they would support two, and he said to come ahead."

Berry, meanwhile, was struggling toward the Old Hen and Chickens group, exhausting himself, unwittingly, in swimming upstream:

"Being now quite despondent, I had about concluded that there was no use of my trying to save myself, that I would drown in spite of my efforts; and that to throw my board away and sink at once would be only to shorten my misery. I was just in the act of doing so when it seemed to me that I was transported for the moment to 'the old house at home,' and that I was wending my way slowly up the path from the road gate to the house, but, strange for me, when I reached the door, instead of entering at once, I sat upon the step.

"My mother was an earnest, devoted Christian; also my father had been, but Father was deaf and dumb, consequently the family devotions fell to Mother, and I knew that in the years of my home life, that if one of the family were away from home during the hour for prayer, nine o'clock in the evening, that one was especially remembered in the prayer. As I sat upon the step I thought it was nine o'clock in the evening, and as plainly as I ever heard my mother's voice, I heard it that evening. I cared but little for the prayer until she reached that portion that referred to the absent one, when all the mother-soul seemed to go up in earnest petition—'God save my boy.'

"For ten long weary months she had received no tidings from her soldier boy, now she had just learned that he was on his way home and her thoughts were almost constantly upon him; and for him her earnest prayer was made. I fiercely clutched the board and hissed between my now firmly set teeth: 'Mother, by the help of God, your prayer shall be answered.' I started out for a grand effort.

"Just then I heard a glad cry from the burning boat and looking around, discovered that past the boat, down the river, two or three miles as near as I could judge, was the bow light of a gunboat."

Ensign Berry, of the *Essex*, trying to bring in another load of survivors in that gunboat's skiff, was encountering opposition once more from Fort Pickering's sentries:

"Before we had taken in half of them another shot was fired from the fort, and came whistling over our heads, and I saw that they were determined to make me come ashore. It was now day-light and though our two boats and a steamboat's yawl, which came out to lend us a hand, made a large mark to shoot at, I would not leave the poor fellows in the water to attend the sentry on shore. When the day began to dawn the cries of the sufferers ceased, and all who had not been rescued had gone down, and I, fearing that I might be fired at again, went to the shore, and when I saw the sentry he had again raised his musket, and I called out to him not to shoot, and at the same time told the sentry, who was a Negro, that if there was an officer there I wished to see him."

Meanwhile, Barden reached a tree on the mid-river island group, Horn was picked up by a river steamer, and Norton broke the death-grip of the man who had been clutching him. But Norton's troubles were not over, as he reported:

"Suffering with a cramp in my stomach, benumbed with the cold, it seemed as if I could go no farther, but if I stopped swim-ming I found myself sinking, and again would try to keep afloat. In this way I kept along. I could hear the cries of those that were burned and scalded screaming with pain at every breath, and men all along the river were calling for help. Away in the dis-tance, floating down the river, was the burning boat with a few brave men fighting the fire with buckets of water. Looking to my left I thought I could see the trees through the darkness. This gave me new courage and I turned in that direction and soon some brush struck me in the face. A little farther on I was washed up against a log which had caught in the young cotton-wood trees."

Lieutenant Joe Elliott, rid of his slipping underwear, had come upon another floating staircase. From its vantage point he watched the death throes of the *Sultana*, which was drifting along beside him, closer than he preferred.

"It looked like a huge bonfire in the middle of the river," he noted. "As the flames ascended, mingled with smoke, and shed their peculiar light on the water, we could see both sides—bluffs on one side and timber on the other, and with no sensation as to the moving current. It was more like one of those beautiful lakes that I have seen in Minnesota, and if it had been only a painting it would have been grand; but, alas! it was all real, and as I floated along with the current this sad picture was before me as a panorama. The men who were afraid to take to the water could be seen clinging to the sides of the boat until they were singed off like flies. Shrieks and cries for mercy were all that could be heard."

With a great hissing, the flaming *Sultana* finally vanished beneath the river waters, ending the sounds and the sights that had so appalled him. He floated on.

"One man who passed us was bobbing up and down in a way that reminded me of the frog in the game of leap-frog. As he came within a few feet of us, I asked him what he was on, and he answered me: 'Don't touch me; I am on a barrel.' He actually was astraddle a barrel, holding on to the rim, and at any other time his queer motion would have been laughable.

"We finally came up with a man who was on the end of a large log, and with his consent we joined forces, one of our men throwing himself partly on the log and partly on the steps. The other man then crawled over onto the log and I crawled up on the steps, where I was when I was picked up. We made no further exertions to get on shore, but floated on down the river with the current. I must have become unconscious or only semiconscious, as I have no recollection of how the steps got separated from the log. I remember passing Memphis, and seeing the gas lights burning in the streets. Then it is all blank until I heard the splash of an oar, and tried to call for help, but my voice seemed to have left me. It was some such feeling as when one tries to call out in a nightmare."

Chester Berry could not reach the gunboat.

"I turned," he continued, "and now was obliged to swim past the burning boat, for I was up the river about eighty rods above it; when nearly past the boat which I kept a safe distance to my left, I ran into the top of a tree that had caved off from the bank and whose roots were now fast in the bed of the stream, upon which I climbed and was nearly asleep when a number of men from the boat came along and climbed upon it, also. Their united weight sank it low into the water, whose icy coldness coming upon my body again awakened me. Then, to more fully arouse me, a man got hold of my board and tried to take it away from me. I remonstrated with him, but he claimed the board belonged to him and that I was trying to steal it. This fully aroused me—it was the straw that broke the camel's back. Giving the board a quick jerk I sprang backward and went swimming down the stream on my back, holding my board high lest I might lose it. I soon turned over and proceeded more slowly. I began again to have an almost irresistible feeling of drowsiness. I was cold and sleepy.

"Just then I came across, or thought I did, a dry black ash sapling about two and one-half or three inches in diameter at the butt and six or eight feet long, that pronged in two branches about three feet from the butt end. I put this with my board and trying them found they would float. I then gave myself up to sleep and did not awake until long after sunrise."

Providentially, the steamer *Pocahontas* arrived and rescued Chester Berry. At the same time, his namesake, Ensign Berry of the *U.S.S. Essex*, was arguing with an officer at Fort Pickering.

"I told him," recorded Ensign Berry, "that these boats were not skiffs, that they were a man-of-war's gig and cutter, and again reminded him of what had happened and of the drowning men whose cries he could not help hearing, and asked him why, for the sake of humanity, he could not execute his orders with

some discretion in a time like this. He said that he had as much
humanity as anyone, and in firing at me he had only obeyed
orders.

"I saw a number of skiffs and other boats laying hauled up out
of the water, and from appearances no one had made any attempt to launch them."

· Barden was rescued from his tree by a steamer. Near him was a
man who had clung all night to a trunk spewed up from the
Sultana's luggage rooms. When he was lifted from it, he was
dead. The trunk itself was found to contain women's clothing.

Nate Wintringer, the chief engineer, was taken from a large
plank, which he had shared with four other men. One of them,
however, slipped off and sank, but a few minutes before rescue.

Norton was saved by a canoeist who paddled out from the
Arkansas shore. Elliott, who had called out to a boatman as
though "in a nightmare," had succeeded in attracting attention,
in spite of his fears that his voice had become paralyzed. It
turned out to be one of the boats from the *Essex*.

He was, however, fired upon by the pickets, as had been the
fortune of Ensign Berry and others, before reaching the final
safety of the ironclad. In fact, not until Colonel Kappner, the
commandant of Fort Pickering, made his presence known in
mid-morning did the over-zealous sentries become convinced of
the folly of their ways.

Now the river fort joined the city of Memphis in an attempt
to treat medically and feed and dress in dry clothing those who
had survived the night's horror. Their condition was "pitiable,"
Surgeon H. H. Hood commented as he commandeered ambu-
lances and spread row upon row of cots in the post hospital.

Survivors such as Chester Berry, however, thought the attention they received was minimum enough. His fractured skull
was not dressed to his satisfaction nor were the "broken pieces"
removed. Worst of all, it seemed to him, the army advised his

mother that he was dead (and no one told her otherwise for
three months, when he himself continued his interrupted
journey to Pennsylvania).

Eleven of the twelve women of the Christian Commission
were lost, including a bride (and her husband) and one who had
refused to jump. She feared that her presence in the water
would result in added panic and confusion on the part of men
swimmers who might try to rescue her.

Captain Mason perished, as did most of the crew. All told, no
less than sixteen hundred lives were lost that night on the
Mississippi, out of the twenty-three hundred or more who had
sailed from Vicksburg on the *Sultana's* last voyage.

Immediately after the tragedy, investigations and court-
martials ensued. But it was too late now to bring back either the
big river packet or the lives of those who had gone with her. The
worst war in history had just ended and peoples' capacity for
shock was dulled.

There remained but the inevitable post-mortems—the forma-
tion of a *Sultana* Survivors Society, the preparation of personal
narratives and, in some cases, of poems. William H. Norton
devoted considerable time to his treatment of this latest of the
tragic lore of the Mississippi:

> On sails the steamer through the gloom,
> On sleep the soldiers to their doom.
> And death's dark angel—oh, so soon,
> Calls loud the muster roll!
> A burst, a crash, and timbers fly,
> And flame—and steam—leap to the sky,
> And men, awakened but to die,
> Commend to God their souls.

And so it went, for many verses, a threnody for a ship disaster
that has not been equaled on America's waterways or upon the
sea off its coasts.

Disaster in '73

THE CIVIL WAR HAD BEEN OVER EIGHT YEARS. COMMERCE WITH the world had not only returned to normal but was mounting to peaks which could not have been predicted at the time of Fort Sumter.

Shipbuilding had to keep pace, in volume as well as quality. Large, faster vessels were coming off the ways in Europe and in America. Two of the greyhounds in 1873 were the *Atlantic*, of the White Star Line, and the *Ville-du-Havre*, of French registry.

Aside from their size and luxury, the two liners shared yet another and far more important common denominator that year. Both had a rendezvous with destiny.

The *Atlantic*, with an overall length of 420 feet, carried 931 persons when she sailed from Liverpool on March 20th. For five days, the big liner's passengers enjoyed smooth sailing. On March 25th, she encountered gales. By the next day, her captain, James A. Williams, recorded that the storms had reduced progress to 118 miles a day.

The weather had a depressing effect on crew as well as passengers, so much so on the former that the tougher members attempted to break into the ship's wine stores. One seaman went so far as to steal the storekeeper's watch out of his pocket.

"On the 31st of March," observed the captain, "the engineer's report showed but about 127 tons of coal on board. We were 460 miles east of Sandy Hook, wind southwest and a high westerly swell and a falling barometer.

"Considered the risk too great to push on as we might find ourselves in the event of a gale shut out from any port of supply, and so decided to bear up for Halifax.

"At 1 p.m. on the 31st, Sambro Island, North 5 degrees East, was distant 170 miles, the ship's speed varying from eight knots to twelve. The wind was south during the first part, with rain, veered to westward at 8 p.m., with clear weather.

"At midnight I judged the ship to have made 122 miles which would place her 48 miles south of Sambro. I then left the deck and went into the chart room, leaving orders about the lookouts, and to let me know if they saw anything, and call me at 3 a.m.— intending to put the ship's head off to southward, and await daylight."

Benjamin Burns, one of the few steerage passengers from Scotland (the majority being German) turned in about 11 p.m., this last Monday in March.

"The night was dark," he recalled, "but starlight, and the weather fine. I knew the ship was going into Halifax for coal.

"The last I remembered was that two bells [one o'clock] struck. I then went to sleep."

At 2 a.m. Quartermaster Thomas Dunn walked onto the bridge in company with the second officer, Henry Metcalf. The wind was blowing, Dunn knew land was near, and altogether he felt there was justifiable cause for concern, even though the captain had not seen fit to remain on his bridge.

"I told him [Metcalf] not to stand into the land," the quartermaster declared, "as the ship had run her distance to make the Sambro light from my calculations.

"He told me that I was neither captain nor mate. I then went to the fourth officer, Mr. John Brown, and asked him if I should go on the main yard, as he could not see the land until he struck on it.

"He told me that it was no use for me to go up. I then relieved the man at the wheel. At 2:30, the second officer told the captain, who was reposing in the chart room, that weather was getting thick.

"The second officer went outside of the chart room, when the man on the lookout called out: 'Land ahead!'

"The second officer ran and told the captain that they were among the ice."

During this time, Quartermaster Charles Raylance, who had been relieved by Thomas Dunn, had gone aft to check the taffrail log, a propeller device towed astern to record the speed of the ship.

"I hove the log," he wrote, "and the ship at that time was going at the rate of twelve knots. I went into the aft wheel house and was looking through one of the windows when I fancied I saw breakers on the starboard side.

"I then ran forward to the lookout man on the bridge and I asked him if he did not think there were breakers on the starboard side."

At this point, Raylance, Dunn, the lookouts, and second officer Metcalf were in agreement that land was looming dead ahead, with the imminence of doom.

"Hard a-starboard!" shouted Metcalf, at the same time grabbing the engine room telegraph lever and pushing it to "full speed astern."

Yet, neither the second officer nor Quartermaster Raylance had much faith that the last-moment commands would save the *Atlantic* from grinding ashore. Reflexively, the two leaped off the bridge and onto the boat deck immediately below.

In steerage, Benjamin Burns awoke "with a shock," still

drugged from sleep. He remarked to the man in the opposite bunk:

"There goes the anchor."

He thought they were safe in Halifax harbor. But as soon as the ship made a second plunge he cried:

"Good God, she's ashore!"

With that, the pair arose and dressed.

John Hinley, twelve, of Lancashire, who was traveling with his mother, father, and younger brother, was awakened by a "great noise." He thought it strange, however, that he did not hear any shouting, or even voices.

Captain Williams insisted his first intimation of the catastrophe was when the *Atlantic* struck. As he came on deck, waves were already tearing at the lifeboats.

The White Star liner was hard on the rocky ledges off Mars Head, an outjutting of Nova Scotia, almost at the mouth of Halifax's broad harbor. Sambro Island's commanding white octagon light would have hove into view in another few minutes.

It was about 3:15 A.M., Tuesday, All Fool's Day.

The two quartermasters were dispatched to summon all hands on deck and to awaken passengers who still slept. Of the latter, there appeared to be very few.

Quartermaster Dunn, who had gone aft to distribute fire axes for hacking through boat tackle, heard a woman shouting over and over, "Robert, where are you?"

She told Dunn her name was Mrs. Munney, from Liverpool, and that she had become separated from her son Robert and brother Alfred. In a moment, Dunn located the child and led him and his mother to the saloon deck. "Wait here," he advised, "until I can get the boats clear and help you into one."

Yet, even as he endeavored to reassure them, the liner suddenly shifted position on its rocky perch, listing so precipitously that mother and son were hurled into the sea.

Quartermaster Raylance ran forward to summon the three other quartermasters. He found they were trapped in their fo'csle behind a jammed door. Raylance, an unusually muscular man for his medium size, battered the door into kindling with his hands and feet, and his associates climbed out.

The four of them then procured rockets and fired them into the gloom. They blossomed prettily in all colors, but brought no answer.

"Get the boats clear and save the passengers!" the captain ordered.

Raylance and Captain Williams then proceeded to the Number 1 boat, already half-filled with passengers.

"Are the plugs in her?" Williams asked.

"They are not," the quartermaster replied.

There were so many frightened women and children—plus a few men—huddled in the bottom of the boat that Raylance was unable to reach the plugs. The captain shrugged in a gesture of hopelessness.

Little John Hinley, of Lancashire, meanwhile stumbled into the passageway. He was swept back by a great rush of people. It seemed some minutes before most of them had fought their way past and he was able to edge his way along the passage until he came to an opened steerage room.

There he observed an incredible spectacle: six men crowding into an upper berth. When he looked closer, he realized they were battering at a porthole in an effort to open it. The men paused long enough to hoist him up, and, as soon as the window was opened, they shoved him through.

Steerage passenger Burns encountered the same impenetrable mass of terrified people in the passageway as the Hinley boy had.

He also noted that the seas were commencing to enter the companionway.

"I got as many as possible to take to the bunks and hold on by the iron stanchions."

In their small cabin they waited, cold and apprehensive, listening, noting the increasing list.

The work of getting boats over the side had to be abandoned. Within ten minutes of striking Mars Head, the *Atlantic* had keeled too far to port to lower either side's boats.

"Seeing that no help could be got from the boats," Captain Williams reported, "I got the passengers into the rigging and outside the rails, and encouraged them to go forward where the ship was highest and less exposed to the water.

"The third officer, Cornelius Brady, and Quartermasters Owens and Speakman, by this time having established communication with the outlying rock, about forty yards distant, by a line got our other lines to the rock."

Quartermaster Dunn himself swam ashore with the three other men who had braved the surf and rocks.

"I traversed from rock to rock, falling sometimes from exhaustion, until I found the signal post, a place where the fishermen have to look out and signalize to the boats. I then called out for help.

"Two old men and a boy came to our assistance. I went to the house with them, and procured a line and retraced my steps to the beach, where I saw a lot of passengers and crew upon the rock.

"Speakman the quartermaster swam toward me with a line from the rock, and I hove my line and caught him and pulled him ashore.

"As soon as I had done this we hauled in the line, which he had from the rock, and made fast the end of my line to it, so as to make it stronger.

"As soon as I got the line made fast, I told those who were on the rock to come on shore one by one, as I would save them.

"The first man saved in this way I don't know, but the second one was Mr. Brady, third officer. I saved in this manner about seventy as near as I can remember. In some instances, as the line was some distance overhead and the persons too exhausted, I had to reach down and pull them up. Some I had to go into the water for, it being out of my depth, with a line fastened around my waist.

"In this manner the two old men would drag me and the man I rescued ashore. I remained there from four until nine, when I fell down through exhaustion."

"Between the rock and the shore was a passage one hundred yards wide," the captain reported. "A rope was successfully passed across this, by which means about fifty got to the land, though many were drowned in the attempt.

"At 5 o'clock A.M. the first boat appeared from the island but she was too small to be of any assistance. Through exertions of Mr. Brady, the islanders were aroused and by 6 o'clock A.M. three large boats came to our assistance.

"By their efforts, all that remained on the side of the ship and on the rock were landed in safety and cared for by a poor fisherman named Clancy and his daughter.

"Before the boats went out I placed two ladies in the lifeboat but finding the boat useless carried them to the main rigging where I left them and went off to encourage the others to go forward on the side of the ship.

"At this juncture the boilers exploded and the boat rolled over to leeward, the ship this time being on her beam ends.

"Finding myself useless there, I went to take the ladies forward, but found them gone, nor did I see them afterward.

"Many passengers at this point could not be stimulated to

any effort to save themselves, but lay in the rigging and died from fright and exposure."

It was bright daylight when Burns, the steerage passenger, decided to quit his bunk. Others had been drowned around him.

"I remained until all who were alive were out. I got out through a port and held fast to the side of the ship for about two hours and then went to the shore by the lifeline."

As he moved to safety, he noticed that many still clung to the rigging, reminding him of large, stunned birds.

The lad John Hinley came ashore at about the same time. He had held to the rope until one of the shore boats came for him.

Captain Williams remained on the side of the almost over-turned vessel, "encouraging, helping and directing until fifteen were landed, when finding my hands and legs were becoming useless, I left the ship, two other boats being close to, and embarked the remainder.

"On reaching shore, I dispatched Mr. Brady, the third officer, off to Halifax across the country to telegraph the news of the disaster and to obtain assistance."

Quartermaster Dunn was relieved by one of the stewards just after the chief steward, Hugh Christie, was drowned within a few feet of safety. Almost ashore, Christie was seized around the neck by a crazed passenger. The two plunged into the cold surf and never reappeared.

Quartermaster Dunn was carried into one of the fishermen's huts, given warm clothing, and put to bed.

By midmorning, one singularly tragic aspect of the sinking became apparent. Not one woman had been helped ashore.

James Bateman, of London, had succeeded in assisting his wife into the rigging, a refuge attained by few other ladies. Weakened by exposure, however, she soon fell off into the sea.

Bateman himself came ashore later in the morning, babbling "like one demented."

Twelve-year-old John Hinley proved to be the only child saved. He solemnly informed the Nova Scotian fishermen that he would continue his journey to New York, for the visit with his two married sisters which his family had planned. He would go alone now, for his mother, father, and little brother were drowned.

"During the day," added Captain Williams, "the survivors to the number of 429 were drafted off to the various houses scattered about, the resident magistrate, Edmund Ryan, rendering valuable assistance.

"The chief officer having got up the mizzen rigging, the sea cut off his retreat. He stood for six hours by a woman who had been placed in the rigging. Sea was too high to attempt his rescue. At 3 P.M. a clergyman, Reverend Mr. Ancient succeeded in getting him a line and getting him off. Many of the passengers, saloon and steerage, died in the rigging, of cold, among the number the purser of the ship."

Stories of individual tragedy were legion. One man, who emigrated to the United States the previous year, had returned to Ireland to fetch his wife and five children. All died in the early morning hours off Nova Scotia. At least twenty persons were crushed when a forward boom swung wild. One man, clad only in a shirt, fastened two life buoys around his waist and jumped, but drowned before reaching shore.

Chief Officer J. W. Firth was one of the last off the ship. He stayed in the rigging with the woman whose child had earlier been swept away. He remained at her side until she was able to hold on no longer, even with assistance, and fell into the sea.

Evening came; the survivors awaited the steamers that were en route to bring them to Halifax—a port they would have made in safety except for a rock and a captain who neglected to take soundings.

Captain Williams' error cost him his master's certificate,

which was suspended, and cost more than five hundred of his passengers their lives.

In Halifax, a reporter several days later penned his own "amen" to the disaster with the laconic item: "A large number of coffins have been made here and sent to the scene of the wreck."

The year moved ahead. On November 15th, 135 passengers (plus six stowaways) walked aboard the "luxury" 5,100-ton steam packet, Ville-du-Havre. She was bound out of New York for the city of her christening.

The crew was large, 172, under the command of Captain Marius Surmonte. On this round trip he had brought along his wife and children. In fact, those who had come to wave at the Hudson River dock commented on how many wives—and youngsters—were sailing that Saturday.

There was a heavy burden of cargo to be lowered into the Ville-du-Havre's cavernous holds—mostly wheat, cotton, and grease—which kept the swift transatlantic ship tethered past her hour of departure. The wait, however, made possible the delivery of late gifts for the voyagers.

Marie, or "Lallie," for example, the daughter of Mrs. Mary Adams Bulkley, of Rye, New York, was "overwhelmed," as her mother mentioned, with "offerings of flowers and fruits." A little friend, Helen Waghstoff, of Long Island, being shepherded to France by Mrs. Bulkley, received almost as many presents.

Passengers such as the Reverend Nathaniel Weiss, of Paris, a delegate to the Evangelical Alliance Conference, just concluded, or the Reverend Emile Cook, consumed the extra time in port by sober reflection and prayer.

Then, when the sun was lower over the Palisades, the Ville-du-Havre was ready. Her lines were cast off. The tired friends on the pier waved. A very few cried. The "magnificent" 403-foot packet was on her way.

At 9 P.M., however, Captain Surmonte, who had cheerily remarked: "It's always good weather when we leave New York," had reason to doubt the propitious qualities of the day. Trouble with the propeller shaft necessitated stopping the steam pistons.

Sails were unfurled from the vessel's fore and aft masts and for nearly five hours these were the Ville-du-Havre's only means of propulsion.

Repairs completed, the liner sailed on. The night sparkled with stars.

Sunday dawned mild. There was praying and hymn-singing as Nathaniel Weiss, Pastor Cook, and others petitioned the Lord for a felicitous passage. Mrs. Mary Bulkley spent her time on deck with the children, drinking in "a delicious atmosphere and sunny sky."

On Monday afternoon, grey fog rolled in from Newfoundland and the Grand Banks. The whistle began to sound lugubriously. As many Cassandras had predicted, wind and rain arrived in the van of fog. Few people appeared for Tuesday breakfast, since the packet was wallowing in a beam sea. It appeared to Mary Bulkley that the "roof" of her cabin leaked. Even so, with her daughter and her charge, she kept close to the little sanctuary.

Nat Weiss, a student of the Old Testament, bundled into his heaviest clothes after breakfast and hurried onto deck. There, fully enjoying the "beauty of the storm," he wrote:

"To be prepared for the constant shocks which the ship receives in forcing her way through the sea, it is necessary to go forward and lean over the guards in the bow and there steady yourself enough to gaze at all this soul-stirring beauty. As the stern rises with difficulty upon the crests of these great waves, you hear the grinding of the screw, which works as if it was breaking stones. Wait a second; the prow sinks now into the sea! The stern rises so that there is a point at which the screw turns in a great space quite free from the water; when it meets the sea again, it seems as if it were cutting through marble— throwing the foam and spray in great spouts up many meters in height, and scattering them like fragments of stone under the chisel of the sculptor. A pitching motion combines with the rolling, when for an instant the ship lies stretched in the trough of a great wave, and this billow surges under the keel, turning the ship over in the opposite direction; when the screw plunges alternately left and right in the water, its movements become irregular, and cause the forward part of the ship to tremble violently. One might say, when these movements are violent and impetuous, that 'the ship was walking upon rocks.' Look back, you will be amazed to see the height and steepness of these mountains of water through which you have just passed.

"The gulls are more numerous than ever. They poise themselves with the same tranquillity above the wake of the ship, which is opal-colored, mingled with large flakes of white foam, like boiling milk. Some of them descend like lightning, having espied a morsel of bread or meat floating on the water, and it is beautiful to see them follow the undulations of the waves and seize their food, without even ruffling the water with their grey, ermine-lined wings. The sky is sombre; the sea is livid."

Few had the stamina of the Reverend Weiss to share in such proximity this "soul-stirring beauty." Judge Rufus H. Peckham, of the New York Appeals Court, perhaps the most distinguished passenger on board, had taken to his stateroom, as had the wealthy Charles Mixter, of Boston. Mixter's wife and two children, Helen and Madeline, were accompanying him to their winter home on the Riviera.

The *Ville-du-Havre*'s punishment continued through the night. The rhythm of the propeller became discordant through the loss of part of a blade. This would not endanger the vessel, the engineers agreed, but merely delay her.

Wednesday found Weiss back on deck and under the spell of the elements, as some latter day Moses on the mount, awaiting a gale-borne message. He gloried anew in the fact that "all the noises on board are swallowed up, completely lost in the screaming of the tempest."

Another passenger, venturing onto the careening, drenched deck for a brief moment, asked: "Well, are you satisfied? Is it not beautiful?"

"It is, indeed, splendid." Weiss then admitted that his lips were chapped and stung by a "very bitter, salt taste."

The other man reported he had been on the stern, which was "entirely inundated and uncomfortable." A gust of wind had caught him and lifted him off his feet "like a feather." He grasped the railing not an instant too soon.

Later in the morning Weiss returned below decks to dry his clothing, and encountered a grim scene:

"The salon looks now like an ambulance or a hospital. The ladies are all pale and weak, but resigned; the conspirators, so active just now, have disappeared one after another, to abandon themselves to quiet meditation. The children, who were lately so noisy a group, are now silently gathered in a corner; in their midst a young lady is seated, the only one to whom the sea has paid proper respect. We have seen her before this morning, gently and kindly going about, taking care of some, amusing and encouraging others, seizing every occasion to make herself useful, and to alleviate the sufferings of those attacked by the common enemy so entirely unlooked for last evening, and from which each one hoped to be exempt. She had been in the midst of the little ones since breakfast, and is telling them in English the fairy tales of Perrault. She tells them so well."

Thursday the winds somewhat abated and a fog came in, acting as a damper on the enraged seas.

"On Thursday night," Mrs. Mary Bulkley wrote, "several of the passengers acknowledged to each other that we had been apprehensive from the very first, as there seemed to be no organized discipline on board; but on Friday the fog dispelled, the young people were on deck again, and after a pleasant evening in the saloon, we all retired to our rest, more quiet in mind than we had been before on the steamer. The night was clear and starry, the sea smooth—what had we now to fear? Just as we went to bed, Lallie came to me and repeated the 'Lord is My Shepherd,' and kissed me two or three times."

At midnight, André Ernault, a Normandy seaman, took the bow watch. Captain Surmonte, exhausted after being on the bridge almost all the week, turned his ship over to the second officer and went to bed. Position was somewhere west of the Azores, he had estimated, and it looked like easy sailing to Le Havre. Auxiliary sails were set. The packet was pushing along at twelve knots.

A few minutes before 2 A.M., Ernault looked up to see a sailing ship bearing down upon the Ville-du-Havre. Since the night was clear, it was incredible to him how the other vessel had suddenly materialized.

He stared, aghast—too amazed to communicate his sighting to the bridge.

The two ships converged, closer, closer . . .

The Reverend Weiss was awakened by what sounded like "two terrific claps of thunder."

Mary Bulkley was thrown from her bunk by "an appalling crash." Next, she heard the "shriek of the whistle and human cries."

She ran, in her nightgown, into the passageway where she met the steward and ship's surgeon. They assured her that "nothing" was the matter, but she wasn't convinced. She hurried back into her cabin and told the children, Lallie, her daughter, and Helen, her young friend, to dress in their warmest clothes.

It occurred to her, even then, that they might finish the night in lifeboats.

Nathaniel Weiss pulled his trousers on and hastened down the passageway past Mary Bulkley's cabin. There the same steward she had spoken to repeated that nothing had happened. He added that the captain himself had said so.

The Paris clergyman was "not at all satisfied" and continued along passageways "already full of people who looked frightened and who were calling to the waiters, 'What has happened? What must we do?' "

Several times he heard the crewmen reply, "It is nothing, it is nothing at all. Stay quietly in your beds."

On deck, Weiss readily observed the inaccuracy of the reassurances.

"Sailors," he noted, "are laboring to loosen the ropes of the small boats; some of the crew rush about the ship in every direction, and passengers, in their nightdresses or partly dressed, are using everything in their reach to loosen the fastenings of the life preservers that are suspended along the guards.

"I approach and place myself by one of them, who is using for this purpose an enormous beam, large enough to demolish the railing. 'What are you about?' I ask; 'Is there a man overboard?'

" 'A man overboard! You do not know, then, that we are sinking?'

" 'It is possible, but you will never detach your life preserver in that way. I will find you a knife.'

"Another passenger is all prepared; he is entirely dressed and

surrounded by a life preserver. I ask him whether he knows what
has happened.

" 'No,' he replies; 'but it is necessary to be ready for anything.' "

Then a man pointed out the silhouette of a large sailing vessel,
three hundred yards distant, and Weiss knew at once what
must have happened. He asked a sailor if there had been a
collision, desiring confirmation of what seemed obvious.

"Do not be anxious, sir." the sailor replied. "If there has, even
if the water did come in through an opening, it would not sink
a ship such as this with so many decks. You need not be
troubled."

Meanwhile, Mary Bulkley, Lallie, and young Helen ran into
the passageway, prepared to abandon ship. Mrs. Bulkley saw:

"a crowd collected around the main staircase. I did not know
then that this was the spot where the collision had taken place,
but instinctively felt we must not get in the crowd, so hurried
back, and went on deck by the steerage staircase; as we reached
the deck, all was darkness and confusion. French sailors were
working at the sail boats, yelling and screaming; great flames
bursting out of the ventilator; *not an officer to be seen, not an
order given*; and very few passengers to be seen.

"We walked toward the stern of the huge vessel, stood in
front of the little saloon cabin on deck; on the right was a lifeboat, black with sailors; here, I thought, there is no hope, for
these men will swamp the boat; still I hoped that under all this
outward confusion there must be some organized system on for
our rescue. Just before us, in the starlight, a ship loomed up
against the sky; surely here must be help; not for one moment
did I suppose we were sinking; at that instant other passengers
joined us; calm and collected we all looked into each others'
faces, but no one could tell us where the danger was."

Charles B. Waite, son of the proprietor of the Brevoort

Hotel, in New York, and his sister, Julia, then arrived at Mary Bulkley's side and told her to stay where she was, and Charles would "try to lower a lifeboat." But Waite and other men attempting to help him experienced insurmountable difficulties, since, as Mrs. Bulkley continues, "not an ax or knife could they find; yet, with three minutes more these brave gentlemen, with their delicate pen knives, and their desperate strength, might have cut the boat (stiffened with recent paint) loose from the steamer; but the next instant the mast fell with crushing noise on the deck."

" 'Good God, we are shipwrecked!' cried a lady near us, a Mrs. Platt, and she burst into an eloquent prayer. Still unconscious of the immediate peril, I exclaimed, 'Perhaps the mast has been cut away purposely.'

"Lallie, Helen, and I clung together. 'Mama,' said Lallie. 'God will never desert Grandma. He has been with her through all her life.' Then she said: 'Let us pray that God will comfort all our's and Helen's friends, and make them all love our Saviour.' Poor Helen, who had never opened her lips, looked up with wondering eyes and said: 'I cannot realize anything and don't believe we can be in danger.'

"As she spoke the waters rolled over the side of the ship and struck us to our knees; still Lallie's calmness did not desert her. 'Now, Mamma, is the time to drop this'—for I still held my bag in my hand; of course, it dropped. We heard Mr. Waite's voice calling out: 'Rush to the upper side of the ship.' Lallie threw her arms around me and said: 'Forgive me, Mamma, if I have ever done wrong.'

"We started in haste for the other side of the ship; water all about us. 'Don't be frightened, Mamma and Helen, it will be only a moment's struggle, and then we will be in Heaven together.' "

"The deck," the Reverend Weiss wrote, "is covered with

frightened passengers, most of whom are in their nightdresses. They run to the right, to the left, in the most helpless way, surrounding the small boats, and questioning every one whom they meet.'

Then he encountered "Madame S., who holds her baby in her arms and is followed by her three other little girls. She comes directly to me, saying, 'You will stay with us, will you not?'

"While I am assuring her that I will not leave her, one of her little girls seizes me, and cries to me, in her terror: 'Oh! You will not leave me; you will take me with you?'

" 'Yes, yes, my child! Do not be afraid. Stay here; I will take care of you. But you are shivering with cold in this little gown; I must look for something to cover you.'

"I go below as rapidly as possible, rush into my stateroom, seize my overcoat, and hasten back, laden with shawls and wraps for the children. In passing the vestibule, I see Cook standing in his nightshirt, and talking in the utmost agitation.

" 'What are you doing there? Why are you not dressed?' I asked.

" 'Why am I not dressed?' he replied, then shrugged in a hopeless gesture of resignation.

Weiss, calmed by the objectivity of the older pastor, made his way slowly back through the passageway. In the grand saloon which had been advertised as a "showplace of the Atlantic," he paused. He looked with renewed incredulity at the marble wainscoting, the velvet upholstery on the chairs, the carpeting, and the gold-lace drapes across the portholes—yes, save for himself, there was none now to appreciate the saloon's extravagant decorations.

Here was the largest and perhaps gaudiest craft since the *Great Eastern*, Nathaniel Weiss reflected—and it was just as perishable as he.

Even as he stared, the stricken *Ville-du-Havre* lurched farther

over on her wounded port side. A chair, a divan, another chair
broke loose and clattered the width of the saloon. The curtains
hung outward at a bizarre angle. The two kerosene lanterns,
which provided the sole remaining illumination, flickered. The
fluid tricked down the marble wainscoting.

It was time, the minister reminded himself, to leave the ship.
No sooner had he re-emerged into the darkness of the decks
than he heard "an awful crash." He saw the shadowy shape of
the bow break from the ship and "disappear in the flood." The
little girl he had been shepherding ran crying back to his side,
looked at him, then, in childish indecision, raced back to her
mother.

Neither the Reverend Weiss nor the captain nor anyone else
aboard the ship could do anything further to help the children
or any other passenger. It was less than twelve minutes since
the collision, and the *Ville-du-Havre* was going.

"The hungry waves," recorded Weiss, "rush suddenly upon
the afterdeck, and in an instant everything is swallowed up in
the yawning gulf, made by the enormous mass of that which we
so proudly called the *Ville-du-Havre*. We feel ourselves whirled
round and round as if in a vast funnel, and roll over in the depths
of an abyss which seems immeasurable. Some, stupefied by the
fall or by the strokes received from the floating pieces which
surround them, or paralyzed with fright, turn over and over in
unconsciousness, and fall asleep, as it were, in the midst of some
frightful nightmare; they are roused for an instant by a sharp
pang, to perish immediately.

"Others, without clothes—Cook is of this number—feel
themselves go down, down, amidst the most frightful min-
gling of arms, legs, and debris. They hold their breath, ask God
to save them, struggle, go up to the surface again; and aided by
their life preservers or floating pieces of the wreck, swim with
all their strength to the side of the sailing ship, or of one of her

small boats, which have just been put into the water, and which they reach breathless and exhausted.

"Others hear the waters boiling noisily around them, stifling their cries, and deadening the sound of their low groans. They see vivid pictures in their imaginations of their friends, their distressed and afflicted relatives; they pray, for they feel themselves lost in this turbulent foam which so closely surrounds them. Two minutes thus passed seem a century; but courage! Eternity is near. The sufferings increase, they collect all their powers for a last struggle, and when that struggle ceases, death has come, and seems almost a desired solace.

"At this awful moment, many experience a sensation of relief—their heads are free, they open their eyes, see the stars looking down upon them with their bright, sparkling light, so cold and unpitying; they see at a distance over the gloomy surface something toward which they are being borne—a great, fantastic shadow which has the form of a ship.

"Unhappy, then, are those who can no longer swim, or those who have not the good fortune to see a plank to cling to or a boat near to save them. Hope comes only to leave them more completely wretched; their heads have already disappeared beneath the waves, but their hands are still held up, imploring, supplicating aid. A sailor sees them—the boat arrives—too late! They are no longer there."

The words of Lallie, "we will be in Heaven together," rang in her mother's ears as a wave surged past the two, rudely breaking their hold upon one another. Mary Bulkley was certain that she had listened to her daughter's last words on earth.

"I clutched desperately to her dress," Mrs. Bulkley wrote, "but it slipped from my fingers and I knew that I was drowning alone; the sufferings of strangulation were upon me, and I thought that I was falling to the very bottom of the sea; with almost a start of horror I found myself rising to the surface. (I ought to mention here that scarcely ten minutes had passed from the moment of the collision until the Ville-du-Havre had disappeared from the view of any who could have looked upon her.) As I arose my hand struck a hard, cold substance; I grasped it, and found it to be an iron chain, suspended from a boat which was upside down in the water; a number of French sailors were clinging to the upraised keel.

"I spoke not a word, as these men shrieked for help, for I felt it was better they should not know a woman was clinging to the bottom of the boat. In a few moments the boat broke to pieces; for a second the shattered fragments held together like a raft, then, scattered by the surging waters, all disappeared. I saw not a human being around me. As the boat broke to pieces a beam struck me in the chest. I remembered that persons could be supported in the water by resting lightly on a plank; so as the chain was drawn from me this beam supported me.

"I was surrounded by barrels, broken timbers, etc., and my faculties were keen enough to distinguish the smell of liquor on the surface of the water; thus I lay on the waters, not struggling for life, but passively waiting God's will. A woman once floated quite near me, and I heard her say 'sauvez moi,' so I knew she was French. I could no longer see the ship, and not a lifeboat had I seen, or knew that one human soul had been rescued. I felt that I was drifting far away into the ocean, and never dreamed of being saved; still physical instinct kept me on the plank. I was alone with my God, and prayed that He might take my soul. I was cold and benumbed, and knew I could not live many minutes; suddenly I felt something under me, and stretching my feet downward, I felt them sustained by a triangular piece of timber; again, with this support under my feet, and the plank at my breast, I raised my head higher above the water, but soon a faintness seemed to come over me. I felt the waters going over my head, and raising my eyes, for the last time as I supposed, toward Heaven, I saw a great white boat above me. Here I screamed for the first time: 'Help a woman!' "

Thrashing to keep afloat himself, Weiss observed those who could not swim at all clinging desperately to pieces of the wreck. Everyone calling for help in a continuous chorus. Many, Weiss noticed, in their terror tended to "hurry too much, their courage fails, their support yields under them, and they are again submerged, then reappear, more and more exhausted, despairing, until someone sees them and comes to deliver them—unless, alas! the boat comes too slowly, or is too full and is obliged to return without them.

He came upon ten or fifteen persons clinging to a log. He went under the water, surfaced, went under again and when the second time he arose, sputtering above the waves and looked at the log, there were no people holding onto it.

Now he saw Madame S. again, clinging to a small plank. He came close enough for her to sob out the tragic news that she had finally lost her baby after the water had wrenched the infant twice from her grasp and twice she had grasped her again.

"Two of her little girls," Weiss continued, "came near an American, to whom they clung; he swam well and hoped to save both, but in the midst of his efforts, the younger one relaxes her hold and disappears; he had almost reached a boat when the elder also sank suddenly. The captain was rescued a few minutes later by this same boat; he had been thrown into the sea from his bridge."

While only the whale boat and captain's gig from the *Ville-du-Havre* had been successfully launched, lifeboats from the other ship appeared among the men and women struggling in the water. The rowers identified their sailing vessel as the *Loch Earn*, bound from London to New York.

"The English sailors work bravely and with the greatest rapidity, and neglect nothing that can help in the rescue. They are obliged to witness the most frightful scenes, and to hear distracting cries for help, which in many cases it is beyond their power to give.

"An American has succeeded in keeping his wife on the surface until they reach a boat. While he is helping her into it, his strength suddenly fails, and he dies at the moment of his rescue.

"Another draws near a boat at the same time with a woman; fright has crazed him, for although sustained by a life preserver, he tries to climb into the boat before her; the sailors beg him to wait one second, but he seizes the woman by the hair, and when his hand is disentangled he bites with rage.

"A feeble cry is heard: they find it is made by a young girl, whom they rescue; she has a large, bleeding gash on her face; a swimmer, raving no doubt, who has seen her approaching his plank, has struck her a violent blow.

"They hear cries from another direction, piercing, repeated, persistent, which the water seems trying to stifle. They approach and see a little girl who is fighting desperately, clinging to a piece of wood and crying, 'I do not wish to be drowned, I will not be drowned.' Happily they are able to save her.

"When the *Ville-du-Havre* sank, she carried with her all who were below at the time of the catastrophe. No one can ever imagine their terror when the water rushed in upon them, disabled in consequence of their wounds perhaps, and prevented by the four walls which surrounded them from seeing even a gleam of hope.

"Many unfortunates were for an hour fighting desperately upon this battefield against the sea, a strong and perfidious enemy, and had almost given up the thought of being saved, but were rescued at last.

"One lady already quite aged, is half dead with cold, when they take her rigid fingers from the piece of wood which sustains her. A young girl who has tried in vain to save her mother, is picked up when quite exhausted from swimming so long; she has some money in a little bag attached to her belt."

Mary Bulkley was pulled aboard one of the boats. Beside her was Miss E. Edgar, of New York.

"We were the last saved," she continued in her letter to her mother, Mrs. Adams, of Augusta, Georgia, "had drifted a mile from the ship, and had been three quarters of an hour in the water. As we came up to the ship an English voice called out: " 'How many have you?'

" 'Six,' was the answer of our brave sailors. 'Good God! Is that all—any women?' 'Two,' was the answer; 'We could find no more.' 'Hurry up with them on deck, and go again.'

"We were utterly helpless, but the men put strong ropes under our arms, and we were hauled up the sides of the ship. As I recognized faces of the passengers about me I felt as if it were a resurrection of the dead. We were taken into a small room; our wet clothes dragged from us, and sailors' flannel shirts, drawers, and socks, put upon us; brandy was given us; and wrapped in blankets, all of the ladies, eleven in number were laid in the cabin of the ship.

"Miss Edgar and I being the last brought in, we were cared for by a young girl, Miss Hunter, of Newport; dear child, she lost her father, mother, and one sister; one sister being saved also. She was one of the first saved, and being one of the first dressed, she was like an angel of light to us all. The ship was the *Loch Earn*, from Glasgow, commanded by Captain Robinson, who says the *Ville-du-Havre* sank in eight minutes after the collision.

"At first, Captain Robinson supposed he only was injured by the collision, and ordered his lifeboats lowered to save his own men; never knew that the steamer was injured, until a boat with twelve of the crew came to the ship; even then, as they approached, he supposed they came to give him help; and not until they rushed with frantic haste aboard did he know the steamer was in danger. These Frenchmen refused to go back in the boat to give help, and then Captain Robinson manned the French boat with his own men, and sent it off with his own boats.

"The Captain of the *Ville-du-Havre* went down with his ship, and was picked up on a plank, with a Mr. Bishop, of Brunswick, New Jersey. This gentleman had been as noble and kind to us all as if he had been related to us; in fact, all the gentlemen have acted as if they had been our natural protectors; and all the ladies, united by common suffering, feel like sisters. Of eighty-nine first class passengers, only twenty-three are saved; and ten of these are women—*not one of the rescued passengers was taken from the steamer in a boat.* Several gentlemen jumped from the deck, just as she was sinking, and saved themselves by swimming; the other gentlemen sank with the ship, as all the ladies did, and were picked up by the French and English boats. Fifty-nine of the French officers and crew are saved."

The death toll was sobering. Of the some three hundred who had sailed, 226 were lost. The captain's wife was among the missing, although two of his daughters had been saved. Judge Peckham had perished, as had Julia Waite, whose father was proprietor of the Brevoort. Her brother survived.

Miss Edgar, who had been plucked from the water together with Mary Bulkley, lost her sister and mother. The Reverend Cook was to die within a month.

"Among the ladies saved," continued Mrs. Bulkley, "is a lovely woman, a Mrs. Spafford, from Chicago, who has seen Josey in Washington, at General Thomas'. She has lost four lovely children, her all; and our miseries bring us close together. She is also alone, but had her husband, who will probably join her as soon as possible. But to return to the narrative: We lay almost unconscious in the cabin of the English ship, when the

news was brought in that a second ship was in sight, this proved
to be the *Tremontain*, of New York, bound for Bristol, England.
Captain Robinson, of the English ship, was very unwilling to
have us leave, but the gentlemen thought as his ship was so
much damaged, it would be best to go on a sound ship, the bow
of the *Loch Earn* being terribly broken by the collision. We lay
so exhausted that it did not seem possible for us to be moved
again; but the gentlemen persisted; talked with Captain Surmonte, of the *Ville-du-Havre*, who gave the necessary orders.
We were taken up, lowered down the sides of the ship, and
placed in the bottom of boats. A few moments rapid rowing,
the sea very high, and we were alongside of this ship. The Captain had a chair lowered for the ladies; we were strapped to it
and drawn up. The last hope was destroyed before we left the
English ship of ever finding any more beloved faces; the boats
cruised for five hours without finding any others, after Miss
Edgar and I were saved. Captain Urquhart, of this ship, also
tacked and cruised over the spot before pursuing his course; so
we have the mournful satisfaction of knowing that everything
was done to look for the lost ones.

"We have been on board this ship a week tomorrow, and
hope to reach land next Monday; we are destitute of money and
clothes; fortunately the Captain is a noble-hearted man, and
does all he can to make us comfortable, and we are grateful
that his sound ship shelters us; but we are leading such an un-
real life, and all feel that we must keep up and not be burthens
upon others—that the very necessity of action acts like a stimu-
lant, and we hardly realize who we are and what the terrible
situation is.

"Imagine eleven ladies and about twelve gentlemen being in
two small cabins, not a tooth brush among us; only such clothing as we had upon us when saved, which has been dried for us,
and the flannel underclothing of the sailors. Only two ladies

have shoes, the rest are in the woolen stockings which the English sailors gave us. I have a pair of gentlemen's slippers, and fortunately had my flannel wrapper on when I went overboard. All must use the Captain's comb; but one of the young girls, a wonderful child of seventeen, Miss Mixter, of Boston, combs our hair every morning—no hair pins, so we must wear it down our shoulders. This poor girl has lost her father, mother, and grandfather. She and her little sister of twelve were both miraculously saved as I was. . . .

"I dare not think of my own future, and only long for my return to you It is mysterious to think why have I been saved, when with Lallie, my life's work is done."

The "Cranky" Atalanta

THE JUNO WAS A LARGE, IMPRESSIVE MAN-OF-WAR WHEN THE Lords of the Admiralty made the tedious journey from London to Portsmouth for her commissioning. The year was 1845, and steam was already supplanting sail in some ships. With Her Majesty's Navy, canvas still had its loyal supporters. They had seen to it that the *Juno* was not encumbered by one piece of machinery in the oaken depths of her hull.

Yet, grossing nearly a thousand tons, she was far more capacious than many of the new iron or semi-iron steamers. She measured exactly 131 feet, 2 inches, from prow to stern (exclusive of figurehead). Three towering masts were calculated as more than sufficient on which to hang her amplitude of canvas. No one—surely not Queen Victoria, who had already reigned eight years—questioned that *H.M.S. Juno* would be one of Britain's swiftest fighting frigates. For her Sunday punch, she mounted a battery of 64-pounders.

In the lifetime of the *Juno*, however, there was no enemy to fight. In the brief Crimean War, soldiers did the dying for Britain. There was nothing reminiscent of a Trafalgar.

With the Channel Squadron, *Juno* guarded the British Isles against incidental damage from Union frigates and Confederate raiders which might join battle. She missed, however, the most famous contest, in 1864, when the *Alabama* was sunk by the *Kearsarge* off Cherbourg.

After the American Civil War ended, *Juno*, the proud queen

82

of the gods, tumbled down the scales of deity, as well as those
of naval registry. Decommissioned as a ship of the line, her
name was changed to *Atalanta*, a lesser heroine of Greek
mythology. However, she was a woman so skilled in archery
that she had slain two centaurs, and was also an accomplished
runner. On the debit side, she was a cruel vixen.

The downgraded *Atalanta* was towed to duty as a "police
hulk" in Portsmouth harbor—prison for erring sailors, barracks
for detachments of Royal Marines. Lashed securely to her
moorings, she had hardly any leeway even to swing with the
tide. Her masts and her yardarms became habitat only for
passing gulls. Her armament—a couple of 9-pounders.

In 1878, England was rocked by a Naval tragedy. The training
ship *Eurydice* foundered in a channel squall between the mouth
of the Solent and the Isle of Wight. Her crew and midshipmen
—three hundred in all—were lost to a man in sight of persons on
shore, who were unable to push through the raging seas to their
aid.

The disaster, nonetheless, was to have its bright side for the
harbor-bound *Atalanta*. The memorial services had hardly faded
into silence when a board of cadet-training inspectors swarmed
onto the police hulk. Much to their surprise, her decade of
navigationless humility had not seriously told on her hull. Her
oak timbers, a third of a century since they had been orphaned
from the forests, seemed as solid as ever.

The next year, with a new suit of canvas and some minor re-
furbishings, the *Atalanta* once more stretched her wings to the
winds. And in October, under command of Captain Stirling, a
naval veteran of "good judgment and high professional qualifications," the recommissioned sailing frigate loaded provisions
for a long training voyage. She was to take a complement of
midshipmen to the West Indies and back, by way of North
Africa, the Azores, and Halifax.

In addition to cargo, her displacement was increased by 109 tons of fresh water and 43 tons of ballast. This was intended to increase the stability of an aging ship which was known to roll.

On November 7th, Captain Stirling certified his command was ready for sea and "in all respects sound, possessed of unusual stability." There were 290 souls aboard, including officers, crew, and midshipmen.

Families had journeyed from all parts of the British Isles to see the *Atalanta* off. They crowded the Portsmouth waterfront and waved hats and handkerchiefs as a steam tug pulled the frigate toward the channel. A band played "Rule Brittania." The Royal Navy personnel stiffened. The women's eyes moistened. Some—and there were mothers of teen-age midshipmen in their number—wept without restraint.

The *Atalanta*, a majestic, almost ancestral sight in this new era of steam and steel, was on her way. Her orders read to be home by mid-April, 1880. As anyone knew, however, a sailing ship was unpredictable. The Admiralty would expect her when the lightkeeper at Bishop's Rock picked her up again with his telescope.

In 1879, she was already an anachronism. As she wallowed southward toward Tenerife, in the Canary Islands, she was passed by one steamship after another. At the mercy of the winds, the slow-sailing *Atalanta* required twenty-one days to swing out around Spain and then south to the little island cluster off the Gold Coast of Africa.

It had not been an auspicious beginning of the training cruise. *Atalanta*, no longer the swift, maneuverable man-of-war of eighteen-forties, was "cranky." She possessed a built-in snap roll, which not only filled her midshipmen with a lurking terror but rendered them frequently too sick to go aloft and work the sails.

Captain Stirling, proving his reputation as a cautious navigator, spent long hours on deck. This concern, however, had an unintended effect on morale.

"Things must be bloody uneasy if the old man can't go below," was the way the cadets reasoned.

John Verling, an able-bodied seaman from Queenstown, decided that his ship was "rather heavily rigged—her spars were too lofty, making her rather top-heavy." It seemed to him that none aboard "had a very good opinion of her."

At Tenerife, however, the men went ashore and temporarily forgot the miseries of the sea. There were women and all the blandishments of a tropical island. On December 4th, the re-provisioned Atalanta set sail. Gradually, the volcanic peaks of El Piton and Chahorra disappeared into the haze of the eastern horizon.

She steered for Barbados across this relatively narrow segment of the Atlantic Ocean. The weather worsened. A week out of Tenerife a seaman, John McClure, plunged into the stormy seas from the top gallant. A boat was put over the side, and a queasy, semi-experienced group of oarsmen strained their backs to his rescue. McClure, however, had gone under forever when the boat reached the spot where he should have been.

With difficulty, the little boat returned to the Atalanta. Trying to bring it aboard, however, other crewmen stove in its sides against the rolling Atalanta. Her occupants struggled out safely. In addition to pointing up the dangers of going aloft in a rough sea, the incident tended to show that Hill and Clark's patented "disengaging gear" for lifeboats, with which the Atalanta had been newly equipped, was more efficient in disengaging than in engaging.

Saddened at the loss of one of his complement and distressed at this apparent weakness in the frigate's life-saving equipment, the captain sat up in the night beside his oil lamp to log the day's tragedy. It was a hapless crossing, altogether. Storms lashed at the *Atalanta* day and night, and she rolled nearly thirty-two degrees. Seaman Verling overheard Captain Stirling make the gloomy forecast: "If she goes over another degree, she'll founder!"

Hanging onto the helm, the binnacle, to sheets and stays, anything he could clutch, Stirling sayed on deck interminably. The wind howled desolately and the Atlantic broke over the ship's decks in swirling green combers. No one wanted to furl or unfurl the canvas. Neither crew nor midshipmen could eat. Sickness, sodden cold, and misery were their unwelcome traveling companions, which seemingly had arrived to stay.

Two ordinary seamen, John Jessop and John McCormack flatly refused to obey orders. They clung to their hammocks as though their only salvation lay within their odorous confines. The commander accused the pair of near-mutiny and locked them in irons.

Christmas and New Year's passed. The year 1880 arrived— bringing welcome warmth and placid seas. The *Atalanta* somehow had thrashed her way across the turbulent ocean. She was, at last, three days out of Barbados. The men swarmed aloft once more, singing—happy. The scuppers and the passageways were swabbed, holystoned, and polished. Torn sails were sewn.

When the *Atalanta* bore down on the little West Indian island, she was again a smart ship. The Governor General's representative was on the dock, waiting to welcome Captain Stirling, as were various inhabitants, especially the dusky young girls of Barbados. The band played "Rule Brittania."

Jessop and McCormack, out of irons but none the less languishing in the brig, begged to be given another chance. Captain Stirling saw no reason why he should do so. As a matter of fact, he had three others of the crew to put ashore at Barbados: the John Verling already mentioned, as well as Thomas Westlake

and Alfred Stansell, both ordinary seamen. They were all suffering from yellow fever, according to the ship's surgeon.

The *Atalanta* remained a week, replenishing food and water,
as well as morale. On January 9th, she sailed for Halifax, leaving
her five crew members behind.

It was winter, once more, when she put into Halifax harbor.
The wharves were covered with snow and ice and the winds
whined continually from out of the North Atlantic. Greenland
was just around the corner. Here she received orders to return to
England by way of Bermuda.

On January 29th, she reached Bermuda after a fast passage,
hurried on her way by northerly gales. *H.M.S. Atalanta* let down
her length of rusty anchor chain opposite Fort Hamilton. April
was approaching, when the training frigate was due back in England. And not a man on board was sorry at the prospect. Soon,
it appeared, their purgatory at sea would be at an end.

She sailed from Bermuda on January 31st.

February, March, and early April, this 1880, were stormy
months on the North Atlantic. The maximum fury of the seas
was centered in the area of the Azores, where dismasted and
sometimes rudderless ships limped into port day after day.
Wreckage washed ashore was testimony to the fate of smaller
craft.

The Royal Mail steamer *Derwent*, for one, thrashed through
gales for the better part of a week in April off the Azores before
she could finally shake them off, as a person would an attacker
in the night, and sail on. A big, powerful vessel, she had suffered
no appreciable damage, though a lifeboat had been swept away.
She had sighted timbers, broken rafts, traces of cargo, and other
ominous hints of what had happened to less fortunate sea-going
craft.

The *H.M.S. Avon*, a gunboat recently detached from the
China Station, warped alongside the Royal piers in Portsmouth

about the same time, bearing reports similar to those of the *Derwent*. Fayal harbor in the Azores, the captain noted, was "full of dismasted ships."

Now the Royal Navy took another look at the calendar and grudgingly conceded that the kinfolk of some three hundred men were not being unduly nervous when they inquired ever more frequently: "Where is the *Atalanta*?"

On April 13th, a navy spokesman admitted it was seventy-two days since the training ship had put out from Bermuda. It was "feared," he added, that she might have been "disabled" by the storms, possibly "dismasted." On the other hand, he re-emphasized that the *Atalanta* was possessed "of unusual stability." He was sure she would turn up somewhere.

Two days later, the Admiralty, besieged with a new flood of letters, telegrams, and personal visitations, confessed to "grave apprehensions." However, "their Lordships regretted they were unable to give any information."

On April 16th, more than two hundred men and women, all related to the men aboard the *Atalanta*, called at Whitehall. Their grief making them bolder, they demanded that something be done at once to discover what had happened to the old training ship.

Britain, dozing pleasantly through routine general elections, was not prepared for a tragedy of national magnitude. Not since the Crimean War had distressing news occupied so much space in the British press. It was all the more surprising in an island kingdom accustomed to disaster at sea.

The Admiralty ordered the stores ship *Wye* to call at the Azores. Perhaps she could obtain news of the missing *Atalanta*. There was momentary exultation in Portsmouth, sparked by a rumor that she had just arrived at Falmouth dockyard. The news was posted in every other shop window and in newspaper offices.

The disappointment, when the falsity of the report was established, was too much to endure. In a seaside community, there
were many others besides relatives who were emotionally af-
fected every time a large vessel was overdue.

The Admiralty, according to a new tidal wave of protest,
should dispatch other vessels besides the *Wye* in search of the
training frigate. The sea lords, uncommonly moved by the surging public opinion, now took a drastic step. They ordered out
the entire Channel Squadron, commanded by Rear Admiral
Hood, of the naval dynasty of Hoods. By May 5th, the fleet was
sailing south, with orders to comb the Atlantic from Bantry
Bay, Ireland, to the Azores, and back again.

The departure left Rear Admiral Ryder, commander-in-chief
at Portsmouth, to fend off the questions which continued like
the insistent buzzing of May flies. For the most part, he was
unable to "confirm or deny" the multitudinous and conflicting
reports as to the *Atalanta's* safety or lack of it.

Throughout April the newspaper carried daily reports on the
Atalanta. Readers, with interest fanned to a fever pitch, wrote
letters to the editors. Thomas Brassey, of Normanhurst Court,
for example, observed aloud to *The Times* that the crew of the
missing ship must have endured "considerable privations."

A correspondent who signed himself "Philomanticus" suggested all sailing ships be fitted with double topmasts.

The stores ship *Wye* returned from her fruitless search. She
had happened across only one oddity of the sea—a tired old fisherman in a rowboat, bobbing about the Bay of Biscay. He died
shortly after being brought aboard, without ever identifying
himself.

On April 27th, the steamer *Tamar* arrived in Portsmouth,
carrying John Verling, one of the five who had been put ashore
by the *Atalanta* in Barbados. His yellow fever had been cured,

but the other two patients had not completed their recovery. The two prisoners still awaited trial.

Verling talked. He told of how the "cranky" *Atalanta* rolled thirty-two degrees, how Captain Stirling supposedly kept to the deck because of his own fears for the ship's safety, and of his allegedly overhearing the captain remark that his command might founder if she rolled one more degree.

His testimony made good reading—so good that Flag Captain Seymour paid a visit to the verbose seaman in the Portsmouth Royal Naval Hospital. Then Seymour himself spoke for publication: "Through no fault of his own, able bodied Seaman John Verling has had distinction thrust upon him."

Seymour was certain that the impertinent Verling was unable "to have distinguished between the roll and the heel of the ship."

But *The Times* rallied to the defense of the sailor and asserted that the Admiralty apparently had now "frightened the man into revoking his former testimony." At the same time, the paper's Portsmouth correspondent published more testimony he had obtained from Verling:

"I do not think any of those on board had a very good opinion of her. . . . During the gale, water went down the main deck, but her lower deck was dry."

Nothing more was seen of or heard from able-bodied Seaman John Verling

By early May, Hood's Channel Squadron was back in Bantry Bay. The depressing conclusion: not a shred of evidence to be found anywhere to solve the riddle of the *Atalanta*.

On May 12th, the Admiralty, officially abandoning hope, announced an inquiry. On May 21st, Queen Victoria's spring message was read in the House of Lords. She was concerned with the Irish famine and with the general topic of burials "in churchyards and cemeteries."

Little by little, the Atalanta was being relegated to the limbo of yesterday's news. The flow of day-to-day events continued in the British Isles. During a severe thunderstorm, at Brierly-Hill, a "young man named Joseph Manning, while backing a horse and cart, was struck by lightning and killed instantly."

On May 29th, a "Select Committee" was appointed to hold public hearings in London as to the missing vessel, while the Lord Mayor of London set up a fund for the widows, orphans, and dependent relatives of the victims of the apparent tragedy.

The fund grew. On one day alone, the Cunard Steamship Company contributed five hundred dollars, which was matched by an equal gift from a Mrs. Philpott, of Ilford. The Admiralty itself offered a reward of one thousand dollars for information as to the Atalanta, then, within a few weeks, withdrew it—thinking it an extravagance. However, a fete at the Alexandra Palace raised nearly one thousand dollars in one evening.

The hearings commenced the first weeks of June, in Westminster. They droned on. Fewer and fewer spectators arrived. For what was there to be said?

The secret, strangely, was to find its most likely key far away on the other side of the Atlantic, even as their lordships alternately mumbled and dozed in the stuffy halls of empire.

On June 14th, the bark Exile arrived in New York from Antwerp. A month before, her captain reported, he had passed a "large boat" bottoms up, covered with barnacles, drifting four hundred miles west of Cape Finisterre, Spain. Shortly afterward, the Exile sighted two heavy deck beams.

Somehow he associated the derelict and the wreckage with the Atalanta.

The same day, Captain Edward Millett, of Rockport, Massachusetts, leaned out of his trawler and picked up a bottle floating a mile offshore. When he uncorked it, he discovered a message, scrawled in "apparent great haste" on a leaf of paper torn from a pocket memorandum book. It read:

"April 17, 1880, training ship *Atalanta*. We are sinking in L. 270, Lat. 32°. Any person finding this note will please advertise in the daily papers. John L. Hutchings. Distress."

The position was just west of Funchal, in the Madeira Islands, and south of Fayal, in the Azores.

Two days later, children playing on the beach at Cow Bay, twelve miles east of Halifax, Nova Scotia, happened on a piece of barrel stave sticking out of the sand. Scrawled on it in pencil was this:

"*Atalanta*: going down, April 15, 1880. No hope. Send this to Mrs. Mary White, Sussex. James White."

Investigators agreed that the stave appeared to have been immersed in salt water for the two months indicated. There seemed every likelihood that top-heavy, "cranky" *Atalanta* at last had had her way and had plunged to the bottom, in the great April storm about the Azores.

But who were John L. Hutchings and James White? The news from America did not reach London in time. By July, the hearings were over. The books were locked, so were the rosters of officers, crew, and midshipmen.

Summer was at hand and their Lordships of the Admiralty, whatever else they might desire, sought passionately to erase the *Atalanta* from memory—forever.

And they did.

Trouble In Vineyard Sound

FOUR YEARS AFTER THE ATALANTA HEARING, ON A JANUARY DAY IN 1884, another maritime hearing was being conducted—this time on the other side of the Atlantic and by the Board of Inspectors of Steam Vessels for the District of Charlestown and Boston. Far removed, in ostentation as well as geography, from Whitehall, the scene was an unadorned room over the Revere Beach and Lynn Railroad offices, 350 Atlantic Avenue, Boston.

Two long tables, running the length of the inner room, were flanked by representatives of the press, attorneys for the Boston and Savannah Steamship Company, and witnesses. An outer office was filled with spectators.

Andrew Burnham, board chairman, sat at the head of one table. He was fifty-eight years old, short, heavy-set, and kindly appearing. He was, by profession, a hull inspector. Andrew J. Savage, a lean down-Easter of few words, sat at the other table. Member of the inspection board, Savage had come ashore after a considerable career at sea as chief engineer.

These two Andrews were judges at the inquiry, without jury. The case to be judged: the loss of the 2,000-ton Boston and Savannah Steamship Company's *City of Columbus* on January 18, 1884, the Friday before the last.

The witnesses were on hand, in answer to their summons.

93

There was but one notable exception: Captain Schuyler E. Wright, master of the liner. This fifty-year-old descendant of a succession of seafarers, who was born in Wareham, Massachusetts, was abed with "low fever and nervous prostration." At that, said his colleagues, he was lucky. The sea had already claimed both his father and elder brother.

Board Chairman Burnham amplified the purposes of the inquiry:

". . . solely and purely in relation to the conduct of the officers . . . admitting only such testimony as has a direct bearing upon the conduct of the officers. There has been no allegation against these officers, only as that it is presumed that there must be neglect or misconduct or otherwise the disaster would not have occurred."

And so the hearing began, though the stories of the witnesses could not very easily keep within the strict bounds defined by the chairman.

It was a cheerful group of eighty-seven passengers who set sail for Georgia and Florida destinations that Thursday afternoon, January 17th, from Boston.

"Almost on our departure," declared John L. Cook, a screenmaker of Portland, Maine, "the passengers began to fraternize together. Everyone liked the pleasant trip."

The sea was relatively calm outside of Boston harbor. The six-year-old coastal ship steamed along comfortably at nearly twelve knots. All on board appeared for dinner. Afterward, in the early evening, babies were tucked in bed so that their elders could play cards. However, with the advent of darkness, the wind freshened from out of the northwest and the ship assumed a gently rolling motion. Almost all the passengers lost interest in pursuits other than betaking themselves to bed. The roll, it was soon evident, was increasing, rather than decreasing.

F. W. Fairbanks of Gorham, Maine, fifty-two-year-old retired engineer, was about to reshape the course of his life at Yalaha, Florida, where he had purchased land. He was now en route to check over his holdings before bringing his wife and five children south.

He began to feel queasy as the waves picked up, and regretted the large dinner he had consumed. He went on deck to taste of the cold, wintry air. Fairbanks walked about, attempting to keep his balance on the careening, slippery decks. Shortly, he decided he did not feel any better and returned to his cabin and lay down, even though he could not sleep.

Captain Wright himself wasn't feeling well. Not seasickness but a recurring malady, chills, was his *bete noire*. There seemed little to be done about the affliction.

By midnight, when almost all passengers were in bed, the sea had swelled to extremely choppy proportions though the skies were clear and the moon out. As the *City of Columbus* left Cross Rip Lightship on her starboard quarter in Nantucket Sound, Quartermaster Roderick A. McDonald came on watch.

He was at the helm, as well, at 1:45 A.M. when the young second mate, Augustus Harding, took the bridge and the master ordered a routine course change, "so'west by west." Nobska Light was astern, Tarpaulin Cove Light would soon be bearing off the port bow—which meant that the ship would soon be clear of treacherous Vineyard Sound and in the open sea.

"I'm going in my room awhile," Captain Wright declared, reminding his mate to alter course again "when Tarpaulin Cove Light bears north."

Wright disappeared into his own cabin, adjoining the wheel house. He lay upon his bunk, sitting up from time to time for the purpose of blasting the overflow from his chewing tobacco at the spittoon against the far bulkhead.

Chewing and resting, he listened to the lowered voices of

McDonald, at the wheel, and Harding, in command of the watch and, technically, of the ship.

The *City of Columbus* continued on her southwesterly course, slowed down to about ten knots by the sea.

As the minutes passed, conditions worsened. The wind approached gale force and the seas mounted. In spite of the thick weather, however, the visibility remained fair.

At 3:20 A.M., the steamer *Panther*, bound for Newburyport, passed the *City of Columbus* about two miles off the latter's starboard beam. Captain Stokely Warrington, of the *Panther*, made out the Boston and Savannah vessel clearly, close to the Martha's Vineyard shore. Warrington, who was steering his ship in mid-channel, thought the other was on a hazardous course.

"She should be out farther on a night like this," he observed to his mate on watch.

Shortly afterward, at 3:42 A.M., Edward Leary, standing lookout aboard the *City of Columbus*, thought he saw the dark form of a buoy bobbing in the foaming sea no more than 150 yards distant.

"Buoy on port bow!" he sang out to Quartermaster McDonald.

It was frightening to Leary, who could recall no buoy in this approximate position. His concern was compounded when the call was not acknowledged.

In the pilot house, behind tightly closed windows, Mate Harding had not heard the call. With the shrieking of the wind, he might not have heard it in any case. He was, just then, advising McDonald not to go even "a hair" to leeward of the course the ship was on.

Leary now ran aft and topsides to the bridge and opened the door, repeating his first message to the helmsman.

"Port!" Harding shouted instinctively.

As he did so, the master ran from his own cabin and onto the bridge.

"Hard aport!" he commanded, thinking, somehow, that the *City of Columbus* was bearing down on another ship coming up the sound.

A minute, perhaps, had passed since the sighting of the buoy, and already it was too late.

In his own cabin, Fairbanks, the Gorham gardener who was going to resettle in Florida, still half-sick and sleepless, heard a "grinding" sound, as if the ship were bumping over rocks.

"What's the trouble?" he asked the man in the upper bunk, sharing the cabin with him.

"Nothing I know of," came the reply.

Even so, Fairbanks didn't like the noise. He left his bed, donned two pair of pants, two vests, an outside coat, and a long rubber coat.

Henry McGarry, berthing in steerage with his brother Eugene, was en route for winter bricklaying work in climates more compatible with mortar's affinity for freezing. Henry slept heavily, but his brother had been restless all night.

"Henry, get up!" Eugene shouted, instantly fully awake at the first jar. "We've struck something."

Both men were dressed except for their shoes and coats. In a few moments, they were up and hurrying out of their cabin.

William C. Spaulding, the purser, was asleep, but was transformed into action at the first shock. He raced out of his cabin on the hurricane deck, and called to the second steward, Charles H. Holmes: "Get the crowd together! If you can't raise them any other way, break in the doors!"

On the bridge, captain, mate, quartermaster, and lookout all knew what had happened. The liner was aground. The particular outcropping here was Devil's Bridge Reef, near Gay Head

Light at the southern tip of Martha's Vineyard Island. She had missed the clear ocean by minutes.

Captain Wright, recovering from the stunning effect of what had happened, ordered: "Full speed astern!"

The ship shuddered, then backed haltingly for perhaps forty feet. She rasped to a stop which had the sound and the feel of finality.

The winds howled about the superstructure and through the rigging. The seas slapped the stricken steamer's sides and sloshed over her canted decks.

The *City of Columbus*, beyond a doubt—and beyond recall— was fast on the reef.

Chief Engineer Archibald Morrison arrived at the wheel house.

"There is water in her, captain," he announced.

"It's all up," Captain Wright told his quartermaster, who let go the wheel. The master then went aft and ordered the mate to get out the boats. He personally advised the passengers to put on life preservers.

The ship was sinking fast. Captain Wright could feel her sliding under even as he walked through the angled passages.

It appeared to him that the "after-part filled with water which came in through the after hatch." On the other hand, he believed the fore hatch was secure and that the vessel's five bulkheads "seemed tight."

Fairbanks, now literally encumbered by his clothing, ran from his cabin, shouting "Come boys, I'm not going to stand this!"

The swish of water sounded as though it were directly under his feet. On deck he encountered Captain Wright, who "looked surprised."

When Fairbanks voiced his belief that the *City of Columbus* was sinking, the captain answered: "I'll do all I can," then exhorted other passengers within hearing to keep calm.

The McGarry brothers, still planning to "tie our shoes up above," met a fireman on deck. They asked him if the vessel had "struck anything."

"Why no," he retorted. "I haven't heard anything."

Eugene McGarry saw men loosening lifeboats. Passengers and crewmen surged around the davits, impeding the efforts of those intent on launching the boats.

"Come away, Henry!" Eugene, disturbed, urged. "That's a poor show."

The vessel was keeling over so far that the brothers were forced to grab the rail to keep their balance. They clambered to the starboard side and struggled upward for the rigging. It seemed that all the other men aboard the doomed ship were pushing and clawing past them.

"Don't let 'em get by you, Harry!" Eugene shouted.

"I'll follow you, go ahead!" Henry yelled back, trying to make himself heard above the roar of the wind and the mounting babble of human terror.

Fairbanks, the Gorham, Maine, passenger, had to confess he was "unprepared" for the sights on deck—women and children as well as men rushing from the passageways only to be swept overboard by the "tremendous cross seas."

"Save us, save us!" implored two women. One held a baby in her arms. Before Fairbanks could assist either of them, the ocean had taken them.

He encountered a man clutching the vessel's rail. His legs dangled free and it appeared as though he would follow the women into eternity at any moment.

"Don't lose your hold!" cautioned the gardener from Gorham, Maine, nimbly starting up the rigging. In a second he looked back, and the other man had disappeared. Showing strength he was unaware he possessed, Fairbanks clambered up the mainmast to the maintop. In his windswept, freezing perch, shared with nine other men, he caught his breath and looked down upon a somewhat unexpected turn of events.

The *City of Columbus*, instead of foundering without trace, had lain at an angle until her hold filled with water, then she righted, as some monstrous, nicely-balanced buoy, and sat on the reef almost level. All of her masts and rigging protruded clear, as well as a foot or two of her superstructure.

Within about twenty-five minutes after striking the reef, the *City of Columbus* had become as much a coffin ship as though she were now at the depths of the Atlantic. To Fairbanks, it looked as though there were no more than three dozen survivors, all frightened, bedraggled birds of refuge in the rigging, as was he.

To the McGarry brothers, the disturbed, frothing surface of the sea was "speckled" with struggling human beings—but only for a few moments. They observed two of the ship's six lifeboats actually start out, heavily loaded with women. But, much less haul survivors out of the water, they could not even keep afloat themselves.

The McGarry's watched one boat turn over and "slide" under the wrecked steamer. The second made a try for it, being rowed nearly fifty feet away from the *City of Columbus*. But the seas were a vastly more powerful adversary. The second boat, too, turned turtle.

Yet, many—both men and women—would not die without a battle. A determined group righted the craft and boarded it, only to be projected into the cold waters once more. There were no more lifeboats left afloat to make for the shores.

One man clung to an outcropping of the superstructure. Each time a wave swept over him, it seemed as though he would surely have lost his valiant fight. But he hung on, sometimes by one hand only.

"Look at that poor fellow; he's there yet!" Eugene at one point observed to his brother.

Yet, as everyone in the rigging knew, the outcome was predetermined. The next time Eugene looked the man was gone. He also noted seven persons clinging to a raft which was fastened to the superstructure by a line. As he marveled that anyone could stick to the wildly careening, half-submerged square of planking, one man was swept off of it.

In a few more minutes, McGarry could count only five persons aboard the raft.

The captain himself was now in the rope webbing. Beside him was a *Boston Globe* reporter, Nathaniel J. Morton, who had been ill. He was sailing for Florida to recuperate from what might be the early stages of tuberculosis.

Captain Wright noted the ailing man was experiencing more and more difficulty in hanging onto the tarred ropes. Finally he cried: "Oh God, remember me!" and fell some fifty feet into the raging seas.

Fairbanks had obtained a miraculous second wind. The fifty-two-year-old Maine gardener was scrambling around the rigging like a youngster, both to keep warm and to encourage others, who, he noted, were "raving cursing and praying."

Night turned into grey, bleak, wind-swept morning. One by one, the survivors fell from the rigging.

About 9:30 A.M. James F. Mosher, postmaster at Squibnocket, Martha's Vineyard—near Gay Head and about five miles inland from Devil's Bridge Reef—was hitching up his horses. Before he could complete this customary morning chore, two neighbors drove by, shouting: "There's a steamer with a red smoke stack ashore on Devil's Bridge! The sea's breaking over it!"

"I'll be with it soon's I get finished with this team," Mosher quickly replied. Wrecks were not uncustomary on the reef and shoals-strewn approaches to this island—graveyard (together with Nantucket Sound) of some one thousand ships. For some reason, he figured this latest stranding was an English steamer, although the other two expressed the opinion it was a collier.

Mosher planned on going over to the Massachusetts Humane Society's lifeboat station near Gay Head, where there was already activity. Word had been relayed from Frederick Poole, assistant keeper of Gay Head Light, that there was a wreck on Devil's Bridge Reef.

A crew of volunteers, mostly Indians and those of Indian descent, dragged the heavy surfboat overland to a spot on the beach where the heavy seas would have the least impeding effect on the launching.

The McGarry brothers, still clutching the tarred ropes, watched that boat approach about ten that morning. Several persons jumped from the wreck and attempted to swim to the rescue craft. Eugene McGarry heard one survivor cry: "Come and take me! Come and take me!" He waved his hands. However, his fear of jumping was involuntarily ended as a piece of the mast tip fell off, knocking him into the sea.

By noon, Postmaster Mosher was manning the boat on its second trip to the wreck. He had been delayed on the beach a few moments by two elderly negro women who berated him for not coming sooner.

Also battling the surf was a skiff from the Coast Guard cutter *Dexter*. A thirty-year-old lieutenant, John Rhodes, was in command of the boat. When he came alongside the *City of Columbus* he found an unexpected ally in Fairbanks, who was still alert and nimble.

"Do what they say!" exhorted the gardener, as some hesitated in obeying Rhodes' command to jump. "Anything is better than this."

Finally, he jumped himself. Weighted as he was by his layers of clothing, he sank so deeply he was convinced "I'd never come up." Yet, he surfaced, and was pulled aboard Mosher's boat.

The McGarrys were less fortunate. They removed their coats and made ready to jump, after shaking hands in a farewell gesture. Henry plunged over the side first. Eugene watched him somersault three times in the air before striking the water. As he surfaced he shouted to his brother: "Is there a rope you can reach me?"

"No, try again, Henry, and keep up if you can!" Eugene called in reply. Realizing that probably nothing could be done to help his brother, he added: "Good-by and God save you!"

Lieutenant Rhodes now plunged from the Coast Guard dory in a last-minute effort to save the bricklayer, who was being swept toward a mass of floating timber.

Eugene jumped, went under, then rose close beside the little boat. He was pulled in. The Coast Guard officer, however, came back to his little craft, blue with cold and breathless, without Henry McGarry who had disappeared under the debris.

Captain Wright was one of the last to leave the rigging. Beside him were two men.

"Jump!" called Lieutenant Rhodes.

"Save those men first!" retorted the master of the wrecked steamer.

"They're frozen!" insisted the lieutenant, certain the two other forms in the rigging were dead.

Finally, Wright, who could not swim, quit what was left of his ship and was pulled onto the dory. Now Lieutneant Rhodes returned to the Dexter and transferred Captain Wright, Eugene McGarry, and others he had saved.

Unwilling to leave the scene if there was a possibility of saving any more lives, Rhodes returned to the wreck once more. Again he plunged into the icy water, slightly injuring himself against a piece of timber.

He ordered his crewmen to row him back to the *Dexter*, where he reclothed himself to continue his unequal fight.

There weren't many more to be saved. Among the exceptions was a man found drifting to sea in a half-awash lifeboat. In surprisingly cheery tones, he told the navy officers aboard the *U.S.S. Speedwell*, who rescued him, that his name was Captain Sherrington Vance, of North Truro, Nova Scotia.

In New Bedford, which had become the nerve center for the operations, the totals were apparent before the week entered its final Saturday night hours: only 29 survived This meant 103 persons had been lost. Sobering, too, was the arithmetic that nearly half of the ship's crew was saved, but not quite fifteen percent of the passengers.

One-third of the original passengers were women and children, not one of whom lived to tell of the terrible night on Devil's Bridge Reef. One older child was rescued: George Farnsworth of Townsend, Massachusetts, who was twelve. His brother perished.

The clergy, as was to be expected, held their own court on the disaster.

"Only four can be responsible for this," ruled the Reverend S. Wright Butler of the North Baptist Church, New Bedford. "They are the captain, the second mate, the quartermaster, and the lookout." He added that the second mate was too young to be responsible, that the quartermaster was merely following a predetermined compass course, while the lookout was expected merely to pass on what he saw.

"The captain was responsible," the minister concluded. "One hour's more watch by him and everything would have gone well. Six score passengers below were asking: 'Wilt thou watch with us one hour?'"

The formal hearing commenced. The witnesses presented their affidavits. The man who might have been the most important witness, however—Second Mate Augustus Harding—was dead.

Finally, Andrew Burnham, chairman of the board of inspectors, adjourned the inquiry until February 5th, so that the next most pertinent witness, the captain should be well enough to attend.

On that day, showing signs of "great mental suffering," Captain Wright appeared in answer to his summons. In a room even more crowded than it was the opening day, the master of the *City of Columbus* nervously kept pressing a hand to his head or half-burying his head in his hands.

"What," asked Burnham, coming quickly to the point, "made the *City of Columbus* hit Devil's Bridge Reef?"

"That I shall leave to a higher power," the captain replied. "I should have been as much surprised if she had struck on the other side of the sound."

In denying that Gay Head Light was an aid to navigation when vessels were hauling close by it, he pointed out: "Bright lights are no benefit to pilots except when the vessels are a great way off. When you're close, they're confusing. Brightness doesn't make any difference in fixing the bearing."

Chairman Burnham was persistent. The steamer was off course, he reminded Wright, then demanded: "How do you account for the ship being so far south?"

"God only knows," answered the man who had gone to sea at thirteen.

"How was the tide?" was the next question.

"High water," the captain responded. "Slack. There was a good breeze blowing but the boat would steam ten miles an hour in it. Ordinarily, she ran about twelve miles an hour at sea."

"Is it usual for you to shave Gay Head?"

"There is nothing to be saved by it. Going south in the summer, I give it a wide berth. The good water here is about three and a half to four miles wide. I had spoken to the second mate but never reprimanded him but once—for getting off his course."

Wright expressed the belief that the *City of Columbus* should have cleared Gay Head by slightly more than three miles on the course as set by himself. He added, on further examination, that he "didn't know" whether his second mate possessed a license to pilot, although the captain had previously asked him to obtain one.

Testimony of a surprise nature was offered. Another master took the stand—Captain Bearse, of the coastal steamer *Glaucus*.

He admitted passing the wrecked *City of Columbus* on the Friday morning, no more than four miles distant. With his telescope, he testified, he scanned the rigging, and felt certain "everyone was dead."

The *Glaucus* sailed on—at about 7:15 A.M., or three hours before the first surf boats appeared. Bearse insisted, however, he would have altered course to study the wreck closer had he thought any survivors were aboard.

"We used the spyglass" he reiterated, with apparent embarrassment. "We saw nobody. We thought the crew and passengers must all be drowned or ashore. With water breaking all over the ship and the ship underwater, we supposed, of course, there could be no one there."

It lent a bitter futility to the whole tragedy, even though the chairman expressed the conviction that the skipper of the *Glaucus* was "sincere" in his original judgment and in his testimony.

Quartermaster McDonald was examined and re-examined. Even though the *City of Columbus* was fast on Devil's Bridge Reef, he asserted, he stayed by the helm just in case the steamer should, by some miracle, be freed. Finally, the captain ordered him to cut the covers and ice lashings from Number 2 boat.

Returning to the stand from time to time, Captain Wright reaffirmed the speed with which the steamer filled. Once he pointed to his shoulder, noting that the water, in a few minutes after striking the rocks, was up to "here."

"It came in so suddenly," he asserted, "that the boats couldn't get off."

The crowds of curious at the hearing dwindled. As one newspaper mentioned, there was more space to breathe at last and "the messenger boys didn't have to come in through the chimney." A heavy snowstorm almost canceled the proceedings one day.

On March 5th, the board's finding was published:

"Only bad steering could have caused the loss of three-quarters of a mile toward the north in a run of only twelve miles. That shift off course toward the south caused the wreck."

Further, the report contended, reversing engines to back off the reef had been a mistake. Only three hundred feet ahead there was a shallow sixteen feet of water, in which the ship could have been safely beached, and "much of the loss of life" possibly prevented.

On the other hand, the captain's decision to reverse was excused as "an honest mistake."

The report of the board continued:

"The ship was allowed to yaw off course. Why didn't the pilot in charge notice this divergence? There was no pilot on duty at an open window. The second mate Harding was young and didn't feel the responsibility that Captain Wright would have if he had been piloting.

"The captain apparently thought it was all right as long as he was on call—but this is not a legal form of piloting. If he was tired because of the long run, he should have rested in other places and been fit for the entire dangerous run through the Sound instead of constantly standing by all the time.

"If a special pilot had been on duty, we believe there would have been no disaster. At the time of the disaster, there was really no legal pilot on duty or experienced officer on deck watch." (Harding, who died in the wreck, was only twenty-one and had no piloting license.)

"The neglect of men to watch the course was the immediate cause of the disaster," the two board members found "Captain Wright was the only legal pilot on duty at the time of the disaster. For at least an hour before the City of Columbus struck, he had not been at the pilot's point of duty.

"Captain Wright illegally delegated the pilot duties to one not authorized. He was inattentive to his own duties as pilot. For these reasons, the license of Schuyler E. Wright as master and pilot is hereby revoked."

As The Century Ended

IN 1898, THE WAR WITH SPAIN OCCUPIED MUCH OF THE NEWS. However, the names of two ships, besides the U.S.S. Maine, also figured in the headlines that fateful year: the La Bourgogne and the Portland.

The three-masted Cromartyshire, out of Dunkirk, was sailing through a fog which her master, Oscar Henderson, thought was thick even for this familiar cauldron of bad weather: the green waters off Sable Island.

The Philadelphia-bound iron-hulled vessel was kept under reduced canvas. She was making, Henderson estimated, four knots. He sounded his fog horn "regularly every minute" as he felt his way through the shrouded North Atlantic, past Nova Scotia's graveyard of ships.

The time was 5 A.M. The date was July 4, 1898—Monday morning.

Mrs. Henderson and her two children were aboard this passage. Awakened by the horn, she was uneasy—uneasy enough to have dressed and gone aft to the poop deck, where she met her husband.

There weren't many others up and about. A. C. Stewart, third mate, had the watch. On the bow, Haley, a seaman, was standing lookout.

As she walked to and fro to keep the chill out of her muscles, Mrs. Henderson became conscious of a sound. It was a faint whistle, she thought—far off. She called it to her husband's attention.

He listened, but he could hear nothing. Stewart could not, either.

Mrs. Henderson remained certain that she had picked up the fog horn of another vessel. It planted sufficient seeds of concern within her that she inched away from the two men to be near her cabin and children "should a disaster occur."

At this moment, the watch on a 7,385-ton French liner, the *La bourgogne*, bound from New York, picked up the warning whistles from the *Cromartyshire*. The four-masted screw steamer was pounding eastward through the opaque dawn at close to top speed—seventeen knots.

Commanded by Captain De Loncie, the big French vessel was solidly booked this crossing, carrying 505 passengers and 220 crew. She had the reputation of a comfortable ship, making her a favorite with the ladies; and this time two hundred of them were proving anew this desirability.

There were also fifty infants and somewhat older children.

Among the passengers were a considerable number going home for visits to the countries of their birth. Fred Nyffeler, twenty-nine-year-old member of a group of Swiss-Americans, was one. A stock raiser from Tacoma, Nyffeler had already commenced a pleasurable flirtation with Elisa Niffemegger, of New York, also Swiss. He had been out on deck most of the night.

A German baker from New York, Charles Duttweiler, was headed toward his fatherland for a summer vacation, as was Christopher Brunen; Patrick McKeown, leather salesman from Wilmington, Delaware, would, of course, tour Ireland before continuing on to his business appointments in France; Anterne Archard was returning to France with his wife and two children, Marie and Anterne, Jr.; A. D. La Casse, Plainfield, New Jersey, language teacher, and Mrs. La Casse were going to Europe simply as tourists.

There were others, all with their own reasons for being aboard this ship at this particular hour in the procession of time: the Reverend Anthony Kesseler, of New York, and two other priests; August Purgi, also of New York, and his mother, who had saved for many years to revisit the Italian hilltown where both had been born; Charles Lisbra, French widower, and his two sons, aged five and seven; Charles Liebre, cook at Philadelphia's Bellevue-Stratford Hotel; a Russian wrestler named Youssof. . . .

The *La Bourgogne* raced ahead on course.

On the *Cromartyshire*, Captain Henderson and Third Mate Stewart now were able to confirm what Mrs. Henderson had noted. The whistle, Henderson believed "to be nearing very fast." He pressed down the leather bellows and the sailing ship's fog horn wailed its mournful warning anew into the gray, early morning.

His wife, morbidly fascinated, kept by the railing, opposite the hatch which led to her cabin, where the children were. Peering into the fog, she sighted the *La Bourgogne* almost at the same time that Haley, the bow lookout, cried: "Ship off port bow!"

To Mrs. Henderson, the liner loomed with the incredibility of a nightmare. She did not wait to see what would happen, but dived down the hatch toward the cabin.

Her skipper husband thought in a flickering that the other vessel was "going at a terrific speed." It was no farther than half a ship's length distant when he first made her out through the mists.

He spun the helm, but it was too late. The *Cromartyshire's* jib boom, jutting from the bow like a slender but inflexible battering ram, smashed into the bridge of the *La Bourgogne*.

"Our foretop mast and main topgallant mast came down," said Henderson, "bringing with it yards and everything attached."

The jib boom did not pull clear until it had punctured the metal plates of the *La Bourgogne* and battered on into her engine room. The two vessels, disengaged, scraped with a weird, wounded sound their lengths, then disappeared from the other's sight once more, as though each had been a wraith and the apparent damage some figment of a warped imagination.

On the *La Bourgogne's* bridge, only Second Officer Delinge survived the impact of the collision. The others had been crushed to death at their posts or in their nearby berths as they slept.

Groping through the wreckage of the wheel house for the engine room telegraph, he managed to signal "Stop!" Then he decided he would run for Sable Island if possible and beach the unwelcome command which had suddenly fallen to him.

Below, Louis LeJulien, a stoker, saw the indicator swing to "Ahead, slow." Many of the crew in the engine and boiler rooms had either been killed by the *Cromartyshire's* executioner bow or scalded by the rampaging steam. None the less, the surviving members of the "black gang" started the pistons throbbing again, at a reduced clip.

LeJulien watched the water "begin to come into the boiler room," and "soon it rushed in great columns." The pumps could not control the flood, which snuffed out the remaining fires amidst choking clouds of sulphurous coal smoke. The propeller stopped.

He believed at least fifteen men were dead in his compartment of the engine room. He looked about for an escape ladder, in order to get out before the water-tight doors would seal him in forever.

Fred Nyffeler, the Swiss stock raiser, was tumbled out of bed

not by the impact but by a "terrible list to port." He threw on
his shirt, jumped into trousers, and hurried on deck, carrying
his shoes.

The first sight that greeted his eyes: "splinters."

August Purgi, an early riser, had been on deck when the ships
collided. Now he raced toward the entrance to the women's
dormitory to save his mother. He passed by one of the lifeboats
around which several sailors were clustered, cursing and clawing
"like maniacs."

They thought that LeJulien was trying to climb in it ahead of
them. The next thing he knew, he was struck over the head with
an oar—or a belaying pin—picked up by at least two of the men
and heaved overboard.

He hit the water, and went under.

The La Casses, like most others who could get out of their
cabins at all, paused only to wrap a life preserver around their
night garments and struggled against the increasing list, toward
the boat deck. Families such as the Archards were frantically
dressing their children.

Pat McKeown, the leather salesman from Wilmington, ran
for an upper deck, took one look at the shouting and confusion
about him, and leaped overboard. The last scene on board to
register with him was that of the three priests holding up their
hands to calm the people.

On the *Cromartyshire*, Captain Henderson "set to work immediately to clear the wreckage and also to ship our starboard
anchor, which was hanging over our starboard bow and in
danger of punching holes in the bow." He heard a steamer blowing, then watched a rocket flaring murkily through the fog. The
evanescent, fiery spectacle was followed by a sound he took to be
a pistol shot.

He replied with rockets and also shots. There was no reply—
only the swish-swish of the ground swells rolling southward

from Sable Island and the creak of rope, canvas and tackle. He then ordered all boats lowered.

Mrs. Henderson had roused the children and was dressing them.

The bows of the sailing ship were "completely cut off," Captain Henderson ascertained. The plates were twisted "into every conceivable shape." But the staunch *Cromartyshire* floated on her collision bulkhead.

To the veteran master she seemed in "no immediate danger of sinking."

On the *La Bourgogne*, the situation was quite the reverse. The big liner, normally low in the water, was settling deeper by the bow with an almost suicidal compulsion.

Her list to port increased and her stern rose higher, ever higher in the air. Fred Nyffeler struggled to maintain his balance as he pushed his way about the decks calling for Elisa Niffemegger. "What's up?" he asked the first officer he saw. The latter replied that everything was "all right." Just the same, Nyffeler looked about for a lifeboat with room in it.

Lisbra, the French widower, put his two sons in a boat. He was shoved back onto deck when he tried to follow, remonstrating that they were but five and seven years old and he was their sole protector.

He watched the boat being lowered, then jumped into the water after it. The North Atlantic was cold. He sank below its surface to such a depth that "I thought I was gone," he said.

Archard assisted his wife and two children into the next boat. But its launching was not successful. One of the falls stuck to the davits and the craft tilted at an angle. At the same time, the *La Bourgogne* lurched farther to port and one of its twin funnels toppled across the lifeboat.

As Archard watched in horror, a stay-chain which had been fastened to the funnel cut his wife in two.

Helping in the loading of the boat was Charles Liebre, who confessed: "It was the most blood-curdling sight I ever saw."

Archard, his sons, and the others who survived the fall of the funnel were dumped into the water. When he surfaced, he could not find his boys. All he saw was wreckage—and bodies.

He struck out for a raft. The sailors on it cursed and beat him off with paddles. He recognized Fourth Engineer Laisne of the *La Bourgogne*, and recalled him saying: "Damn the passengers! Let them save themselves. We save ourselves first. If I had a revolver I would shoot the passengers!"

Purgi, Lisbra, and others who had jumped into the water were having similar experiences. Purgi, as Archard, was beaten away from one raft and lifeboat after another by the "inhuman savages" who had minutes before been the crew of the French liner. He finally grasped a lifeline, trailing a safe ten feet behind one boat. He watched, helpless, a sight that defied comprehension— his mother being pushed from the bow of another boat.

However, the sailors were impartial. The same tactics were repeated with another woman, the aged mother of a passenger, John Burig. Mother and son had successfully clambered into a lifeboat, only to be picked up and hurled out again.

His mother floated out of sight. Burig tried four more times to struggle aboard, was beaten back at each attempt.

Youssof, the wrestler, was observed thrashing about the water, grasping planks, barrels, any bit of wreckage which drifted close. He held a stiletto in one hand and struck out at any one who approached him.

Soon the powerful man, who could not swim a stroke, disappeared. Charles Liebre, the Philadelphia hotel cook, was apparently the last to see the well-known wrestler alive.

Lisbra could neither find his children, a refuge, or a lifeline. He had been smashed over the head and shoulders so cruelly by men on the boats and rafts that he had resolved to keep dog-paddling about the ocean.

It seemed the safest course, cold or not.

Christopher Brunen, a second class passenger, witnessed considerable savagery, which commenced when he saw a seaman belonging to the liner clout a passenger over the head with a bar of iron and kill him. His body was dumped into the water. Brunen reported:

"Men fought for positions in the boats like raving maniacs, women were forced back from the boats and trampled on by the human beasts who invoked the first law of nature and made self-preservation their first object. On board were a large number of Italians who care little for human life. These fiends stopped at nothing. In one boat was a party of forty women, but so great was the panic that not a hand was raised to assist in her launching.

"So desperate was the situation that an Italian passenger drew his knife and made a thrust at one who, like himself, was endeavoring to reach the boats. Immediately the action was imitated in every direction. Knives were flourished in every direction and used with deadly effect.

"Women and children were driven back to an inevitable death at the point of weapons, the owners of which were expert in their use. Even sickness was not respected and according to the stories of some of the survivors, women were stabbed like so many sheep.

"The scene in the water was even worse. Many of the unfortunates who were struggling in the water attempted to drag themselves into the boats and on rafts. These were rudely pushed back to their watery grave."

Brunen finally reached an upturned boat. With the assistance of another man he righted it and found wedged under the seats the bodies of four men and three women.

On the decks of the *La Bourgogne*, afloat, though barely so, men still fought for the remaining boats or rafts. A steerage passenger, Mehelini Secondo, was locked in a life and death struggle with two or three other men—whether sailors or passengers he did not know—to free a raft that was chained to the decking. None seemed to realize that all the group was working for the same end.

Finally, he gave up and leaped overboard.

There was still a small cluster of kneeling figures, mostly women with their children, at the feet of the three priests. The trio kept calling on the passengers to make "acts of contrition."

La Casse, the language teacher from Plainfield, assisted his wife into a boat. It was lowered before they discovered there were no oars in it.

In the adjoining boat, Karl Elkoory was grabbed by several men whom he took to be crewmen. They lifted him above their shoulders, suddenly paused, as he was suspended, kicking. When he looked, he saw a French passenger was leveling a revolver at his assailants, threatening to shoot them all if they didn't let go of their intended victim. Elkoory was saved.

Two waiters, however, in the opposite end of the same boat were intimidated by knife-brandishing fellow crewmen and some others they took to be "Austrians." Terland and Mons Lucas had no stomach for it, and leaped overboard.

Nyffeler, the Swiss, in another boat, already launched, watched the end of the *La Bourgogne*—"A sudden crack and the ship went down."

It happened that suddenly and completely. She had survived the fatal collision about fifteen minutes.

Dozens of passengers still on the decks jumped as the liner made her death plunge, in a hissing cloud of steam. Several, landing in the La Casse's boat, capsized it. Mr. and Mrs. La

Casse swam to a raft. It was designed for eight persons, though there were already twenty on it.

The raft settled to knee-depth as Mrs. La Casse crawled onto it. Her husband clung to its lifeline.

It was not so easy a matter to come aboard other rafts. Patrick McKeown observed an "American from Philadelphia" being beaten over the head with oars on one raft. Finally, his limp form was picked up and tossed into the Atlantic.

It was "murder," thought McKeown.

Charles Lisbra, who had already abandoned hope for his sons, saw sailors cut the lifeline trailing behind a small raft. Five women had been clutching it in a death grasp.

Lisbra himself was indifferent to survival. He was already a widower. Now he had no children. The world was ended for him.

Mehelini Secondo, who had abandoned his efforts to free a liferaft from the deck, finally crawled into a boat. He was not a large man but he was wiry and strong. The crew had slashed and jabbed viciously at him with boathooks. He was cut and bruised from his forehead to his waist.

He had picked an oar out of the debris-choked water and fought back like a cornered tiger. He cowed the crew into glum submission. They put down their boathooks and sat glowering. His oar blade, Secondo noted, had taken its toll on several foreheads, from which blood trickled.

The fighting, the insane fear continued into the morning. Some passengers shared desperation for survival with the crew.

The first boat arrived at the side of the *Cromartyshire* about 5:30 A.M., as the fog began to lift.

"We saw two boats pulling towards us with the French flag flying," noted Captain Henderson. "We signaled them to come alongside and found that the steamer was the *La Bourgogne* from New York for Havre and that she had gone down."

"Men were seen in every direction clinging to wreckage," Mrs. Henderson wrote. "It was a terrible sight. No pen can picture the appalling sight revealed to the onlookers when the curtain of mist arose."

Little by little, as the drenched, bruised, and dazed survivors came aboard, the bizarre, hateful story came out.

"I am heartbroken and wretched," sobbed Archard. In his money belt he carried twenty thousand dollars, soaked but otherwise intact. And yet, that was all he had left in the world.

Nyfeller, Henderson reported, cursed "the fiendish French sailors with passionate earnestness." He never found his girl friend, Elisa Niffemegger; indeed, he soon concluded that he alone survived of the original Swiss party of fifteen.

McKeown came aboard babbling about "three or four women" who had been struck and tossed into the water. He cried: "It was a terrible sight and I hope to God I never witness another like it."

Charles Duttweiller, the German baker, did not need to explain. The deep wound over his left ear and purple contusions on his forehead spoke for him.

"I am thoroughly ashamed of my countrymen," declared Charles Lisbra, who had lost his two motherless boys.

Mrs. Henderson was soon aware that "No effort was made to save the women."

Her husband wrote:

"We laid to all day and received on board about two hundred survivors from among the passengers and crew, reported to be in all about six hundred. Several of the passengers were on life rafts without oars and I called for volunteers from among my crew and the surviving French seamen to bring those rafts alongside of the ship. Some of the passengers and seamen from the sunken steamer assisted us and we jettisoned some thirty tons of cargo from our fore hold in order to lighten the ship. About 1

P.M. another steamer hove in sight bound westward. We put up our signal 'N. C.'—'Want assistance!' "

She was the *Grecian*, bound from Glasgow to New York. The captain said he would take the survivors and tow the crippled sailing ship to Halifax. The latter had fourteen feet of water in her hold.

About the time the *Grecian* hove into view, the last raft was picked up. On it were the La Casses, from Plainfield, and six others.

Captain Henderson's first count was in error. As the officers of the *Grecian* tallied their lists and retallied them, they could find just 164 on board, no more. Of that number 105 were *La Bourgogne* crewmen.

The fact which appalled the officers of the rescue vessel—Mrs. La Casse was the only woman who had been saved. There were no children.

Here was one of the shocking tragedies of the sea, they realized—561 souls having perished in these waters of the North Atlantic that very morning.

It was even more difficult for the nation's press to comprehend the actions.

"Whatever the verdict concerning the management of the steamer," editorialized the *New York Mail and Express*, "both before and after the collision may be, the fact will remain that never in all the tragedies of the deep which memory marshals before us has so utterly shameful and cowardly a climax been enacted as that on Monday morning off Sable Island."

The *New York Times* put it even more succinctly: "It was a French ship and only one woman was saved."

The magnitude and peculiarly depraved nature of the disaster even dampened rejoicing over the fall of Santiago and destruction of Admiral Cervera's fleet in the rapidly concluding Spanish-American War.

In New York, Paul Faguet, general agent for the *Com-pagnie General Transatlantique*, better known as the French Line, understandably refused to accept what had happened. "We do not believe the charges to be true," he reiterated to reporters.

But the next of kin, who were making his own life a special purgatory, did believe it. The brother of Miss Gertrude Steel, who was lost, reiterated the survivors' observation: "It was no less than murder!"

Even M. Faguet could not escape soul-wracking doubts as he supervised the preparation of the final list of the dead:

> Mrs. R. Hyman, and child
> Mr. and Mrs. Richard Jacob, and child
> Mrs. Osgood, and child
> Mrs. Whitney, child and maid. . . .

And so it read, like something imagined by a mad teller of nursery tales.

When the survivors arrived at Grand Central Station, New York, still bearing the marks of their pummeling, even policemen were misty-eyed. As one patrolman noted the cluster of crewmen huddled together in a rear coach, every ounce of aggressiveness gone, he remarked: "What cattle they are!"

That Second Officer Delinge—whose conduct was praised—was the only surviving senior officer of the ship's company did not seem to help much in Faguet's attempts to point out self-sacrifice on the part of the crew. After all, 725 souls had been aboard the *La Bourgogne* on her recent departure from New York. A handful had returned. And only 59 were passengers.

In Glen Ridge, New Jersey, John Phelps Firing hugged and kissed his wife. With her daughter, Bessie, she had been booked to sail on the *La Bourgogne*. She hadn't been able to pack in time, so canceled her passage.

She sailed the following week on another liner.

The summer wore on. Clara Barton wired President McKinley that hospital accommodations in Siboney, Cuba, were "inadequate . . . many of the wounded lie on the water-soaked ground." On August 12th, an armistice ended hostilities.

In Halifax, a Canadian court of inquiry met to ponder the *Cromartyshire-La Bourgogne* disaster. On September 25th, the judges "entirely exonerated from all blame" Captain Henderson, while refusing to pass on the guilt or lack of guilt on the part of officers and crew of the French vessel.

On October 14, 1898, the 8500-ton Atlantic transport liner *Mohegan* smashed ashore off Lizard Head, England, in a fog reminiscent of that near Sable Island earlier in the year. A total of 150 persons were lost amid tales of great heroism by the crew in an effort to save the passengers from rocks and surf at this southwest England land tip.

Among those who perished were Mrs. John Phelps Firing, of Glen Ridge, New Jersey, and her daughter Bessie. She had finished her Paris shopping and laughingly vowed to her friends that she wouldn't miss *this* sailing.

The next month, on a Saturday afternoon—November 26th—people were hurrying through a light snow in Boston, resolved not to miss yet another sailing. Warped alongside the old India Wharf was the pride of the Boston and Portland Steam Packet Company: the *Portland*. She was receiving passengers and freight before casting off for "down East."

Grossing 2,300 tons, she was 281 feet long and could make twelve knots or better. Plush and trim, she was equipped with electric lights and intercommunication phones, and was even steered electrically. She was one of the largest, most comfortable and—they said—safest coastal vessels to ply American waters.

The paddle wheels themselves were inclined to make her ride more smoothly than many propeller-type vessels. Lounges were furnished richly: overstuffed Victorian chairs and sofas, deep, red carpeting. Many of her staterooms boasted actual brass poster beds, instead of bunks, and washing facilities.

Her owners had built up such a reputation for caution that their company was often called "the old granny line." The *Portland* had hugged dock so often at the least sign of a blow that her eight lifeboats suggested an extravagance.

But tonight, she would sail. It was the end of the Thanksgiving weekend—also of the yearly Mechanics Fair in Boston—and people were hurrying to get aboard her. They wanted to be home in Maine for Sunday, and ready and rested to start a new week.

There were men, women, and children, of all ages, all social and financial levels. Perhaps the wealthiest was Oren Hooper, owner of Portland's large house furnishings store, which bore his name. With him was his fourteen-year-old son, Karl. Considering his affluence, his presence on the night boat was somewhat surprising. With the uncertain weather, threatening all afternoon in Boston, he could have taken the evening train and been in Portland before midnight.

But he had a reason, and it seemed logical to him—he possessed a pass for the Boston and Portland Steam Packet Company. He would save a few dollars train fare.

Perhaps the most impoverished was Lewis Metcalfe, twenty-seven, who was returning to Lewiston, Maine, after a fruitless job quest in Brockton, Massachusetts. His wife Nora had "an awful feeling" about his going away, especially over Thanksgiving. But the lumber mill where he had worked was shut down. What could he do? she asked herself.

Between the extremes of Oren Hooper and Lewis Metcalfe was an almost random assortment of passengers:

Miss Maud Sykes, of Portland, whose fiance had died two

weeks before of fever contracted in the recently-ended Spanish-American War.

Charles Thompson, of Portland, traveling with his wife and baby, Gladys.

Miss Emily Cobb, of Portland, choir singer in the First Parish Church.

Madge Ingraham, Negro servant, of Portland.

Mrs. Daniel Rounds, wife of a Portland cobbler, and her daughter.

No one knew just how many were on board—possibly two hundred, counting passengers and crew.

This Saturday the papers were filled with a normal quota of trivia as well as more important news, covering a range which commenced with the haggling over conquered Spain's ceding the Philippines to the United States and ended, possibly, with the advertisement which promised "nervous, sick-headache cured for 10 cents."

There was also the weather forecast: "Heavy snow and warmer tonight. Sunday, snow and much colder. Southeasterly winds shifting by tonight to northwesterly gales."

One prospective passenger, Captain C. H. Leighton, of Rockland, had read the warning and didn't like it. He clomped up to the cabin of Captain Hollis Henry Blanchard, fifty-five-year-old skipper of the *Portland*, and asked his old friend if he really was going to sail.

"I shall," was Blanchard's curt reply.

"By George," Leighton asserted, "I don't think this is a fit night to leave port." With that, he picked up his satchel and hurried down the gangplank and back onto India Wharf.

In a few minutes a long distance call was received on the wharf telephone. It was from Captain Alexander Dennison, of the sister *Bay State*, warped to its dock in Portland. He informed

Blanchard: "I'm not sailing tonight. It's blowin' like sixty down here!"

Blanchard informed the other captain bluntly that he would sail. At Sunday dinner in his Yarmouth home two of his three children would be present for a family reunion . . . He added before hanging up that he was in receipt of a weather advisory from New York which indicated the storm would back around to the northwest. He would be sheltered "in a lee" all the way up the coast.

In his early thirties, Dennison, of the *Bay State*, was one of the youngest New England skippers. Gruff and considered exceptionally stubborn by associates, Blanchard was not one to take advice from a junior.

Meanwhile, on the *Portland*, J. Frank Hunt, second clerk, closed his books, switched off his desk lamp and said goodnight to Purser F. A. Ingraham. Hunt would be ashore to attend the funeral Monday of Captain Charles Deering, former master of the *Bay State*, whom Dennison has succeeded. First Mate Edward Deering, a relative of the deceased, and First Pilot Lewis F. Strout were also taking a short leave from their side-wheeler to attend the funeral.

At 6:40 p.m. the wind was picking up, although the snow was desultory and inconsequential. It barely fringed in white the mahogany railings, the lifeboat covers, and the *Portland's* distinctive mascot: the large gilded eagle atop the wheel house.

Five minutes later, as the cargo holds were being closed and the machinery tested, Captain Blanchard had a visitor, his oldest son Charles, who worked in Boston. He happened to be passing along Atlantic Avenue and noted with some disbelief that his father's ship was preparing to sail.

Charles hurried aboard, to be informed by his elder: "I have my orders to sail. I am going."

After the younger Blanchard had gone back ashore, it seemed

to him that his father had alluded to routine instructions from John Liscomb, manager of the line.

At 6:55 p.m. the stern hawser splashed into the debris-choked water of the slip and was hauled onto the deck. Blanchard spoke from the bridge to George Barton, wharf watchman: "Keep an eye out for me. I might come back."

The gangplank was removed and the *Portland* started from the wharf.

At this juncture, a nineteen-year-old North Billerica (Massachusetts) man, Clyde Doyle, arrived breathlessly at India Wharf, hoping to put his half-sister, Florence Pierce, aboard. Florence taught school in Vassalboro, Maine. He recalls:

"As I walked to the edge of the wharf the signal was given to change from reverse to go ahead; and as the bow was turned out, the stern came within a foot of the landing, and I walked along side with my hand on the rail while I turned to ask my sister if she would like to jump aboard.

"The captain laughed and told me to be careful not to fall in —to which I replied that I wouldn't, and the five people on the upper deck just above me were enjoying it all.

"They were a girl about eighteen, a man and woman about thirty-five, and another couple in their fifties. They appeared to be one family. And as the *Portland* gained speed the younger man waved to me and said: 'Better luck next time!'

"I waved back to them and all five waved and turned to go inside. The boat was out of sight at three or four hundred yards down the harbor in the blowing snow."

There were several other persons who just missed the sailing. Like Clyde Doyle and his half-sister, they walked back to Atlantic Avenue to hail a cab for North Station.

There was one man, at least, on India Wharf, on whose ears their laments rang flatly—Charles F. Williams, the stocky, bald passenger agent at Boston. Earlier he had received a telephone message from Liscomb, in Portland.

Liscomb had a bad cold and was on his way to The Hub by train. He told Williams that the *Portland* should "wait till nine for a weather report." In his own mind, Williams was sure he had "said to Blanchard all that a man could say" to convey the message. He had also passed the order on to Barton, the watchman.

Yet, the great side-wheeler was sailing. In the confusion, had he, Williams, not made himself clear? Had he perhaps been guilty of the unthinkable: of having imagined he had relayed the instructions?

Williams tugged at his moustache as he pondered and worried, and pondered some more. Blanchard was stubborn, difficult. His manager, Liscomb, had a temper, was known to go "wild" when disobeyed. The passenger agent listened to the wind whine across the wharf's dried shingle roofing and decided he was in an unenviable position.

With Second Pilot Lewis M. Nelson, fifty-six, at the helm, the *Portland* pushed across the choppy harbor waters. A massive mahogany wheel, the helm was a scientific wonder in itself: it was hooked up electrically to the rudder, through a maze of cables and junction boxes.

Because of similar modern devices throughout the vessel, a degree of semi-automation was effected.

At 7:20 P.M. Wesley Pingree, keeper of Deer Island light, at the harbor entrance, logged the *Portland's* passing. A few minutes later, the *Kennebec*, serving Bath, Boothbay, and other Maine ports, blew her whistle in greeting to the *Portland*. Captain Jason Collins, of the *Kennebec*, had tested the seas beyond Deer Island. He decided to put back to dock for the night.

Blanchard kept on. With Boston Light winking to starboard,

the *Portland* swung up the coast, so as to pass clear of Graves Ledges.

And, at this time, the final late arrivals had reached India Wharf. There was, for one, an angry Saco, Maine, shoe worker, Leonard Dora. He had been aboard the *Portland* earlier in the afternoon, then returned to his hotel for his forgotten luggage.

Another was Harry Sylvester, fourteen, of Portland, who had been spending Thanksgiving with an aunt in East Boston. He had missed the sailing because the rough harbor had delayed his ferry boat from East Boston to Atlantic Avenue, Boston, near the North Station.

Now, abeam of Graves Ledges, the *Portland* was signaled by Captain William A. Roix, of the *Mt. Desert*, as well as by the tug *Sylph No. 8.*

The night boat to Maine continued along the coast as northeast winds blew with mounting force and snow cascaded seaward in ever-thickening sheets.

In Boston the evening had not commenced with sufficient severity to keep people home. The cry of the wind and the sight of slanting snow on thoroughfares such as Tremont Street were not unfamiliar to Bostonians.

Some were at the theater, attending De Wolf Hopper's performance of *The Charlatan*. For the students of the numerous universities and colleges in the area, it was Saturday night and a time to dance and sing. "By The Sea" was a smash hit—in fact the Globe this Sunday was printing its full verses in the feature section.

In the same issue, those irrepressible cartoon characters, the Brownies, were up to new antics. Their creator this Sunday had them sailing in the Killarney Lakes, Ireland. So as not to disappoint his readers, he saw to it that their boats were capsized before the end of the comic strip.

By 9 P.M., those students who poked their noses outside the

doors of Boston drinking places knew the night was worsening. The words of their song suddenly assumed ridiculous overtones: ". . . by the sea, by the sea, by the beautiful sea!"

And just after nine the *Portland* had struggled past Gloucester and was hauling in closer to shore, two or three miles off a boarded-up summer resort section known as Bass Rocks.

Aboard the fishing schooner, *Maude S.*, Captain Bill Thomas perceived the *Portland* night boat's "dim, white form." She appeared on course and navigating routinely. Thomas, however, was more concerned for the safety of his own command as he tacked this way and that through the angry seas, trying to make Gloucester harbor.

A few minutes later, on nearby Thatcher's Island, William Harrington, who was visiting his friend the lightkeeper, stared out of the streaked window of the island's one house. He squinted, looked again, then remarked: "There goes the *Portland!*"

He thought the time was shortly after nine-thirty when he finally lost track of her. The *Portland* and *Bay State* were familiar sights, churning nightly past the twin lights of Thatcher's Island.

By 11 P.M., however, the *Portland*—strangely—was still abeam of Gloucester's rocky and storm-lashed shores. At this hour, some twelve miles southeast of Thatcher's Island, Reuben Cameron, kipper of the schooner *Grayling*, saw the wraith-like white bulk of the *Portland*. She was bearing down on his small craft with such speed that he shot off a flare to warn her away.

As the towering steamer swept perilously close to him, he could see that she was "pitching and rolling badly." Nonetheless, he did not consider her out of control.

At approximately 11:15 P.M., the schooner *Florence E. Stearns* found the *Portland* in approximately the same position. Frank Stearns, the *Florence E. Stearns'* owner, was not certain whether the massive side-wheeler was underway or not. It occurred to him that she merely might be heading into the seas, trying to ride out the gale.

At 11:45 P.M., Captain D. J. Pellier, of the schooner *Edgar Randall*, glimpsed the *Portland* through thick snow and spray some fourteen miles southeast of Eastern Point Light, at the mouth of Gloucester harbor.

The night boat, these various reportings meant, was being driven back, back away from the coast.

Pellier kept her in view for several minutes. He felt concern for the steamer's safety, since it looked as though her superstructure had been damaged. He blew his signal horn and fired several rockets, trying to attract her attention and possibly to offer his assistance.

She either did not see him or did not need help. At any rate, the *Edgar Randall* was becoming top-heavy with ice, and Pellier could not delay longer his own attempts to reach shelter.

In Boston, meanwhile, the winds had picked up to fifty miles an hour, and the snow was heavy. Shortly before midnight, Edward Proffet, a thirty-year-old Negro steward on the fivemaster *Governor Ames*, anchored off Commercial Wharf, ventured from a hatchway to throw garbage overboard. A surging wave just then swept the decks, taking Proffet with it.

Inbound from England, the steamship *Ohio* had almost made port when the bow watch sang out: "Land dead ahead!"

It was too late. The mammoth vessel ground across the beach and part way across narrow Spectacle Island before coming to rest. She was still on even keel, as though in dry dock.

Three horses slipped, rounding a curve on the Boston elevated, tore loose from their harness, and plunged fifty feet to the cobblestones below.

The Park Street subway station, piling up with snow which poured down through the entrance and gratings, was closed.

The tug *Cumberland* finally made her moorings in South Boston. But she had lost her tow, a barge from Baltimore with three men aboard, near Boston Light.

In Providence, Rhode Island, the afternoon train from New York finally bedded down. For ten hours the engineer had butted winds and drifts in a losing battle to reach Boston.

The storm, however, was only teasing, at Portland. Even as the audience walked home from the Jefferson Theater, where Rose Colgan had been performing in *The White Heather*, it did not seem as though there would be enough snow by breakfast time worth shoveling.

But one Portland resident, John Liscomb, had no illusions about the intensity of the storm. Sick with his cold, he went to a hotel room in Boston for the night, both disquieted and surprised to learn that the *Portland* had sailed.

By 2 A.M. the blizzard was pummeling Maine. Off Wiscasset, surfboat crews struggled to reach a two-master pounding helplessly on the rocks.

Another schooner, the *Fred A. Emerson*, out of Boothbay, crashed ashore on Thompson's Island, at the approaches to Boston. She was a total loss, but her crew survived.

By 5 A.M. the full venom of the storm was being hurled at Martha's Vineyard. It was now classed by weather observers as a "blizzard of hurricane intensity." As it swept the little island, it toppled trees and utility poles, sliced off roofs, demolished small buildings, and sank almost every lobster boat at mooring.

As a dark, howling dawn arrived over the tip of Cape Cod, at least six vessels were in distress somewhere off treacherous Race Point: the schooner *King Philip*, heavy with eighteen hundred tons of coal, in command of Captain A. A. Duncan, of Portland; the *Pentagoet*, of the Manhattan Line, and former Civil War gunboat, bound for Bangor; the small schooners *Ruth M.*

Martin, F. R. Walker and *Addie E. Snow,* and—the steamer *Portland.*

About 7 A.M. this bleak Sunday, Michael Hogan, master of the *Ruth M. Martin,* which had lost her sails, boats and anchor, spotted "a big side-wheeler" through a rift in the clouds and snow. He figured she was trying to round the tip of Cape Cod, as was he, to reach Provincetown harbor.

Hogan thought the steamer was "drifting with the wind, but keeping her head with the storm, indicating that she was under steam." He could not possibly have reached the *Portland,* since she was to windward.

He had also seen "a propeller steamer," presumed to be the *Pentagoet* "to leeward." He started for her in hopes of transferring his crew and himself aboard. In moments, his little schooner was swallowed in the trough of a giant wave.

When he bobbed to a crest again, no vessel was in sight. The *Ruth M. Martin,* caught in a series of combers, was shortly saved through fantastic good fortune. She was swept clear over Peaked Hill Bar, off the tip of Cape Cod, and finally onto the beach at Provincetown.

At the Race Point Life Saving Station, meanwhile, winds were being clocked at ninety miles per hour. The keeper, Samuel O. Fisher, heard four distant blasts of a steamer's whistle, which signified to him there was a sizable steamer in distress. He rang the station's bell, finally donned oilskins and walked outside where he shot up rockets. Yet he saw nothing and heard no further whistle signals.

The day wore on. Little by little, the storm abated.

In Portland it was still snowing heavily as men and women crunched their way to Franklin Wharf to meet relatives and friends. There was Henry Hooper, twenty, waiting for his father and brother; Daniel Rounds, the cobbler, looking for his wife and daughter; Mrs. Isaiah Frye, whose husband, a wealthy mer-

chant, and eight-year-old daughter Ruth and niece Maud Sykes
(whose fiance had just died) were all aboard; and George
Loring, a Portland printer, delivering printed invitations to
Henry De Merritt Young, the Boston artist, who was to have
an exhibit Monday at the Falmouth Hotel. The M. M. Baileys
had sent their coachman for Madge Ingraham, their Negro
servant.

They waited.

In Boston, others besieged Agent Williams on India Wharf
for news. He could only surmise that the *Portland* was safe in
Gloucester harbor. Telegraph lines were down. He could not
be sure.

For that matter, some trains were yet unreported by mid-
afternoon Sunday. Where was the express due in from Montreal
at 8 A.M.? The Flying Yankee, from Portland, had flown no
closer than Lynn. Passengers attempted to complete their journey from Lynn to Boston by trolleys.

Roosting on almost every island in Boston harbor was a ship
or the wreckage of ships, of all sizes and shapes, from the transatlantic liner *Ohio* to lesser schooners. The militia was mobi-
lized for rescue work.

Sunday passed to the echoing symphony of tens of thousands
of snow shovels. Evening came on.

In the waning light over Cape Cod, surfboat crewmen were
patrolling the beaches. John J. Johnson was half a mile east
of his Race Point station when he spied a life preserver. He
picked it up and read:

"Steamer *Portland* of Portland."

Nearby was wreckage: creamery cans, a splintered oar, wood
paneling, a barrel, green and pink tissue paper . . .

Gideon Bouley was walking near Highland Light, about five
miles from Johnson, when he saw a body in the surf. It proved

to be that of a Negro. A badge on the dead man's clothing indicated he had been a steward on the *Portland*.

At Nauset, still farther down the seaward side of the Cape, Daniel Gould recovered another corpse. It was wrapped in a life preserver from the *Portland*.

By midnight, the fate of the Boston-Portland night boat was apparent to Cape Cod.

The remnants of what the advertisements had proclaimed a "new and palatial steamer" surged ashore for the next twenty-four hours: barrels of lard and sausage, piano keys, the heavily lashed helm, still dangling its electric controls, an ornament from the paddle-wheel boxing, mahogany table legs, the binnacle stand, door locks, part of the main companionway, paneling, toys . . .

Mingled with the wreckage was that of another ship, the coal schooner *King Philip*.

Bodies continued to float to the beaches, some clothed, some nude, most of them surprisingly free of bruises. A number, including that of Oren Hooper, were clad in night garments, indicating to the searchers that the disaster had somehow not been anticipated by those on board.

At Orleans, Mayo's blacksmith shop was converted into a morgue. Carpenters were hastily called out to help alleviate the shortage of coffins.

Workers, who found bodies and debris along a six-mile stretch of shore, scribbled brief descriptions:

"A woman of fifty-three . . . large and somewhat stout."

"Body of a girl about twenty years of age. Gold watch and a ring marked 'J.G.E.' Dark hair and a full set of teeth."

"A man well dressed in black suit and overcoat, light hair and moustache."

A trunk was found. Among its contents was a Bible and a

letter addressed to Miss Madge Ingraham, 190 Middle St., Portland.

There were odd, disconnected bits, like torn fragments from the chapters in the passengers' lives: a photograph of a man, with the stamp of the photographer's shop on the back: "Rue Bismarck, Posen," an empty wallet, a woman's hat, a baby's rattle . . .

In Portland, the people had all gone home from Franklin Wharf, even Daniel Rounds, who had refused many previous offers of assistance. All day he had sat on a bench in the steamship waiting room, his head sunken into his hands—as though from the very first the little cobbler knew that never, never would he see his wife Anna or his little daughter again.

George Loring, the printer, had tossed the invitations into a trash can on his way home. Even should the *Portland*, by some miracle, arrive tomorrow, he knew it would be too late for the art exhibit.

The family reunion at the Blanchards in Yarmouth was over. It had been a silent one. A seafaring brother of the *Portland's* master, G. D. Blanchard, had been buried at sea only the previous month, just east of Hong Kong.

On Monday, the *Portland Press* commenced a lead article: "There is no denying that considerable anxiety is felt for the safety of the steamer *Portland*. . . . Nothing has been heard from her yet."

In Boston, Manager Liscomb was quoted concerning Captain Blanchard: "It is clearly a case of bad judgment and disobedience of orders on his part." Agent Williams had inserted a notice in the newspapers of Boston:

"Note: People having friends on board the steamer *Portland* when she sailed from Boston Saturday evening should not become alarmed for the safety of the vessel as yet."

In Orleans, Mayo's blacksmith shop was stacked with freshly-made coffins. Bodies and debris from the *Portland* continued to come ashore, as did planking from the *King Philip*. This circumstantial evidence caused some to theorize that the two ships had collided.

Of the *Pentagoet*, her crew of fifteen, or her cargo, which was said to include tons of Christmas toys, there was not a trace. To deepen her mystery, it was reported in Maine that she had been sighted Saturday off Cape Elizabeth.

Not until Tuesday afternoon, three days after the *Portland* had sailed, did the news of the side-wheeler's disaster spread beyond Cape Cod. Harry Sparrow, a "stringer" for the *Boston Herald*, finally got word through to Charlie Ward, the regular Cape Cod correspondent. Ward managed to find a telegraph station on the South Shore side of the Cape that was in operation.

The flash electrified the city room. The city editor called for "second coming" type and hurried the dramatic story into print: "ALL PERISHED! The Steamer *Portland* carried 140 souls to death on Cape Cod!"

As perhaps an afterthought, the editors inserted a small note on the bottom of page one: "The *Herald* . . . again vindicated its right to the title of New England's Greatest Newspaper."

The gentlemen of the fourth estate, however, were talking to themselves. Few in New England cared that week which was the greatest—or the worst—paper. Hope and self-deception were at an end.

"Grief has stricken our city," wrote the *Portland Press*.

At 44 Bowdoin Street, the family of Oren Hooper had lost a father as well as a son. In the stable, Oren's prized pair of bay mares had become a confounding reminder of their late owner's measure of—things. He had paid six hundred dollars for them, and his wife had labeled it extravagance.

And yet, even on a threatening night, he apparently would not pay the few dollars' train fare back to Portland.

He had a pass for the night boat.

Daniel Rounds had far fewer and less valuable personal possessions. There were only the tools in his cobbler's shop—his meager house furniture, his clothes and those of his wife Anna and daughter, not packed for their trip to Boston.

Thursday night came, and time for the regular choir rehearsal in the First Parish Church. But one of the voices would be absent—that of Emily Cobb.

In Lewiston, Nora Metcalfe finally was back home. She had been with her sister in the country and was snowbound since the "electrics" could not get through until tracks were plowed.

Nora remembers to this day how she was baking chicken, with the neighbors' cats watching just outside the window, when someone brought her a newspaper telling of the *Portland's* loss. She did not know on what steamer Lewis was returning, but as soon as she saw the headlines, somehow she knew that she was a widow.

Lewis, the good-looking young man whom Nora always thought of as "full of fun," was gone.

And on Cape Cod, Agent Williams identified George Watson, fifty, a Negro second cook, as he blurted excitedly: "I've complimented that man many times on the excellent soup he made!"

The strain had told on Charles Williams.

"God forgive me," he cried out to reporters, "if I gave out information in Boston that was not true. I told the newspapermen that the *Portland* was all right in Gloucester. No men could have stood what the men in the Boston office have been obliged to go through the past few days. It is horrible."

New England's ministers regarded the tragedy with somewhat balanced emotions. The Lord, inscrutably, had struck down the innocent. Speculation as to why was the proper subject for a sermon of considerable duration.

The Reverend E. Leishof, of the Universalist Church, Orleans, apex of the disaster's backwash, announced on Saturday that he would attempt from his pulpit "to lighten the grief of the relatives of the unfortunates."

Yet the newspaper reporters wondered if the well-intentioned efforts of even hundreds of Leishofs could possibly lighten the ache which dwelt within so many hearts. They would perhaps be as effective as the pills which, for a modest ten cents, would cure "nervous sick-headache" and purportedly a long list of unrelated ailments and symptoms.

The year 1898 was coming to an end, the year which started out with the sinking of the *Maine* and, before it was half over, had witnessed America's emergence as an empire-nation. The headiness which the victory over Spain had imparted to a youthful United States had found, in New England at least, a coldly sobering antidote.

Never again in their lives would the men and women of Boston who had sung "By the sea, by the sea, by the beautiful sea" that Saturday night think of the verses without a peculiar mixture of nostalgia and loathing.

Hints of the *Portland's* whereabouts—dinnerware, a lantern, keys, bits of paneling, a chandelier—were to be brought from the bottom of Cape Cod Bay in subsequent years in fishermen's nets. But, now, it hardly mattered where her remains or those of her passengers and crew rested.

The *S.S. Portland* had made her final departure from old India Wharf, and all the singing or sermoning or hoping could not, in the measure of time, resummon the two hundred souls who had sailed cheerfully aboard her—to oblivion.

The Lonely Men

NEARLY TWO HUNDRED MILES OFF THE SCOTTISH COAST, WEST OF the Hebrides, even west of St. Kilda Island, there juts a reef: Rockall.

Shafting above the surface to a maximum height of seventy-five feet, its underwater length measures a treacherous five miles. Sailors of many generations have shunned Rockall for the certain destruction it holds for the unwary. Except that it is stationary, the massive outcropping of granite is as menacing as an iceberg.

Because of its own visible danger, Rockall claimed very few ships. The chances of colliding with it were seemingly and mathematically slim. But one summer morning in 1904, an immigrant ship had a rendezvous with the off-shore reef—and kept that rendezvous.

The Norge was old, smallish, grossing 3,318 tons, in the Scandinavian-American Line service from Copenhagen to New York. Glasgow-built in 1881, she was strengthened by six watertight bulkheads and considered a very safe ship for her size.

She could, nonetheless, carry a disproportionately large passenger list. Since her owners were engaged in the "cut rate immigrant war" with other lines, 703 low-fare passengers, most of them bound for America for the first time, were aboard on this crossing. The crew numbered seventy-one, under the command of Captain Gundell.

The trip had been uneventful, the weather fair. Tuesday, June

28th, dawned cloudy, mild, with a gentle southerly breeze teasing the grey-blue waters. Katerina Sillander, of North Franklin Street, Chicago, going home to join her husband, had awakened and was preparing to dress her baby.

The morning appeared "quiet" and she thought that "most of the passengers were sleeping."

Pedre Nelsen, recently naturalized, was returning to South Dakota from a visit to his homeland. He had arisen early, washed and dressed, and was now lying on his bunk, waiting for the breakfast gong.

To Gundell, the master, all seemed to be going well. At 7:45 A.M. the visibility was good in spite of the overcast. The steam engines were thumping their customary slow, rhythmical beat, driving the blunt-prowed vessel at a plodding eight knots.

There was just one thing wrong. The master obviously did not know where he was, having possibly neglected star sights during the night. He was on the bridge talking to Chief Officer Carpenter when he felt his ship "strike heavily forward."

He surmised at once, from the jar and the crunching sound, that the Norge had smashed into a "sunken rock."

Katerina Sillander, almost finished with clothing her baby, thought the vessel had hit twice. On the second shock, she grabbed the child "by the hair and ran up the companionway."

A man was already shouting in a loud, authoritative voice: "All hands on deck! Hurry or you may sink!"

To Nelsen, waiting, dressed for breakfast, the first bump was "slight," the second more definite. He reported:

"I rushed on deck and saw that something serious had happened. I made a dash to return in order to collect my few belongings. Scores were rushing on deck and the hatchway was crowded with immigrants.

"They were launching boats and I rushed to get into one.

There was no panic. There were four or five people in the boat when I got in."

Captain Gundell watched the smashed prow of the *Norge* sticking fast against the rock, standing rugged and implacable out of the water. He gave orders to reverse engines and the ship careened slowly back from the pile of granite, accompanied by an almost agonized "grinding." Once completely free from the ledges, the noise ceased, but the steamer commenced to fill with incredible speed. Soundings revealed that there were already five feet of water forward.

Pumps were started, but they could not control the flow of the cold Green North Atlantic.

The launching was not going well, since neither crew nor passengers had been familiarized with boat or fire drills. Few knew how to fasten a lifebelt, and some who learned under the stimulus of necessity found that the cords tore as if they were rotten.

Karl Mathieson, a Danish seaman who had signed on at Copenhagen just before sailing, had never in his life been taught how to abandon ship. But he was willing.

"I worked with the third mate," he recalled, "and followed him to the different boats. The first we attempted to lower fouled her tackle, keeping her stern fixed, while her bow fell and shot the occupants into the water. A heavy sea washed the boat against the ship's side.

"We went to another. A crowd of shrieking women and children following. The launching operations were not conducted simultaneously, the officers and crew going from one to another. Some of the crew were worse than the passengers, and but for the officers would have been put off in the boats themselves. These were driven back and threatened with death unless they obeyed orders.

"The captain never left the bridge but shouted so many orders that the crew did not know what to do."

The scenes in the cramped passageways had become ones of horror as it appeared that the Norge was rapidly sinking. Those who were not pushing and clawing toward the open decks, now virtually impossible to attain because of the packed mass of frightened humanity, were on their knees, praying. Children huddled close to mothers.

From her own lifeboat, as it hung swaying from the davits, Mrs. Sillander, holding her child tightly to her, watched the scene at the edges of the decks and in the doorways, observing some "supplicating aid from any one and shrieking for permission to enter the boats, elbowing, fighting their way to the places from which the boats were being lowered."

She watched the first lifeboat, just ahead of hers, being launched. The job, complicated by the presence of interfering male passengers, was done improperly and in seconds the boat hung perpendicularly, spewing some of its occupants into the sea, leaving others to hang to the ropes or upended seats like terrorized hotel guests fleeing in a fire. All were torn loose and dashed into the sea as a wave surged along the sides of the listing, stricken Norge.

The second boat miraculously reached the water on even keel. Oarsmen commenced to row away as a small cheer went up from those on deck. Then, as Katerina Sillander noted, "waves picked up the small craft as if it had been a feather, and dashed it against the side of the ship, in spite of the frantic efforts of the passengers to fend it off.

"The crash was heard on deck. Then the sea swallowed more victims and pieces of wreckage slowly drifted toward the rock."

She put her child in the bottom of the boat, by her feet, deciding that this was the safest place during the perilous launching. She found herself worrying about the mothers on the vessel whom she knew "had seven or eight children." Now she heard some of the mothers calling for the little ones from whom they had been separated. Altogether, it was "heart-rending."

As her own boat finally touched the water she observed men and women left behind "with hands outstretched."

Now, as the end seemed near, to sailor and passenger alike, a phenomenon happened. Where men had been shouting and often cursing and women wailing for their children, there came a sobering quieting, not a silence, but a dampening upon the crescendo of panic.

Katerina Sillander remarked upon this transition to a woman sitting next to her in the crowded boat.

"Seven boats got safely away," Captain Gundell reported. "The life rafts were cut adrift, and the steamer went down by the bow. The chief officer [Carpenter] told me she was sinking and I told him to jump overboard which he did. I did not see him again."

Katerina Sillander watched the Norge plunging down by the bow:

"One man threw himself overboard and another followed his example. Still another jumped into the water, and soon around the ship hundreds of persons were struggling in the sea, having preferred death in the open than being submerged with the ship. Others determined to stand by the ship, hoping against hope that she would remain afloat."

Her sinking, twelve minutes after she struck the rock, was abrupt. After her bow had been completely submerged for a few moments, her stern shot up in the air. She rushed down—and was gone.

"I went down with the steamer," reported Captain Gundell. "My right leg got jammed between two stanchions and was very much injured. When I rose to the surface I noticed a number of bodies floating.

"I swam for about twenty minutes and came across Second Engineer Brunn, who is a good swimmer."

Nelsen's boat cleared the ship, as "dozens" of passengers, though wearing belts, drowned "before our eyes."

"Fortunately," he continued, "our party included the only seaman of the Norge who was saved and he was able to navigate our little boat. We saw two other boats capsize owing to the heavy weather and because nobody could navigate them."

Karl Mathieson, the Danish sailor, together with the third mate, had found a small utility boat nestled abaft the funnels seconds before the steamer's death plunge. What amazed him, once they were struggling in the water, was the number of people who had been left behind, "chiefly women and children."

He could see only two other boats afloat, carrying perhaps a hundred persons.

The boats pulled away. The sights dimmed in the distance, the sounds quieted, then stopped. Once again, around Rockall, there was only water—and the circling gulls. Only small bits of wreckage and floating corpses hinted at the morning's tragedy.

The captain and the chief engineer swam for an hour and a half before they arrived at one of the lifeboats.

"I was hindered by my sore leg," said Gundell, "and the engineer reached the boat first. Both of us were taken on board quite exhausted. We found that it was lifeboat Number 1. It was crowded and under the charge of Able Seaman Peter Olsen."

It was also the boat carrying Pedre Nelsen.

"After recovering a little," the captain added, "I took charge of the boat and the provisions, which consisted only of a box with bread and two casks of water. The boat was steered for St. Kilda, 150 miles distant."

Out of sight sailed the other two boats on their separate

course—the tiny one with Mathieson and the third mate, the lifeboat with Katerina Sillander, which was jammed with sixty persons.

A baby died and was buried at sea. The day wore on, night came. Wednesday dawned. There were only the sea, the cold winds—and hunger, thirst, and a numbing all-pervading fear.

Late that afternoon the trawler *Sylvia* out of Grimsby was pulling in her nets at a position southwest of Rockall. She had cruised somewhat further to sea than customary. The fishing fleet had been goaded on by the vagaries of the herring and haddock, which this week had forsaken their usual offshore grounds.

Henry Glover, second engineer on the big trawler, was on the bridge, watching the long swells sweeping under the ship and listening to the gulls cry, when he thought he saw a buoy. He had never observed one this far out in the Atlantic.

"Is that a buoy out of place?" he asked the cook who was standing near him.

"You don't see no buoy," the cook answered.

Glover hurried below and returned with his glasses.

"It's a small boat!" he exclaimed. "And they have got a jacket flying at the bow. They've been shipwrecked."

The *Sylvia* cast loose the nets not already hauled in and steamed toward the boat. Soon the survivors, "a terrible sight," were being taken aboard.

"Men and women insufficiently clothed," declared Glover, "and so cramped that they could hardly come on board. We could not start immediately for we still had our nets out but as soon as they were stowed in we went directly to where the *Norge* went down.

"There was no trace of the ship, but awashing in the water back of the rocks were bodies of more than a hundred men, women, and little children."

The lifeboat commanded by Captain Gundell was less fortunate. On Saturday morning a large steamer passed them about four miles distant. The survivors fastened a blanket to an oar and waved it to and fro without attracting attention. Another ship sailed tauntingly by without noticing the lifeboat.

"At about noon Sunday," the master reported, "land was sighted and the drooping spirits of all were revived. It proved to be St. Kilda.

"Sometime afterward a steamer was noticed coming from the west, bearing down upon our boat. She proved to be the *Energie* [a German steamer] and at six o'clock we were safe on board."

All the survivors were now accounted for, and their number was pitifully small. Of the 774 who had sailed on the *Norge*, only 120 lived to tell of the experience.

At the line's New York offices on Whitehall Street, the relatives and friends waited for information: fathers, mothers, husbands, wives, and children. One of them, Max Brandenburg, of Graham Avenue, Brooklyn, learned that his wife and eight children, as well as his mother and father, had perished on the *Norge*.

Loneliness came to dwell in many hearts—especially in that of Captain Gundell, who had made the fatal error on a June morning of not knowing where he was. His remaining life was spent in a solitude as profound as that of Rockall itself, and he was to speculate bitterly on the dubious blessing of his survival.

Yet, loneliness was not peculiar to a time, to a place, to a person, or even to a category of persons. On October, 1937, at his estate in Costelloe, County Galway, Ireland, death finally came to a tired and profoundly sad little man—as much alone as any mortal could be, and because the Atlantic had proven as implacable in 1912 as it had in 1904.

Joseph Bruce Ismay, seventy-five, had been an influential figure once: president of the International Mercantile Marine

Burning of the *Ocean Monarch*, 1848.

Explosion of the *Sultana*, 1865.

The New York Times reports the wreck of the *Atlantic*, 1873.

The training ship *Atalanta,* which vanished off the Azores in 1880.

The liner *La Bourgogne,* victim of a North Atlantic collision, 1898.
(The Mariners Museum, Newport News, Virginia.)

The *Portland,* which was lost in a storm off the coast of Massachusetts,
1898. *(The Peabody Museum of Salem.)*

FIRE ON THE EAST RIVER

It was 8:30 A.M., Wednesday, June 15, 1904, when the 250-foot excursion boat *General Slocum* cast off from her pier at East 23rd Street, New York City. On board were nearly two thousand people, mostly women and children, en route to attend the annual picnic of the Sunday School of St. Marks German Lutheran Church.

"When we left the pier the decks were packed to capacity," recalled twenty-one-year-old John Eiell who was aboard the sidewheeler with his mother and younger brother. "A band was playing, the children frolicking about and we were having a fine time."

Nearing 125th Street, at an area of boiling river currents known as Hell Gate, the *General Slocum* gave totally unexpected hints of terrible difficulties. "Suddenly and without warning," Eiell continued, "there was a burst of flame from the furnace room . . . the flames spread with the rapidity of an explosion, setting fire to the clothing of the women and children who were grouped about the engine room watching the machinery."

Captain William H. Van Schaick, sixty-seven-year-old master of the steamer, sounded the fire alarm and sent his twenty-three-man crew to unreel the hoses. Rotted, they burst when water gushed into them. In desperation, Captain Van Schaick kept the *General Slocum* headed up the river toward North Brother Island, hoping to beach her. A brisk wind fanned the mounting flames.

"They all rushed to the after part of the ship," Eiell's narrative went on, "in a stampede that carried those who were near the rail overboard against their will. At one time it seemed to me as if the women and children were pouring over the sides like a waterfall."

The flaming excursion craft never made North Brother Island. Her prow grounded on sand flats. Passengers who leaped off her stern, thinking they would wade the remaining distance to the land, drowned in water well over their heads. Those more or less out of reach of the flames on upper decks perished in the roaring inferno below when the deck supports collapsed under the incandescent heat. Eiell swam to safety, though his brother and mother died.

Why the fire had broken out in the first place, why the fire fighting equipment was defective, or why a veteran skipper had allowed continuing headway of his command to fan the flames into the fury of a blast furnace all proved to be questions that would never be answered. All that was known for certain—all that really mattered—was that 1,030 victims perished that terrible Wednesday on the East River.

The *General Slocum,* built in 1891, was one of the largest excursion boats in New York waters. *(The New-York Historical Society.)*

The flaming wreckage of the *General Slocum* off North Brother Island. *(The New-York Historical Society.)*

DISASTER IN CHICAGO

The *Eastland* disaster was surely one which never should have happened. On July 24, 1915, she was boarded from her pier in Chicago by 2,400 persons, all headed for a Western Electric Company picnic. Never an overly stable steamer, the *Eastland* showed signs of listing that morning even as she was berthed in the Chicago River at La Salle Street. As a tug started to pull the *Eastland* off for the excursion, a woman stumbled on the already sloping deck, screamed, and the swarm of holiday-seekers rushed in unison to the port side. Like a weary monster lying down to die, the *Eastland* did not stop her roll until she was flat in the river mud on her port side.

Women and children—trapped below decks—accounted for the vast majority of the more than eight hundred victims of the strange tragedy. The capsizing was especially incredible since some hawsers were still secured to the bollards on the pier. Entire households were wiped out by the calamity. Early the next morning, when divers had recovered most of the bodies, a horse and wagon, bearing two newly closed coffins, stopped at a house on the near South Side. Two Western Electric families, comprising seven persons, had dwelt in the residence. The driver, needing burial instructions, knocked on the door, and knocked again. But there was no one to answer. Every soul from this home had died on the *Eastland*.

(In this photograph, probably made on the afternoon of the capsizing, the masts which had been hastily installed can easily be seen. It was hoped to affix cables to the tops of the masts and right the steamer by windlasses on the pier. Note the life preservers still piled in the storage house).

The *Eastland* lying in the mud of the Chicago River, 1915. *(Chicago Historical Society.)*

TROPICAL HURRICANE

"The warships," noted Robert Louis Stevenson, who happened to be in Samoa, "were thrown upon the beach as schoolboys' caps tossed on a shelf." The author was speaking of the hurricane in 1889 which altered the course of history.

A German fleet had been sent by empire-minded Chancellor Bismarck with the ostensible purpose of seizing the Samoan Islands. The U. S. dispatched a similar number of warships to prevent such a grab. While opposing guns faced each other in Apia harbor and Berlin and Washington exchanged notes of mounting heat, a providential storm arose—one of the worst to sweep the islands.

In its wake three American and three German warships were wrecked, 147 lives lost. The photograph above shows the beached and damaged *U.S.S. Trenton.* As a result of this storm, the Navy department was made strongly aware of the obsolescence of its ships, almost all of which were Civil War vintage. The next year, shipyards began turning out fighting vessels of completely altered and "modern" design such as the *U.S.S. Maine.*

The *Volturno* burning at sea, 1913. (*The Mariners Museum, Newport News, Virginia.*)

The *Titanic,* which sank after colliding with an iceberg on her maiden voyage, 1912. *(The Mariners Museum, Newport News, Virginia.)*

The *Empress of Ireland,* which carried 1,027 passengers to their deaths after a collision in the St. Lawrence River, 1914. *(The Mariners Museum, Newport News, Virginia.)*

The *Lusitania* arriving in New York harbor on her maiden voyage in 1907. Six years later, a German torpedo sent the liner to a watery grave. *(National Archives.)*

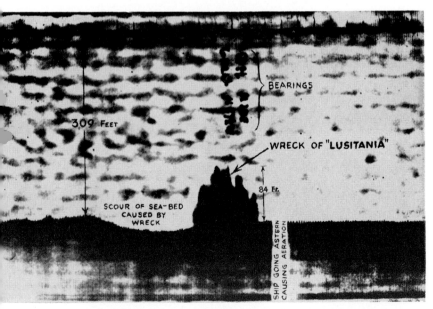

"Picture" of the wreck of the *Lusitania* made by a straight-scale recorder, a kind of underwater echo sound "camera." *(Kelvin & Hughes.)*

View of Halifax on the morning after the French ammunition ship *Mont Blanc* blew up in 1917 and destroyed large sections of this Nova Scotian city.

The naval collier *U.S.S. Cyclops,* which vanished mysteriously on a cruise in 1918. *(Official U.S. Navy Photo.)*

Terrified passengers aboard the *Vestris,* which sank after developing
a severe list because of overloading cargo, 1928. *(The Mariners Museum,
Newport News, Virginia.)*

The charred hulk of the *Morro Castle* lies in shallow water off Asbury Park, New Jersey, 1934. (*The Mariners Museum,*

The Army transport *Dorchester* a year before she was torpedoed off the coast of Greenland in 1943. *(U.S. Army Photo.)*

Artist's conception of the last moments of the heroic "Four Chaplains" aboard the ill-fated *Dorchester (Reproduction by U.S. Army.)*

The *Andrea Doria*, which collided with the *Stockholm* and sank in 1956. (*The Mariners Museum, Newport News, Virginia. Phillip R. Meyers Photo.*)

Company; director of such substantial organizations as the London Midland and Scottish Railroad and the Birmingham Canal Navigation Company.

Son of the shipping pioneer, Thomas Henry Ismay, he himself held one special position of honor and responsibility. That was the managing directorship of the White Star Line. Ostensibly, it was all the more surprising that, at fifty-one, he should retire to his barren, coastal hideaway in Ireland, with his wife, the former Julia Schieffelin, of New York, his two sons, and two daughters. As far as the world of directorships was concerned, Bruce Ismay was dead.

His life in the world of men, and in the less tangible realm of moral values, had ceased on a cold, starry night, April 14, 1912, just a year before his self-imposed exile.

Children coming home from school had chanted as they passed his house: "coward—coward—coward." That was before he fled to County Galway. Newspaper editors had shrilled much the same vilification at him, going even further to place the blame for the loss of the steamship *Titanic* solely upon him.

It didn't help that Lord Mersey, the wreck commissioner, had exonerated him at the Westminster hearings. It only mattered that he, Joseph Bruce Ismay, had climbed into a lifeboat from his own sinking liner with the words from Captain Edward J. ("Smitty") Smith ringing from the bridge: "Be British my men!"

Most had been. Others, such as John Jacob Astor, Major Archie Butt, Isidor Straus, and Harry Widener, had also shown how Americans could die.

The world had never seen anything like the *Titanic*, in size or grandeur. She displaced sixty-six thousand tons, featured turkish baths, period furnishings, and de luxe suites, themselves as extensive as some mansions. There was another exclusive quality claimed for her—she was "unsinkable."

When she sailed from Southampton April 10, 1912, on her first crossing for America, an assemblage of 2,201 persons, including 1,316 passengers, were aboard. About one-half the passenger complement was in third class. One third of the total in all classes were women.

She was not the fastest liner in the North Atlantic service, and not even White Star attempted to boast that she was. The rival Cunard's two greyhounds, the *Lusitania* and *Mauretania*, could exceed the *Titanic's* estimated top speed of twenty-four knots by a comfortable three-knot margin.

And, yet, Bruce Ismay made it clear to fellow passengers that he had no desire for his most monstrous and altogether wonderful liner to waste time on this, her maiden voyage. While white-bearded old-timer Smith was the captain, Ismay was "Mr. White Star." His word carried authority.

The fifteen-story-high ship had sailed on Wednesday. By Sunday her three enormous propeller shafts were clocking 75 of a maximum 80 rpm's. This drove her through the Atlantic at twenty-two knots, even though all of the twenty-nine boilers were never under steam simultaneously.

Ismay had alternated his time between the passenger portions of this world-afloat and Smitty's own domain of splendid navigation equipment: the bridge. On the latter he had assumed executive prerogatives, to discuss speed and optimum arrival time in New York.

"It was our intention," he explained, "to speed the boat up to her full quota on Tuesday."

The *Titanic* should raise Ambrose Lightship, he told Captain Smith, at 5 A.M., Wednesday, but not before. If necessary, speed should be reduced, in order to adhere to this schedule. In many respects, the White Star Line's managing director professed interest in his beautiful and gargantuan "boat." He wished, he confided, to study the *Titanic* thoroughly and ascertain "in what manner she could be improved upon."

By Sunday afternoon, neither Ismay nor anyone else on board in the employ of White Star saw how the splendid ship could really be improved upon. Yet, this same day, a trickle, but a vaguely disturbing trickle, of wireless messages was received from other ships. The *Caronia*, the *Baltic*, and a much smaller vessel, the *Californian*, of the British Leyland Line, all warned of ice fields along the *Titanic's* track.

The *Caronia* had specifically mentioned "growlers," bergs of insidious menace, since the greater proportion of their mass lay under water. At lunch time, Smith had handed Ismay the message from the *Baltic*.

It read: "Have had moderate variable winds and clear, fine weather since leaving. Greek steamer *Athenai* reports passing icebergs and large quantities of field ice today in Lat. 41° 51′ N., Long. 49° 52′ W. . . ."

It also touched on other subjects. Ismay pocketed the dispatch and continued walking along the promenade deck.

Before he finished his constitutional, he took the message out of his pocket and showed it to two ladies. They did not think it was his intent to make a point of the warning. Later, the captain asked for the return of the message, so he could post it in the chart room. This was done at 7:15 P.M., nearly six hours after its receipt.

On the other hand, neither Captain Smith nor Ismay attached sufficient importance to the warnings to reduce speed, although course was altered a few degrees south, as routine on the New York track.

The *Titanic* plowed on through the calm but bitterly cold evening. In one hour the temperature dropped ten degrees, to thirty-three. There was no moon, but the sky was brilliant with stars.

At 7:30 P.M. a radio message was intercepted from the *Californian* addressed to the steamer *Antillian*, reporting "three large bergs."

Dinner hour was characteristically gay in the Jacobean dining room of first class. In second class, meal time over early, there was hymn-singing. As to what the immigrants in third class were doing, no one cared. Doors not only shut them out from the remainder of the four-block-long ship but locked them out.

At 9:40 P.M. the vessel *Mesaba* flashed the *Titanic*: "Much heavy pack ice and great number of large icebergs."

The wireless operators were busy pumping commercial traffic to Cape Race and spiked the warning on a hook, intending to deliver it eventually.

The majority of the passengers, including Ismay, were in bed and asleep by ten o'clock. There were six lookouts stationed about the ship, in addition to the duty watch on the bridge. Each officer and seaman had been advised to "keep a sharp lookout for all ice."

But even as Ismay had said, the *Titanic* "was the last word in shipbuilding." No one worried that anything could happen to her. In testimony to this faith, White Star had equipped its queen with lifeboats sufficient to carry less than one-half the number now on board.

At 11 P.M. the *Californian*, which the *Titanic* had "read" earlier, sparked a message to the big ship: "We are stopped and surrounded by ice."

Yet the evening wireless traffic was voluminous. Passengers were communicating arrival plans to America, business memoranda, and simply "hello" greetings from the greatest and gaudiest liner afloat. First Marconi operator John Phillips, overworked and irritable, wanted clear channels.

"Keep out!" he snapped to the *Californian*.

At this same hour, the *Titanic's* lights were observed by the

Californian, whose officers were in mistaken agreement that such lights were coming from a much lesser vessel, "about our own size."

Rebuffed and weary from a day-long wireless watch, Cyril Evans, the *Californian's* sole radio operator, pulled off his earphones and went to bed.

Outside, the air surrounding both the *Californian* and the *Titanic* was like a refrigerator, thirty-two degrees or lower.

The latter, far from hove to as was the smaller steamer, was sprinting westward at twenty-two and a half knots, gradually accelerating toward what might have been her greatest day's run. The additional half-knot was even at this hour giving the mighty vessel her fastest speed of the voyage.

But, at 11:40 P.M. Ismays' world commenced to crumble. He was awakened in his suite on B-deck.

Instinctively he knew the ship had struck something, though the jar had been slight. He flicked on the light-switch and reached for his bathrobe. On the thick carpeting next to his bed were his slippers.

Lookouts had seen the iceberg and telephoned the alarm to the bridge. The helm was spun hard a-starboard. The engines were reversed, but too late.

The razor edge of the growler had slashed a wound one-third the 882-foot length of the *Titanic*. Bits of ice tumbled onto the forward deck. Yet so ponderous was her bulk that the shock had been negligible—everywhere except in the engine room, into which a cataract of water gushed.

Slowly, the massive ship drifted to a stop.

Harold Bride, second Marconi operator, who had transferred from the *Lusitania* to make the maiden crossing, was sleepily relieving Phillips. Captain Smith stuck his head into the radio room.

"We've struck an iceberg," he announced matter-of-factly,

then added there would be no request for assistance until his engineers had completed an inspection of the *Titanic's* vitals.

The bearded, patrician Smitty padded out of the Marconi "shack." Back on his bridge, he met Ismay, who had drawn a suit of clothes and overcoat over his pajamas. He wore the carpet slippers which had been beside his bed.

"What has happened?" asked the managing director of the line. The captain told him, and Ismay inquired if he thought the *Titanic* was seriously damaged.

"I'm afraid she is," answered the captain.

Ismay hurried below to the first stages of engine room gratings, where one engineer after another corroborated Smitty's pessimistic opinion. Steam was escaping from boilers wet with sea water. In some compartments, fourteen feet of water surged over the decking.

It was about 11:50 P.M., Bride estimated, when Captain Smith ordered a call for help. Still, neither operator was particularly alarmed. Phillips dot-dashed the international "C.Q.D." for assistance. The two joked between one another for five minutes as they repeated the message, coupled with the *Titanic's* position, which was south of the Grand Banks and nearly fifteen hundred miles east of New York.

Then Smith returned and asked Phillips what he was sending. The latter told him, as Bride interrupted:

"Send 'S.O.S.' It's the new call and it may be your last chance to send it!"

Bride noted that even the captain joined in the laughter which followed. And when the latter left the room, the two operators, while continuing to work the key, "said a lot of funny things to each other."

The steamship *Frankfurt* was the first to acknowledge. The operator on the German vessel proved to be interested solely in haranguing by short wave, finally asking them to stand by while he relayed the messages to his captain.

By twelve-thirty o'clock, Monday morning, Bride and Phillips had raised the Carpathia, about sixty miles distant.

Captain Arthur Rostron, astounded at the news, asked if the Titanic's master were "absolutely certain" immediate aid was needed. Phillips was now able to report, as emphasis, that the Titanic was low by the head and apparently "sinking."

Joking had come to an end in the radio quarters.

It was minutes past twelve-thirty, and already the command "women and children in the boats" was being passed down the long decks and through passageways. Many were not awakened until stewards pounded on cabin doors. Still they were as incredulous as the captain of the Carpathia. Those on deck even wondered why rockets were being fired from the bridge.

To be sure, the Titanic had developed a port list. Otherwise, there seemed no manifestation that anything was seriously wrong.

Ismay himself was on the boat deck, "standing still" as the small wooden craft were being uncovered. Second Officer Charles Lightoller observed to himself how quiet the managing director was, talking with no one, near no one.

Ismay had been on the bridge when Captain Smith ordered the boats lowered. He then walked aft, as others remarked, like a man in a dream.

While lifeboat Number 3, was being filled and then lowered from the starboard side, Ismay watched, transfixed.

In the radio room, Phillips noted the ammeter needle waver: lower, lower. Power was failing. Smith returned and advised that the engine rooms were "taking water—the dynamos might not last much longer."

While Bride dressed, now convinced he would have to swim

this cold night, Phillips flashed to the *Carpathia* that transmission might soon cease for lack of electricity.

After Bride had put on warm clothing, he brought an overcoat to Phillips since it had become "very cold." The first operator kept to his key, scribbling position reports from the *Carpathia* as she neared the *Titanic* at flank speed, disregarding her own peril from the ice. He tore off the messages every few minutes, and Bride would run to the bridge to give them to the captain.

"I noticed as I came back from one trip," Bride recalled, "that they were putting off women and children in lifeboats. I noticed that the list forward was increasing.

"I went out on deck and looked around. The water was pretty close up to the boat deck. There was a great scramble aft and how poor Phillips worked through it I don't know."

Ismay, impelled to greater activity, urged the crewmen who were loading the Number 5 boat to hurry up. Not recognized, he was informed curtly that they took their orders from the captain. Yet the director of the steamship line continued to hover about the lifeboat. Finally, in his impatience, he cried out: "Lower away!"

This was too much for Fifth Officer Harold G. Lowe, who was working the davits. Convinced that Ismay, whom he *did* recognize, was interfering with the launching and might endanger the lives of the passengers already aboard, he shouted to Ismay to "get the hell out of the way!"

Ismay was stunned. He lingered for another moment, then shuffled away.

Lowe finally put off in command of boat Number 14, loaded with fifty-five women and children and a few crewmen (as rowers). He had to fire his pistol to prevent any more from swarming aboard and capsizing the heavily-loaded boat.

Nearly two hours after the *Titanic* had struck the iceberg,

Bride decided "it was about time to look about and see if there was anything detached that would float. I remembered that every member of the crew had a special life belt and ought to know where it was. I remembered mine was under my bunk. I went and got it. Then I thought how cold the water was."

Phillips had contacted the sister ship, *Olympic*, five hundred miles distant. It seemed hopeless, but she promised she would plow to the rescue as fast as her engines would permit. While the senior Marconi man was communicating with the *Olympic*, Bride put a life belt on Phillips' back.

Then, the junior radio man walked outside again along the sloping deck and watched twelve men trying to launch a collapsible. It occurred to him that this was the last boat left on board.

Bride lent his muscle to the task, and the craft slipped into the water with a slight splash. All twelve "started to scramble in."

The radio officer, however, knew that his duty was still on board the doomed liner. He looked "longingly" at the collapsible, insubstantial as it was, then returned to his transmitting compartment. He saw Captain Smith beside Phillips.

"Men, you have done your full duty," he announced. "You can do no more. Abandon your cabin. Now it's every man for himself."

It was 2:10 A.M. and a new ship, the *Virginian* was responding. But she was one hundred fifty miles distant—too far away to be of any help.

Around collapsible lifeboat "C" on the starboard deck, a little knot of passengers and crewmen exchanged glances. The water was nearly over their feet. The bow was far under water, and from the *Titanic's* submerged vitals the ruptured steam lines sent forth a roaring, gurgling crescendo. The noise, all left aboard agreed, "was terrifying."

In the group stood Ismay, still wearing his overcoat and shod in carpet slippers, no longer excited or imperious. He looked and decided that "there were no women and children around." This impelled the conclusion: "I thought they had all been saved."

He had considered himself, sometimes on the voyage, as a "voluntary passenger." He did so now. Four crewmen and forty-five passengers stepped into the boat. Hidden under the seats already were four Chinese steerage passengers.

"The boat was being filled," Ismay recalled. "The officer called out to know if there were any more women to go. There were none. No passengers were on the deck. So as the boat was being lowered I got into it."

He asserted: "My conscience is clear."

But it wasn't.

In the radio shack, Phillips and Bride had no disposition to obey Smitty's last order. As long as there was a sputter of electricity, Phillips would keep tapping the key.

As he was doing so, Bride observed "a stoker or somebody" trying to steal Phillips' life belt from his back. In a blind rage at the man's cowardice, the junior operator seized an object he did not even stop to identify and smashed the would-be thief over the head, thinking: "I hope I finished him."

It was now 2:18 A.M., and the *Titanic* was going fast. Bride tugged at Phillips and told him he had not much more time.

"From aft," continued Bride, "came the tunes of the band. It was a ragtime tune. I don't know what. Then there was 'Autumn.'

"Phillips ran aft and that was the last I ever saw of him alive."

Bride went aft to where he had helped launch the collapsible and "to my surprise" found the men still struggling to get it completely afloat. Before Bride could lend assistance this second time, a huge wave—produced by the vessel's own death plunge—surged around the group and knocked them off their feet.

"I had hold of an oarlock and I went off with it. The next I knew I was in the boat . . . the boat was upside down and I was under it."

He kept reminding himself: "I must not breathe."

Now safely away from the *Titanic*, the passengers in collapsible "C" watched a terrible sight: the great liner tilting, bow first, until she was perpendicular. Her porthole lights flashed off, flashed on again—then as she slid under, they winked out forever.

A loud rumble of cargo, machinery, and furniture breaking loose, a final eruption of steam and sparks—and the *Titanic* was gone.

"I turned my back," Ismay admitted. "I did not want to see the end."

Bride thrashed his way up into the open air from his inverted lifeboat to see men, "hundreds of them," dotting the night seas. He swam hard to get away from the plunging liner. Even in the last seconds he thought he heard the band still playing "Autumn."

Then came the long wait, for Bride, for Ismay, for all in the lifeboats. The suggestion from a man in the Marconi operator's craft was a typical one: "Don't the rest of you think we ought to pray?"

A few minutes after 4 A.M. prayers were answered with the arrival of the *Carpathia*. Her record dash had been too late for those in the water, unable to find lifeboat space. Other lifeboats had rowed off half empty.

About an hour later, the *Californian*, drifting in the ice fields no more than twenty miles from the spot where the *Titanic* had disappeared, resumed radio watch. Only then did those of her

crew who had actually observed a number of the White Star
Liner's rockets comprehend the stunning significance.

When the *Carpathia* made her final count, the pitiful total of
saved stood at 711 persons, or a mere 32.3 percent of those who
had sailed from Southampton. There were other statistics; for
example, while 62 percent of the first class passengers had survived, only 25 percent of third class had been rescued. And third
accounted for some 33 percent of the of the total complement
of the *Titanic*.

Ismay sought refuge in the cabin of the ship's surgeon on
board the *Carpathia*. He did not emerge until Thursday, when
the vessel docked at Pier 54, New York. He was able, by then, to
make brief statements to the small army of newspapermen who
surrounded him:

"She hit the iceberg a glancing blow. . . . What kind of a
man do you think I am? Certainly there were no women and
children around. . . .

"I can only say that the White Star Line officers and em-
ployees will do everything humanly possible to alleviate the
suffering and sorrow of the relatives and friends of those who
perished. . . .

"I was rowing the lifeboat all the time until we were picked
up. . . . I turned back only once after we left the vessel. I saw
her green light and never turned back again. I did not see the
Titanic go down."

There remained, now, only the post-mortems. They were
bitterly eloquent, both for their anguish and their recrimina-
tions.

A United States Senate investigating committee conducted
hearings in the Waldorf Astoria Hotel. Bruce Ismay, looking
"wan and haggard," reviewed the voyage. He disclaimed any
intent of urging the late Captain Smith on to a speed record.
He found an all-absorbing interest centered about his survival.

It did not seem to mollify the inquisitors, official and unofficial, that he kept repeating, tirelessly, that his conscience was clear, that there were no other women in sight when he stepped into his lifeboat.

The dispassionate omega—1503 souls left to drown—persisted. There seemed no rational basis of refutation.

In his own country, Joseph Bruce Ismay was absolved, morally and professionally. In blaming the catastrophe, possibly in over-simplification, on "excessive speed," Lord Mersey said of Ismay:

"Had he not jumped in [the lifeboat] he would merely have added one more life, namely his own, to the number of those lost."

Lawrence Beesley, a passenger from second class, believed the sinking to be the captain's responsibility, asserting: "Nor would any officer connected with the management of the line—Mr. Ismay for example—be allowed to direct the captain in these matters."

Ismay inspired some of the bitterest invective ever leveled against a fellow human being. It reached an epitome in a poem, more renowned for its hate than literary qualities, by Ben Hecht. Titled "Master and Man," it was published that April in the *Chicago Record-Herald:*

> The captain stood where a captain should,
> For the law of the sea is grim,
> The owner romped ere his ship was swamped
> And no law bothered him.

> The captain stood where the captain should,
> When a captain's boat goes down,
> But the owner led when the women fled,
> For an owner must not drown.

> The captain sank as a man of rank,
> While his owner turned away,

The captain's grave was his bridge, and brave
He earned his seaman's pay.

To hold your place in the ghastly face
Of death on the sea of night
Is a seaman's job, but to flee with the mob
Is an owner's noble right.

It endured as a terrible epitaph, for a terribly lonely man.

Fire on the Atlantic

ON A STORMY FALL DAY IN 1913, THE 3,600-TON VOLTURNO, OUT of Rotterdam, butted through the North Atlantic. New York-bound, she was loaded to her Plimsoll with oils, wines, gin, burlap, rags, peat moss, chemicals, and other cargo.

She also carried 564 passengers mostly immigrants. They came from the Balkans, from the Levant, from Poland, and, in lesser numbers, from Germany. Those of the Jewish faith, accompanied by a rabbi, were awaiting Yom Kippur, the fast of atonement.

The crew totalled ninety-three on this seven-year-old Canadian Northern Steamship Company vessel, currently chartered by the Uranium Line. Her first port of call was Halifax, yet twelve hundred miles distant.

Thursday, October 9th, dawned wild and grey. Few could sleep through the ship's contortions, much as the youthful skipper, J. D. Inch, tried to find a comfortable course.

In the limited first class accommodations, Mrs. F. W. Alexander, of New York, a previous traveler aboard the *Volturno*, was awake and troubled. She had been talking the past night to C. J. Pennington, junior wireless operator. In a recurrent dream, he saw the ship ablaze, as he worked the Morse key, calling for help. He had even written a letter to London, requesting reassignment, he confided to Mrs. Alexander.

Dawn came and went, with no change in the leaden skies or the wind velocity. Until a few minutes before 7 A.M., however,

161

it was just "another bad day on the North Atlantic," thought Second Officer Lloyd.

At just 6:55 A.M. by the bridge clock, he spotted yellowish smoke curling from the canvas of a forward hatch.

In this wind Lloyd knew how rapidly flames could spread—especially when the cargo included chemicals and liquor. Advising Captain Inch, he raced forward against the gale and combers which swept the decks. He was a big, powerful man and it required but a few swings of an ax to crash a hole through the hatch planking.

He trained a fire hose into the opening and called for full pressure. But even as the salt water gushed into the black abyss he suspected the *Volturno* was doomed. The volume of smoke and the intensity of the heat were omen enough.

This standard procedure of fighting shipboard fire had unorthodox results. An explosion in the hold scattered and spread the fire and widened the opening in the hatch to the Atlantic gale.

The combination was converting the forward portion of the *Volturno* into a blast furnace. Nor could the flood valves be turned on. The ship was too heavily loaded already.

The fire could no longer be hidden from the passengers. Captain Inch sent crewmen to every cabin and steerage compartment to advise of the peril.

Pennington, the junior Marconi operator, commenced tapping out the call which the *Titanic* had dramatized—S.O.S., S.O.S.—Save our Souls!

Pennington could not believe it. He wondered whether he were asleep dreaming his terrible dream once more, or awake and recalling the dream in such realism that he believed the ship actually ablaze.

Dramatically, almost within seconds, an answer—the *Carmania* was less than eighty miles distant.

"Hold on, chaps!" reassured the radio operator aboard the big Cunarder. "We're coming!"

Captain Barr ordered all off-duty stokers out of their bunks. They heaved coal into the glowing furnaces of the *Carmania* until the boilers' safety valves hissed. Her speed, however, had been increased from fifteen to nearly twenty-two knots.

On the *Volturno* there was dismay. The flames were spreading, fanned by the gale into incandescent intensity. They burned through the antenna stays on the foremast, and consumed a stack of life rafts nested at the mast's base.

Officer Lloyd climbed up the shrouds. With tongues of flame licking about him and half-blinded by smoke, he succeeded in refastening the antenna. When he was almost down again, the ship lurched and a blast of wind snatched him and hurled him to the deck. Dazed from concussion, he picked himself up and limped to the bridge.

Passengers, having donned their life belts, arrived on deck. They looked at the seas, saw and heard the ever-engulfing fire forward, then returned into their cabins and compartments.

With the aerial lashed back in place, Pennington was receiving messages from other ships: the *Czar*, the *Rappahannock*, the *Kroonland*, the *Minneapolis*, the *Devonian*, the *Grosser Kurfuerst*—all were within a day's steaming or less of the *Volturno* and were coming as fast as their propellers would drive them.

Yet, even though the fastest and nearest of this fleet, the *Carmania*, should be alongside by noon, it began to appear that the *Volturno* could not survive the next three or four hours. And if she did, Captain Inch wondered, could boats navigate the seething water between the two vessels?

He ordered one boat over the side, in command of the chief officer and containing two dozen passengers, mostly women, in addition to other crewmen. Almost on the water, it capsized, spewing out its occupants. None was saved, although the chief officer, the chief steward, and several others were seen clambering into the boat after it righted. It vanished into the rain.

"Prepare Number 6 boat for lowering!" ordered Inch, believing, even after the first tragedy, that the sea presented less certain menace than the blazing ship.

Passengers on deck cheered as their erstwhile shipmates safely reached the water. Then Number 6 sailed out of sight.

Number 7 lifeboat was next. It, too, was launched successfully in spite of thirty-foot waves which smashed against its sides. It was, however, swept aft. Those on the big ship watched as the stern of the Volturno smashed down from the crest of a wave and crushed the boat and all in it.

More than a hundred had now perished. French newlyweds clasped hands and jumped over the side together. The young pair preferred death by drowning to suffocation.

One man rushed toward a lifeboat still secured to its falls. He had broken into a linen locker and stolen an officer's coat, which he was wearing. He was knocked to the deck by one of the crew.

Near the stern, a group of equally terrified passengers, men and women with babies in their arms, were trying to steal a lifeboat. They hoped to launch it and row away before the officers should notice.

They, too, were restrained before they succeeded in what promised to be their self-destruction.

Shortly before noon, the Carmania completed her dash and hove to alongside the Volturno. Captain Barr ordered Chief Officer Gardiner and his most proficient oarsmen into the water. He knew the seas were too high for safe lifeboat work, but the sight of the smoke and flames from the Volturno told him there was not much more time, if any.

For nearly two hours, Gardiner fought to come beside the Volturno. The seas hurled his little boat away each time. He gave up and was hoisted back aboard the big *Carmania*, which could make her own lee from the storm.

Barr circled the *Volturno* as close as he dared, wondering if perhaps he could lay his vessel to for brief periods, allowing the passengers to jump. He looked at them, trussed in their life belts, huddled on the stern, staring at his liner. But he realized he would have to devise other means of rescue.

The fire was spreading amidships. The navigation bridge was abandoned. The radio shack was unbearably hot.

"Can't you string a breeches buoy?" Captain Inch signalled the *Carmania*.

Barr knew that he could not. Yet, to demonstrate the futility of such an effort, he ordered one to be floated from the *Carmania*. The wind and sea drifted it astern. There was no chance of its spanning the frothing channel between the two vessels.

At 3:30 P.M. the German freighter *Seydlitz* poked out of the murk. By blinker, semaphore, and radio she added her voice to the mid-ocean consultation.

Within the hour the *Grosser Kurfuerst* was on the scene, followed almost at once by the *Kroonland*.

The *Seydlitz* put over a boat at 4:30, which was no more successful than that from the *Carmania*.

At the same time, Captain Inch, commanding his furiously-blazing ship from an aft post on the boat deck, ordered a radio plea for a tanker. If oil could only be pumped onto the seas. . . .

The master's shoes, as those of all his officers and crew, were seared almost through by the scorching decks. His uniform was greasy and torn. He saw no hope of salvation. And yet, a weary resignation had taken possession of him.

Even the passengers had become calmer. Their hysteria, as exemplified by the abortive attempt to commandeer and launch a lifeboat by themselves, had palliated into the same cowed sense of hopelessness.

Those of the Hebrew faith were gathered on their knees around their rabbi. They had appropriated a small segment of the fantail on the port side. They clung to it tenaciously as though this were a plot of earth and here they expected to go to their final rest.

Shortly after six o'clock, Pennington received a message in response to his captain's call for a tanker. It was from Charles Harwood, master of the Anglo-American tanker *Narragansett*, a night's steaming distance away. However, he promised: "Will come with the milk in the morning!"

Its optimistic spontaneity had a cheering effect on Captain Inch's spirits.

Darkness came, stabbed only by flarings from the blazing ship. Inch radioed: "Cannot something be done to help us? We must abandon ship. Her plates are buckling. Stand close, as I may have to jump for it."

Somehow, he stuck to his ship.

Second Officer Lloyd decided to demonstrate to the circling rescue fleet that a small boat *could* navigate. Though burned and half-crippled from his fall, he commanded a small gig, with three other crewmen. He put out into the darkness, using only running lights for identification and steering by the searchlights of the other ships.

In forty-five minutes he had done the "impossible." Half-filled with cold sea water, his boat came alongside the *Grosser Kurfuerst* and was hauled up. All four men were safe.

Even so, the captains of the waiting ships—now joined by the *Devonian* and *La Touraine*—did not think it prudent to attempt to move passengers off the *Volturno* until morning.

About 9 P.M., Captain Barr himself was to record the scene:

"When darkness was at its blackest, the flames burst through amidships of the Volturno from her engine room and coal bunkers. As the fire lighted up the ship there came an explosion which sent into the air burning wreckage like the flight of rockets. It lit the surrounding ships."

Yet, those who still lived aboard the Volturno kept to their uncertain bit of steel. The rabbi prayed. Mothers held their babies. Strong men were tormented by frustration.

At midnight, the Grosser Kurfuerst could not watch the spectacle any longer. A hardy group of seamen from Kiel stripped to their undershirts and manned a lifeboat.

Meanwhile, the tanker Narragansett was taking the seas. No one could stand on her pipe-latticed decks. Captain Harwood, refusing to sleep, stood by the helm, hanging onto an upright for support, peering into the blackness of the Atlantic night. He confided to his mate on watch that he would be at his destination in the morning, as promised, with the "milk," if he had to "crack every frame in the ship!"

Captain Inch, about 2 A.M., sent the despairing entreaty dot-dashing through the air: "For God's sake, do something!"

As if in punctuation, a new explosion tore the radio mast from the Volturno. It was the end of her transmission.

The boat from the Grosser Kurfuerst circled the fiercely-blazing steamer, as its officer in charge shouted to the passengers to jump.

But no one obeyed—no one except Pennington, the wireless operator, who now had no more duties to perform. After his nightmares, he was sure he would die, although there was a pyrrhic satisfaction in cheating destiny in the manner of his going.

"I went down so far, I didn't care whether I came up again," he told his rescuers a few minutes later. He missed the nearer boat from the *Grosser Kurfuerst*, however, being hauled in by the *Kroonland.*

Just before dawn, all the passengers began jumping into the sea. The smoke and flames were blinding, suffocating even on the stern. There was a new element, now, but a welcome one— oil.

The *Narragansett*, just as Captain Harwood had promised, had arrived. She was pumping her greasy, irridescent "milk" onto the writhing seas as fast as her machinery would permit.

It helped. There were eleven rescue vessels now on hand, and all were able to launch boats and ring the stricken liner close to.

With brightening skies in the east, it was at one time possible to count thirty-five such lifeboats rowing over the seas which the heavy oily coating was blanketing into a mere chop. Among the last to leave the *Volturno* was an opera singer from Moscow, who first sought out Inch and asked permission to leave the ship. The singer then took off his coat and jumped.

Sailors formed human ladders down lines and cargo nets strung over the sides. Older women and babies were passed from hand to hand into the cluster of boats waiting beneath.

Aboard the rescue fleet was a retired newspaperman, Arthur Spurgeon, formerly managing editor of the National Press Agency of Great Britain. He started a wireless to London:

"It was a strange company that filled the last boat to put off from the side of the flame-swept *Volturno.* It carried Captain Inch. It carried the officers. It carried a dog. And it carried a cook who was one of the big heroes of the tragedy, for he stood at his post and baked and made coffee until the flames were so close that his shoes were literally burned off."

One by one, the survivors were brought onto the rescue ships. The *Grosser Kurfuerst* held the greatest number—105. When the tally had been decided after much signaling between the rescue fleet, 133 lives had certainly been lost out of the 657 who sailed from Rotterdam.

It was Friday, the commencement of Yom Kippur. To many, many Americans, however, it was Friday, the day of the fourth game of the World Series.

Till We Meet Again

IN MID-AFTERNOON, MAY 29, 1914, A HASTILY-PRINTED BULLETIN was posted in the windows of the Canadian Pacific Railway's London and Liverpool offices:

NOTICE TO THE PUBLIC

We are deeply distressed to have to announce that at 2:30 this morning the *Empress of Ireland*, homeward-bound from Canada, was in collision with the collier *Storstad* off Father Point, in the St. Lawrence River. She sank immediately. Two steamers were at once on the scene. A large number of passengers were picked up and landed at Rimouski. This is the extent of the information so far. Further particulars will be advised to the public as received.

The crowds, this warm Sunday, milled about the two build-ings—on Cockspur Street, in London, near the Mersey docks in Liverpool. There were those personally involved, as well as the idly curious, recounting, like a cinema's second showing, scenes after the *Titanic* went down. To the Liverpool-Bootle-Birkenhead area, the announcement was especially sepulchral. The majority of the *Empress of Ireland's* crew of nearly seven hundred lived in these Merseyside communities.

Only that morning, the *Aquitania* had sailed from Liverpool on her maiden voyage. Grossing forty-seven thousand tons, she

170

was England's largest liner, though she yielded topmost honors to the German *Vaterland*, of fifty-eight thousand tons, which made her first Atlantic crossing just a week ago.

When word reached the London hotels, there were many who opened their Bibles or hurried to St. Paul's, St. Martin's, St. Pancras, or whatever church was nearest, to pray. Men and women, already several thousand in number, they were the delegates to the Salvation Army's international congress, the largest ever held.

Major nations, as well as minor protectorates and insignificant South Pacific islands, were represented.

Canada had sent 171 delegates, plus their families, under the leadership of Commissioner Davis Rees, veteran Salvation Army worker and a tireless "servant of the Lord," as he described himself. The elderly Rees, distinguished by an ample beard, had yielded to the entreaties of Mrs. Rees and his three children to accompany him to London. It would be in the nature of a convalescence for Mrs. Rees who had been ill.

The Rees family was among the 1,479 who had sailed on the *Empress of Ireland* the preceding afternoon from Quebec. The Salvation Army band, numbering forty-three musicians, also en route to the congress, played a hymn as the liner drew away from the pier. It was the same familiar hymn the musicians had chosen for their concluding number in a farewell concert at the Salvation Army Temple, Toronto: "God be with you 'till we meet again."

The 14,191-ton ship, but eight years old, was exceedingly comfortable. In addition to Victorian lounges for first class accommodations, she featured such refinements as a children's dining room and even a spacious sand pit on deck for the same kiddies.

She was an unvarying choice of seasoned and often distinguished transatlantic voyagers. The Duke and Duchess of Connaught had crossed on her in 1912 when the Duke was commencing his Governor Generalship of Canada.

The peerage this late May, 1914, was represented by Sir Henry Seton-Karr, sixty-one-year-old big game hunter, politician, and author.

Eminent in the world of the theater was Laurence Irving, forty-three-year-old actor, son of the famed Sir Henry Irving. With him was his wife, ten years younger than he, whose stage name was Mabel Hackney. Accompanying Irving were other actors and actresses of lesser billing, including Harold Neville and Mrs. Neville, and a relative newcomer, Isabel Strong.

The entire troupe, having completed a tour of Canada, presenting *Typhoon* and other plays, had been booked on the *Teutonic*, sailing the same Saturday but due in Liverpool three days later. Passage on the *Empress* had been a last-minute decision.

The actor and his actress-wife, posing for photographs, were still clad in the beaver overcoats and caps they had worn in the western provinces. Laurence, with his sharp features and pincenez glasses, was often reminded that he resembled an English Woodrow Wilson.

Also on board was L. E. Gosselin, prominent Montreal attorney; Leonard Palmer, of the *London Financial News*, and Mrs. Palmer. The newspaperman was returning from conducting a group of British manufacturers about the United States and Canada.

There were lesser people aboard: R. A. Cunningham, for one, elderly professor at the Manitoba Agricultural College and Salvation Army delegate.

On the bridge, as the *Empress of Ireland* left the spires of Quebec and the Ile d'Orleans farther and farther astern, was her captain, tall, handsome forty-one-year-old Henry George Kendall. Native of Blundellsands, Liverpool suburb, Kendall,

who somehow looked the part of a British seafarer, had cut his
nautical teeth on sailing ships.

Known as an expert navigator and efficient commander, Kendall achieved international fame in 1910 when he figured in
the first transatlantic use of wireless to solve a murder. Dr. Haw-
ley Harvey Crippen, Michigan-born London dentist, was fleeing
in disguise to Canada aboard Kendall's command—then the
Montrose—after killing his wife.

From "wanted" posters, sharp-eyed Kendall recognized both
Crippen and his girl friend, though she was dressed as a young
boy. His radio message to Scotland Yard, while the *Montrose*
was nearing mid-Atlantic, sent Inspector Walter Dew racing
westward on a faster liner. At a spot 185 miles down the St.
Lawrence from Quebec—Father Point, where pilots come
aboard—Dew, whose vessel had overtaken the *Montrose* by
hours, "got his man," in the best traditions of the Yard.

Supper time neared this Saturday, when the liner, in a wide,
clear channel accelerated to eighteen knots and churned down
the St. Lawrence toward the Gulf.

What had been a mild afternoon, with a high haze, turned
into a cool evening as Cape St. Ignace came abeam. But few
lingered on deck to watch the shoreline or smell the pine forests.
The passengers ate dinner and went to bed.

Cunningham, the professor from Manitoba, was among the
latter number. He made a habit of retiring early, wherever he
was, thus providing more time to read his Bible. For awhile he
had counted the revolutions as the twin propellers thumped and
thumped their even, heavy rhythm.

"The ship was as still as a dish on a shelf," he recalled. "I
was lying next the outer wall of the cabin, where I could hear
the engines beating sleepily down below. I could hear the quiet
splashing of the water from the bow and every little while a sort
of crash as a bigger wave rose and hit her on the nose.

"She was a pretty ship. There was a little motion, a little heave now and again, but nothing else. . . . I read my Testament in the music room of the second class. There was some singing going on, but it never disturbs me. I was reading about our Lord in the garden but I was thinking about the noises of the ship, quiet, sleepy noises, dreamy, faraway noises that should have put me to sleep."

Soon, the old Salvation Army delegate nodded.

The *Empress* sailed on. The shore lights dwindled to infrequent yellow blobs bordering the river wilderness. At midnight the temperature dropped to a few degrees above freezing. One hardy passenger, Thomas Smart, of Toronto, was making a final turn around the upper deck preparatory to going to bed, when he encountered the captain.

"It is nice and light," Kendall observed pleasantly, "but it looks to me as though a fog is coming up. You never know how soon a fog drops its pall upon you at this part of the river."

The Canadian Pacific liner passed the lighted channel buoys, which resembled distantly-spaced traffic lights along a rain-soaked boulevard, as she was near Father Point. Already, the running lights of two smaller vessels were sweeping into view off the starboard bow. They were the pilot boat *Eureka* which would debark Camille Bernier, who had guided the *Empress* up from Quebec, and the *Lady Evelyn*, a government postal steamer.

The latter would remove mail and put aboard final items for England and the continent which had been rushed by train to this last Canadian stop, only three miles east of the city of Rimouski.

Below decks, there was little else to do this night. Assistant Purser Ernest Hayes closed his books and spun the dial of his office safe. Dr. James F. Grant, ship's surgeon and a poker player, cashed in his chips and went to his cabin. The youthful

Grant had graduated from McGill University Medical School
only the preceding year.

Rowland Ferguson, a senior wireless operator, awaited his
"dog watch" relief, Edward Bamford.

In the engine room a new shift was also going on duty. Among
its number was an oiler, Frank Tower. His associates in this
world of grease and steam called him "Lucky" Tower, since he
had swum away from the *Titanic* in 1912.

At 1:30 A.M. Kendall stopped the engines, and the *Lady
Evelyn* swung alongside. She was secured only by a bow line
while the sacks were pitched onto and off from the towering
liner. Pilot Bernier climbed down the rope ladder to his little
craft and waved good-by.

Soon, both the *Lady Evelyn* and the *Eureka* were steaming
back toward shore, leaving Kendall the sole responsibility for
piloting his ship. As he ordered her underway again, fog wisped
across the river, intermittently obscuring the channel buoys. He
slowed the *Empress* to about fifteen knots, which seemed con-
servative enough to him in view of his familiarity with the St.
Lawrence, broadening rapidly before it finally widened into the
Gulf. He told First Officer Edward Jones, who had the watch, to
keep a sharp lookout, and then went to his own cabin, aft of
the bridge, to have a cup of tea and warm up.

It was bitter. He had been standing on one bridge wing or
the other almost since sailing from Quebec. His hands and face
were cold.

Shortly after 2 A.M., Cock Point gas buoy came in sight
through low-lying fog patches. It was positioned about seven
miles down the river from Father Point.

First Officer Jones didn't like the way the buoy kept appearing
and then disappearing. It was a poor night for navigation, he
concluded, and he didn't want the responsibility for the liner.

He sent his quartermaster to summon Kendall back to the bridge.

And at this time the watch officer of another vessel was observing the light buoy from its opposite side. Chief Officer Alfred Tuftenes, of the Norwegian collier *Storstad*, grossing seventeen thousand tons under her capacity load of coal, had not seen fit to call his master, moustached, heavy-set Captain Thomas Anderson.

Mrs. Anderson happened to be aboard this trip, another reason Tuftenes had tried to shoulder more than his customary share of navigating the collier.

While the chief officer realized the fog was worsening, he also estimated the ship should be off Father Point within the hour, where a pilot would take over the tricky navigation of night-time St. Lawrence.

On the *Empress*, Ed Bamford had relieved Ferguson for the wireless watch.

Back on the bridge, Kendall picked up his binoculars and stared ahead. He estimated the other ship was "about one point on my starboard bow. . . . I saw a slight fog bank coming gradually from the land." He knew it was going to "pass between" the two vessels. He judged the ship to be two miles distant.

However, as an experienced navigator, Kendall knew that two miles between two large approaching vessels was no distance at all. Acting instinctively, he first reversed his engines, blowing the customary three blasts on the whistle as he did so. Then he ordered the engines stopped altogether.

He blew one long blast, to signify, in this case, that he had turned the helm to starboard. The *Empress'* momentum was carrying her past Cock Point buoy.

Hayes, the purser, looked up in the act of closing his office door. He had noticed the change in pitch of the propeller throb, then its cessation altogether, and heard the horn blasts. Some passengers were awakened by this same disquieting combination: the abrupt end of the engines' lullaby, subconsciously heard though it generally was, and the whistle.

Kendall looked over the bridge wing at the black, night waters and saw "my ship was stopped."

On the *Storstad*, Chief Officer Tuftenes reacted at the sound of the other steamer's horn. He summoned the master, who happened to be up and dressed in his quarters, since he was preparing to greet the Canadian pilot.

Captain Anderson of the *Storstad*, immediately picked out the starboard running light of the *Empress* and replied with one blast. The green light signified to him that the *Storstad* possessed the right of way.

Satisfied that his big liner had stopped, other than her normal drift with the current, Captain Kendall blew two long blasts meaning, in the language of water-borne traffic: "My ship is under way but stopped and has no way upon her."

The *Storstad* answered with one "prolonged blast."

The massively-laden collier, with most of her bulk under water, was swallowed up again in the fog. However, Kendall estimated her position, from the horn signal, at about "four points upon my starboard bow." He started his engines up again, full speed ahead, but only momentarily.

In the next few moments the *Storstad*'s prow broke through the fog. Kendall snatched his megaphone from an overhead rack in the wheel house and shouted as loud as he could: "Ahoy! Go full speed astern!"

Realizing "the danger of collision" to be "inevitable," he ordered his engines full speed astern, his helm hard aport.

On the *Storstad*, Anderson ordered his own engines reversed. It was too late.

"I was sort of sleeping down into a doze," Cunningham, the

professor, reported. "There was a bump. It did not seem to me a very bad bump. Then a crash and things began tearing.

"The steel seemed to bend and twist under my hand as I touched the cabin wall getting out of the bunk. It made a shrieking noise.

"I did not wait for anything. I ran out and before I reached the stairs the floor seemed to drop under me, and instead of being level under my feet, rose like a hill.

"I could hear a tremendous roar of water rushing in somewhere and at the same time a tremendous sweep of wind."

Holding onto the bridge wing, Captain Kendall called again through his megaphone, this time for the *Storstad* to keep her prow inside the twelve-foot-deep gash in the *Empress'* starboard side, between her two funnels. The collier's anchor had acted like a can opener as the heavy ship bore in.

But this expedient was not effected. Either the ship's own propulsion, in reverse, or the momentum of the two vessels and the river current parted them. Soon, the *Storstad* vanished into the fog.

In his radio shack, Ed Bamford did not wait for orders. He flashed: "SOS—in collision."

He repeated it.

Marconiman Whiteside, on watch at the Father Point station, received the distress message with particular disbelief. He had watched the lights of the *Empress of Ireland* glide past only an hour ago. However, he reacted with much the same speed as his radio apparatus.

He ordered his two assistants to dispatch the nearest river craft immediately. One of them was the *Lady Evelyn*, just warped to her pier at Rimouski after delivering the mail to the *Empress*. The other was the *Eureka*, back at Father Point and waiting to take a pilot on board the incoming *Storstad*.

In minutes, lines were cast off. The *Lady Evelyn* was boiling back down Rimouski Roads into the St. Lawrence. Captain Boulanger personally took the helm of the *Eureka* and drove her hard.

First Officer Jones calmly wrote down the *Empress'* position —some three miles beyond Cocks Point buoy—and handed it to Bamford. He observed that the liner was but two miles off shore.

Captain Kendall knew that the water was 120 feet deep here and that he would have to run almost to the river's bank to beach his ship. Nonetheless, he decided to try for it.

In the engine room, "Lucky" Tower and the rest of the "black gang," officers and men, were scrambling up ladders toward what they hoped would be safety. Steam pipes were split and water was cascading in. Even if a man had been at the throttle, the pumps could not have been started.

The *Empress*, listing twenty degrees, was obviously going fast. Kendall, fully aware of this fact, since his orders "full speed ahead" had not been obeyed or even acknowledged, leaned over the bridge and shouted through his megaphone to the gathering passengers, who were mostly clad in their night garments: "Keep your heads there, and don't get excited!"

Down below, most of the people were excited. F. E. Abbott, of Toronto, was one. As he ran into the passageway, he met Laurence Irving, the actor. The latter asked Abbott: "Is the boat going down?"

"It looks like it," replied Abbott.

"Dearie," Irving remarked, turning to his wife, "hurry. There is not time to lose."

"Mrs. Irving began to cry," Abbott recalled, "and as the actor reached for a life belt the boat suddenly lurched forward and he was thrown against the door of his cabin.

"His face was covered with blood and Mrs. Irving became frantic.

"'Keep cool,'" he warned her.

"But she persisted in holding her arms around him. He forced a life belt over her head and pushed her out of the door. He then practically carried her up the stairs. I said:

" 'Can I help you?'

"Mr. Irving said, 'Look after yourself first, old man. God bless you all the same.' "

Abbott decided he would look after himself. He raced for the deck and leaped into the river, without waiting to look for a boat. He clutched a piece of lumber floating by.

Sir Henry Seton-Karr, the big game hunter, was seen trying to persuade another man, M. D. A. Darling, of Shanghai, to accept his life belt. The argument was resolved when a second belt was procured from an overhead rack. The two helped each other into the lifesaving devices, then hurried their separate ways.

Frail old Commissioner Rees, of the Salvation Army, was observed on the shoulders of one of his deputies, Major Frank Morris, of London, Ontario, who was struggling upward against the list of a stairway.

Dr. Grant, the ship's surgeon, could not unbolt the door, which had become jammed by the collision. Finally he opened his porthole and was pulled up and onto the side of the vessel, which was becoming more and more horizontal.

He was struck by the scene silhouetted before him in the night's gloom. Passengers, in a variety of attire and disattire, some screaming, some moaning in a low key, others remarkable for their very lack of sound, were moving across the sloping side of the Empress "as though they were walking down a sandy beach into the water to bathe."

Cunningham, meanwhile, was continuing his battle for life.

"The air of the ship," he noted, "came up from below as the water rushed in. I scrambled up the tilting floor and reached the balustrade companionway. There was a sudden sort of 'glug' like water coming out of a near empty water bottle. She twisted again and the stairs were at a crazy angle. But I scrambled up."

It was then that he was thankful for the dumbbell exercises he took every morning of his life, keeping his muscles fit.

"I got up somehow to the level of the saloon deck. I went like mad. I scrambled up the sloping floor to the high side and I knew by instinct there would be rising water on the other side, and I got on deck.

"She began to turn over like you see a horse rolling in a field. Her great big whitish-looking belly turned slowly upward and I jumped far, because, as she slewed over, her length of side increased."

"Hurry up there everybody!" Captain Kendall shouted through his megaphone. "There is not a minute to lose. Get the stewards through the corridors. If there are people locked in, break the doors. Get people out, and don't forget that women and children come first!"

Bandsman Green, of the Salvation Army, noticed one man who paid no attention to Kendall's orders. While he was trying to shoulder his way into a lifeboat, ahead of the women and children, another man, also a passenger, swung and flattened him.

Many of the women, not realizing how few minutes remained to the Empress, had yielded to their normal modesty. They lingered in their cabins, listing as the liner was, to dress.

However, Gracie Hannagan, seven, daughter of Bandmaster Hannagan, was being shepherded outside by a Mrs. Atwell, whose upper-lower bunk cabin she shared. Her parents, who had been in another cabin, were nowhere to be seen.

"I came up on deck with Mrs. Atwell," the child recalled. "I was only frightened when I saw Mr. and Mrs. Atwell go into the cold water. Then I went away down deep, oh so deep, into the water, too. I was hanging onto a black rope. When I came up again after a long time, I looked around and saw a light in front of me.

"Then when I looked a second time I saw mama and papa. They were swimming."

Kendall, shedding his coat, shouted to those left aboard: "Heaven help us because we cannot help ourselves!"

C. H. Bristow and his wife thought they saw the *Storstad* heave to about half a mile distant. Bristow noted her red port running-light.

The couple joined the "long line" of passengers hanging onto the remaining above-water portions of the *Empress*. Bristow heard a "loud roaring" which he attributed to a ruptured boiler tube. He decided no time was to be lost and goaded his wife along by the arm toward the water.

He helped another woman and her two children down the sloping side, only to watch them lose their hold and slip into the water. Next, his own wife tumbled into the river and was gone. He watched other passengers clutch onto deck chairs and plunge into the dark nothingness of the river.

Staff Captain McCameron, of the Salvation Army, had scrambled out of his cabin and on deck to find "unspeakable confusion." The official recalled:

"With every lurch of the steamer we had to take a step higher and higher on the upper side and finally I gained the rail and stuck to it. In a breathless moment I felt the last rush to the bottom. A moment we hung on the surface. Then an endless, dreadful force dragged us down. How deep we went I cannot know—it was yards and yards. Then came the cresting of the wave and I was buoyed up on it."

He reached an overturned lifeboat, helped right it, and then assisted others aboard.

The *Storstad* had put over all her lifeboats. Her seamen were rowing desperately through the fog, guided by the sound of people screaming.

Everyone who was able was jumping into the water. Purser Hayes leaped from the promenade deck and pulled himself up over the gunwales of Number 3 lifeboat.

Major Morris had almost succeeded in walking, with Commissioner Rees still upon his shoulders, into the water when the *Empress* started her final plunge. At the same time, the boilers blew up, as if to end the suffering of the many who either could not swim or who could not endure the bitter cold of the St. Lawrence.

Morris, losing Rees, was himself projected into the water. One arm had been severely scalded by steam, but he stroked on, anyhow, to put all possible distance between himself and the whirlpool he was certain would follow the sinking of so heavy a ship.

In less than fifteen minutes the big liner had been swallowed by the waters.

Captain Kendall, who had jumped from the bridge, was assisted by Hayes into the lifeboat. The radio operators, Bamford and Ferguson, had tumbled into the waters moments ahead of their captain. They struck out for shore—or, more properly, where they thought the shore should be.

The *Storstad's* boats were already in the area and beginning to pull survivors aboard.

Cunningham, as he swam like one possessed, recalled a millrace into which he was once tumbled. He saved himself then, since he was "the best swimmer in town." He was determined, in spite of the many years which had intervened, that he would save himself once more.

"I saw just the greyness and that damned water lapping, lapping like a fool dog that has ruined a flower bed and then stands sniffing at it, wondering what made things look so untidy. I never hated water so in my life before.

"It didn't seem wicked or vicious, or menacing or cruel, but just foolish, like an idiot fooling with a double-barrelled shotgun and hopping around and laughing about it.

"There was a bit of wind and it tittered and there was a bit of sea and it hopped up and down sort of carefree, and aimless, as though to say:

" 'Oh see what I done. Ain't it awful?'

"At first I swam because I was excited and had lost my head; then I floated and got my mind. Then I shouted. The wind just snickered around and I began to meet my Maker—but it was willed for me to be spared.

"I was picked up by a lifeboat—a big Swede dragged me in."

Little Gracie Hannagan recalled going under again. "And I swallowed a lot of nasty salt water this time. When I came up the next time I saw a light again and it was very near. In about a minute a man put out a board to me and yelled to me to grab it and I tried to take hold of it.

"I slid down the rope. My hands were all black as tar. The man helped me to get into his boat by holding the board under my arm."

An eight-year-old girl, Florence Barbour, of Silverstone, British Columbia, was saved by a man, Robert W. Crellin, who lived next door to her. He swam with her on his back until they reached a collapsible boat.

"The child was pluckier than a stout man," he observed. Her father had died a year ago and she was en route to England with her mother and sister.

Bandsman Green, as he swam, heard a remarkable as well as "inspiring" sound. He was not sure whether it emanated from a group in the water or in a boat. It was the hymn the band had played at its final concert in Toronto:

God be with you 'till we meet again.
By his counsels guide, uphold you,
With his sheep securely fold you,
God be with you 'till we meet again.

Tears came to his eyes and welling emotion combined with
the river water to choke him up. Then he dived under and surfaced again several yards farther on. Now the singing had ceased.
There were only the diminishing moans of the dying.

Odd companions of fate, L. E. Gosselin, the Montreal lawyer,
and "Lucky" Tower, the oiler,—survivor of the *Titanic*, clung
to a raft until rescued by the *Eureka*, first on the scene. Tower
swore he would never go to sea again; but he did not mean it.

The *Lady Evelyn* arrived off Cock Point buoy in another
fifteen minutes and commenced searching through the darkness
for additional survivors.

Shortly after 3 A.M. the pilot boat tied up once more at
Father Point, with thirty-two men, women, and children
aboard. She also carried several bodies, which were disembarked
at Rimouski. The *Eureka* then turned her prow back toward the
scene of the disaster.

The famous were going with the unknown. Laurence Irving,
his wife, his entire troupe perished, as did Sir Henry Seton-Karr.
Leonard Palmer, the London newspaperman, and Mrs. Palmer
were lost. The Salvation Army had suffered the worst single
tragedy in its history. Of the 171 who had embarked, only 26
were saved. Commissioner Rees and his family had been wiped
out. The band, save for one or two, had been lost.

One of its members, without family, mother or father, son
or daughter, survived as a scanty, broken reminder of a ship and
its people.

The fleet of fishing craft which gathered near Cock Point gas
buoy at dawn saw a desolation of "wreckage, strewn for thousands of yards along the river."

At Rimouski pier, a reporter for the *L'Echo du Bas St. Laurent* wrote: "One of the saddest sights at Rimouski pier is the number of children among the dead. Babies in arms and boys and girls of eight or nine years of age were there. Near one of the doors was a little girl of perhaps ten years old. Her brown hair was quite dry and blew across her face. Just beside her was a young mother, some twenty-five years old, with her little baby clasped tight in her arms close to her breast."

The *Storstad*, a cabin plate from the sunken liner still dangling from her smashed bow, continued to Quebec. Below decks, Dr. Grant worked on the survivors, some with broken limbs, some with mortal gashes, some coughing out their lives because of the oil and coal dust they had inhaled.

Nearly twenty succumbed before the collier could make port.

Captain Kendall had given way under his night's ordeal. When Pilot Nault visited him aboard the *Lady Evelyn* he found a sunken-eyed man, sipping brandy and sobbing into a piece of dirty tarpaulin, as he repeated: "Where's the ship?"

It was to be a day of tears—in Rimouski, in Quebec, in Montreal, Toronto, in far corners of the Empire.

By afternoon this somber Sunday, coffins lined the Canadian Pacific Railway's shed at Rimouski, as survivors sought to identify lost kin or friends.

One coffin was tagged: "No. 1—Woman on bottom, baby on top."

Another bore a scribbled label: "*Ne pleurez pas sur moi!*"

But the otherwise hardened stevedores who were carrying these burdens paid no attention to the entreaty, apparently written by some priest. Tears rolled down their cheeks in an incongruous fashion. Such scenes were repeated when the "morgue ship" *Lady Grey* arrived in Quebec, bearing 188 bodies.

In Toronto, friends of the Salvation Army delegates returned to the organization's temple, scene of the farewell, to pray. Into the Union Station of the same city, rolled the first train of survivors on Monday morning. A reporter noted a "feeble cheer" as the cars clattered into the station, then a sudden, almost "shameful" silence, as if those waiting realized that cheers were inappropriate.

As the broken, haunted-eyed people, dressed in all sorts of makeshift garments, limped off the train, those on the platform started singing "Oh God our help in ages past."

Gracie Hannagan, the seven-year-old bandsman's daughter, was on the train, along with a ten-year-old friend, Helen O'Hara, also of Toronto, and Florence Barbour, eight, of Silverstone, British Columbia.

"Do you think I'll get home before Father and Mother?" Gracie asked a reporter, then observed: "They are not on the train now. They are coming on the next one."

But neither the reporter nor anyone else on the windy, lonely platform had the heart to tell Gracie or Helen or Florence that each one was now an orphan.

The dead totaled 1,027, the saved, 452. The toll seemed out of all proportion in this, the worst ship tragedy since the *Titanic*.

Mayor Napolean Druin, of Quebec, with the cooperation of the Canadian Pacific, promised an "imposing funeral" for nine of the crewmen whose bodies had been borne to his city.

And, presently, the steamship operators announced they would maintain in perpetuity a small cemetery at Father Point for the unidentified dead, as well as continue diving operations in search of additional bodies.

Lord Mersey, wreck commissioner and former presiding justice in British Admiralty Court, who had conducted the *Titanic* inquiry, speedily fixed blame on Chief Officer Tuftenes of the *Storstad*. He had, ruled the jurist, been guilty of not advising his captain of the approach of fog as well as of altering course in a fog in the presence of an approaching ship.

Tuftenes' license was suspended for two years.

In London, where the *Empress* had now replaced the *Titanic* as "the great disaster," the Salvation Army congress commenced session under a pall of sorrow. Bramwell Booth, son of the illustrious founder who had died only two years before, was hard put to reconcile or ever interpret the loss of so many of their members.

Evangeline Booth, heading the American delegation, gave thanks that she and her co-workers were spared. They had decided to cross on the *Olympic* after originally planning to travel with their Canadian colleagues.

Yet, not the prayers and tears in London, the ruling of Lord Mersey, the cemetery plot at Father Point, nor, indeed, Mayor Druin's "imposing funeral" in Quebec could ever balance out the tragedy for the many who had been bereaved because of it.

The bands could play and choirs sing "God be with you till we meet again," yet the sick heartaches would linger and, for some, fear would give way to conviction that never, never would they meet their loved ones again.

Flotsam of the Great War

THE EUROPEAN WAR BEGAN IN THE SUMMER OF 1914 AS A GIANT struggle to the death between opposing armies, numbered in the millions. There had been nothing remotely like it in history.

Yet the fight at sea, while less known or even less understood, was in many ways to be the decisive phase. The U-boats, which nearly isolated Britain as an island kingdom, indirectly hastened America's entry. Jutland, the last great contest between naval juggernauts of the line, was to end—apparently forever—German aspirations as a sea power, as well as an empire.

The war afloat was unique in many phases, not the least of which was the role played by merchant vessels.

On a humid September morning, as the second month of the Great War commenced, the new superliner *Cap Trafalgar* was beating homeward from Buenos Aires. Caught in Argentina at the end of her maiden voyage by the war's outbreak, the 20,000-ton Hamburg-South America vessel was too swift and altogether too lavish in her appointments to languish at a foreign quayside for the duration.

Responding to urgent wireless orders from the Reichsmarine in Berlin, Commodore Julius Wirth, her captain, turned his crew of nearly four hundred to, with a passionate haste. Inflammable draperies were removed and stowed away. The furniture from the gaudy, overstuffed lounges, which resembled Potsdam's royal salons, was dumped unceremoniously into cargo holds to make room for hospital wards—"just in case."

The woodcarvings of Hansel and Gretel in the first class nursery looked gravely down now on cases of ammunition.

The telephone circuits remained in operation but in the handsome cabins of this "finest vessel in the South American trade" there were no longer passengers to answer or to call up.

Meeting the old German gunboat *Eber* off Bahia, she obtained meager enough armament—two 4.1-inch cannon, six pom-poms, and two machineguns, plus several petty officers to head the gun crews. Her third funnel was removed in an effort to obscure her identity.

A small, impulsive, often irascible man, Commodore Wirth was far from satisfied. His sealed, secret orders revealed he should sail as a "raider." However, he believed he would be fortunate to cross the Atlantic undetected and tie up in Kiel, where he could obtain proper weapons.

On September 12th, the *Cap Trafalgar* dropped anchor at Trinidad, and commenced coaling from two supply ships. During the tedious operations, seamen went aloft and painted her remaining two funnels red and black, her hull light gray—the colors of the Union Castle Line.

Now Julius Wirth was more satisfied. He might outfox King George's Navy after all, he concluded, and bag a stray British or French merchantman, as bonus, on the long voyage across the North Atlantic, up past Iceland, and north even of the northerly Faeroes, where, surely, he could elude His Majesty's men-of-war.

During the time that the *Cap Trafalgar* was readying for possible action, King George's Navy was doing the same thing. The Admiralty's activity, also extending to merchant ships, included by chance a liner of the same tonnage as the *Cap Trafalgar* and of very similar outlines. The *Carmania*, which had raced to the aid of the *Volturno* the previous year, was, however, an older ship. Launched shortly after the turn of the century, the large

Cunarder was the first modern liner to be fitted with steam turbines. She proved their efficiency to such an extent that the *Lusitania*, the biggest ship afloat when she sailed on her maiden voyage in 1908, had been equipped with them.

Although the Admiralty was in almost as much haste as its German counterpart, the naval yards at Liverpool took enough time to arm the *Carmania* with the best weapons available for these so-called "auxiliary cruisers." When she sailed the first day of September, commanded by Captain Noel Grant, R.N., she mounted eight 4.7-inch guns, nests of rapid-firing small-caliber guns, in addition to a range finder, searchlights, and secondary fighting equipment.

Captain Grant himself, a tall, hearty, rather deliberate Briton, knew that the pick of the Kaiser's liners, headed in size and Wagnerian grandeur by the 54,000-ton *Vaterland* were bottled up in United States ports. It was impossible for them to elude the offshore patrol already established by British cruisers and destroyers. On the other hand, Grant considered it more than likely that enemy merchantmen on South Atlantic runs would try to slip homeward through the blockade.

He set his initial course for the Caribbean, although he could not possibly divine his first exact zone of action. The wireless was a confusing jumble of reported enemy sightings. The cruisers *Karlsruhe* and *Dresden*, for two, were on the prowl, probably between Africa and South America. The *Emden* had already struck, and struck hard, in the Indian Ocean. The *Konigsberg* was playing cat-and-mouse with a disproportionately large part of the British fleet off West Africa.

And von Spee's mighty Far East squadron? Some reports had it already in South American waters, where it could knock off Allied freighters like ten-pins.

The whereabouts of the scrappy little *Goeben* and *Breslau* was another serious headache in naval intelligence chambers at Whitehall.

On the morning of September 14th, Captain Grant unexpectedly came upon the answer to one of the Admiralty's puzzles. Raising Trinidad at dawn, he was scanning the greenish-brown slopes of Mount Aripo, dominating the island's northern coast, when an alert signalman put aside his telescope and shouted: "There's a German auxiliary!"

At about the same moment, Commander Wirth recognized the inbound Carmania. He had maintained a full head of steam during coaling operations for just such an eventuality. In no longer than was required to weigh anchor, his Cap Trafalgar was pounding away from Trinidad and out into the Atlantic, to meet this hulking Britisher which might by her silhouette be an older sister.

Battle stations were sounded on both ships. The Carmania, now manned largely by naval reservists, was in every way ready for action. The Cap Trafalgar was not. Chinese cooks, ship's musicians, waiters, and pursers must "fight" this ship, auxiliary cruiser in name only.

With a range of several hundred yards because of his slightly larger guns, Grant opened fire first. His salvo fell short, though it projected towering water spouts in a neat line off the Cap Trafalgar's starboard beam.

Faster than the aging Carmania, the Cap Trafalgar arrowed pluckily in at nearly twenty knots toward her harder-hitting adversary, kicking up a wake like that of a destroyer. As the second salvo from the Britisher whistled through his rigging, Wirth replied with his two guns. The shells straddled the Carmania.

A second round from the Cap Trafalgar, and the Carmania was hit. A puff of smoke billowed from her port waterline.

In the engine room of the Cunard liner, which had already

carried a quarter of a million passengers, several merchant firemen, jarred by the hit, had "gotten their wind up," and wanted out. A five-foot fourth engineer, Fraser, succeeded in bolstering their courage and thereby keeping the fires hot and steam up.

Wirth kept boring in, closing the range finally to 3500 yards. He tried to sweep the *Carmania's* decks with pom-poms, in addition to working his pair of 4.1-inch cannon as fast as they could be reloaded.

Captain Grant was admittedly filled with admiration for the German as he ordered every gun trained on the Hamburg-South America liner. A shattering broadside rattled the portholes in the British auxiliary, and when the smoke cleared, the gunners could see that they had taken terrible toll.

Visibly, the *Cap Trafalgar* had been torn at the waterline. Two-thirds of her lifeboats had been blasted into splinters. Her decks and superstructure were riddled.

Within her vitals, the havoc was even worse. The engine crew had suffered casualties. Seas were pouring in. Forward, a fire blazed.

Gunners dropped at their posts, to be replaced by others.

Commander Wirth ordered a distress call in the German naval code: "Cap Trafalgar on fire! SOS!"

It was repeated, then sent in international Morse in the hope a neutral American ship would pick it up.

"Cap Trafalgar on fire!" the cry was sparked across the waters of the Atlantic, over and over, together with the vessel's position.

A sister raider, the converted *Kronprinz Wilhelm*, one hundred miles to the south, heard the call. For the last three days, her captain, Paul Thierfelder, had been more concerned with hunting rats than enemy ships. The rodents had taken possession of his wallowing old liner, and they were so large and ferocious that cats or even ferrets were no match. As a last

resort, he had equipped his stealthiest seamen with tennis shoes
and sent them into the cargo holds, armed with baseball bats
and planks of wood. The toll had already been several bashed
skulls, but no vermin.

Now Captain Thierfelder called off the strange quest and
set course for his countryman in distress.

Wirth's command was still under control, although her speed
was cut and she was blazing in many sections. He had succeeded
in starting lesser fires on the Carmania, in addition to shooting
away her range finder and peppering her bridge with machinegun bullets and shrapnel.

Casualties were mounting on both vessels. On the Cap Trafalgar, the surgeon could not keep up with the quantities of
wounded and dying demanding his attention.

For two hours the carnage continued. The Cap Trafalgar, at
last halted, blazing virtually from fore to aft, her guns out of
action, would not surrender. The Carmania, hit seventy-three
times, was also burning, her funnels tottering and almost ready
to fall off, her booms gone.

In her sick bay, the surgeon counted nine dead, twenty-six
officers and men severely wounded, as they wondered if the
cruisers Bristol and Cornwall, which had responded to the
Carmania's own plea for assistance, would arrive in time.

With the Cap Trafalgar, however, it was all over. Wirth
transmitted one final plea: "Am afire and sinking! Enemy also
on fire!"

The new liner listed heavily to starboard. Her bow dipped
under the blue waters adjacent to the Caribbean. Her German
eagle ensign flying at the stern and one machinegun still crackling, the Cap Trafalgar plunged down, down—carrying Commander Julius Wirth with her.

The smoke and the steam cleared from the spot where the
great ship had vanished. A life jacket, torn and scorched, a

crate, a plank, a gathering, morbid assortment of flotsam floated away in the currents.

The *Carmania*, too badly hurt to pick up the *Cap Trafalgar* survivors and fearing other German ships were close by, set course for Gibraltar, crippled and leaking though she was.

Another three hours steaming to the south, Captain Thierfelder turned his *Kronprinz Wilhelm* around. There was nothing he could do but resume the rat hunt. And, anyhow, one of the *Cap Trafalgar's* two colliers, the *Eleonore Woermann*, was almost at the scene.

As fall turned into winter, the survivors of the lost German liner settled down for a long respite at Buenos Aires. The *Carmania*, which barely had made the "Gib," licked her many wounds. It would be spring before she was ready to fight again.

And that spring of 1915, in London on a balmy bright May 7th, Colonel E. M. ("Ed") House, President Wilson's special adviser, was calling on King George at Buckingham Palace. "We fell to talking, strangely enough," recalled the colonel, "of the probability of Germany sinking a transatlantic liner. He said: 'Suppose they should sink the *Lusitania* with American passengers on board.'"

By coincidence, possibly, the 32,000-ton Cunarder was nearing the Irish coast that Friday noon, even as Ed House and His Majesty conversed informally. On board the graceful four-stacker were 1,257 passengers and a crew of nearly eight hundred. Elbert Hubbard, the writer-philosopher, Alfred Gwynne Vanderbilt, the millionaire, and Charles Frohman, the theatrical producer, were among the approximately 160 Americans who were sailing on this, the fastest liner remaining in the transatlantic passenger service.

All had embarked in New York the Saturday before in the face of a warning inserted in the newspapers as an advertisement:

Travelers intending to embark on the Atlantic voyage are reminded that a state of war exists between Germany and her allies and Great Britain and her allies. That the zone of war includes the waters adjacent to the British Isles. That in accordance with formal notice given by the Imperial German Government, vessels flying the flag of Great Britain or of any of her allies are liable to destruction in those waters, and that travelers sailing in the war zone on ships of Great Britain or her allies do so at their own risk.

IMPERIAL GERMAN EMBASSY

April 22, 1915　　　Washington, D. C.

The voyage was uneventful until May 6th. On approaching Ireland, sixty-three-year-old Captain William T. Turner ordered all the boats hanging on the davits to be swung out and lowered to the promenade deckrail. All bulkhead doors which were not necessary for the working of the ship were closed, and it was reported to Captain Turner that this had been done. Lookouts were doubled and two extra ones were put forward and one on each side of the bridge.

Directions were given to the engine room to keep the highest steam they could possibly get on the boilers and, in case the bridge rang for full speed, to give as much as they possibly could. Orders were also given that ports should be kept closed.

In taking these precautionary measures, "Will" Turner was mindful of recent warnings, such as this one transmitted to him by the British Admiralty:

PROCLAMATION

1. The waters surrounding Great Britain and Ireland, including the whole English Channel, are hereby declared to be war zone. On and after the 18th of February, 1915, every enemy merchant ship found in the said war zone will be destroyed without its being always possible to avert the dangers threatening the crews and passengers on that account.

2. Even neutral ships are exposed to danger in the war zone, as in view of the misuse of neutral flags ordered on Jan. 31 by the British Government and of the accidents of naval war, it cannot always be avoided to strike even neutral ships in attacks that are directed at enemy ships.

3. Northward navigation around the Shetland Islands, in the eastern waters of the North Sea and in a strip of not less than thirty miles width along the Netherlands coast is in no danger.

VON POHL

Chief of the Admiral Staff of the Navy.
   Berlin, Feb. 4, 1915.

This was accompanied by a so-called memorial:

Just as England declared the whole North Sea between Scotland and Norway to be comprised within the seat of war, so does Germany now declare the waters surrounding Great Britain and Ireland, including the whole English Channel, to be comprised within the seat of war, and will prevent by all the military means at its disposal all navigation by the enemy in these waters. To this end it will endeavor to destroy, after Feb. 18 next, any merchant vessels of the enemy which present themselves that area will be destroyed, and that neutral vessels may be exposed to danger. This is in effect a claim to torpedo at sight, without regard to the safety of the crew or passengers, any merchant vessel under any flag. As it is not in the power of the German Admiralty to maintain any surface craft in these waters, this attack can only be delivered by submarine agency.

At 7:50 P.M., on May 6th, the *Lusitania* received a wireless message from Admiral H. L. A. Hood, at Queenstown, commanding the Irish Coast Patrol: "Submarines active off south coast of Ireland." At 7:56 P.M., the vessel asked for and received a repetition of his message. The ship was pounding along at twenty-one knots.

At 8:30 P.M. a message crackled in from the British Admiralty:

To All British Ships 0005:
Take Liverpool pilot at bar and avoid headlands. Pass harbors at full speed; steer mid-channel course. Submarines off Fastnet.

At 8:32, the *Lusitania* acknowledged. The same message was offered to the vessel seven times between midnight of May 6th and 10 A.M. of May 7th.

At about 8 A.M. May 7, on approaching the Irish coast, the big vessel encountered fog banks, or "Scotch mist," and the speed was reduced to fifteen knots. Previously the speed had been reduced to eighteen knots. This adjustment was due to the fact that Captain Turner wished to run the last 150 miles of the voyage in the dark, so as to make Liverpool early on the morning of May 8th, at the earliest time when he could cross the bar without a pilot.

From the location of previous submarine attacks, the most dangerous waters in the *Lusitania's* course were from the entrance to St. George's Channel to Liverpool Bar.

On the morning of May 7, 1915, the ship passed at least eighteen and a half miles south of Fastnet Rock, which was not in sight. The course was then held up slightly, to bring the ship closer to land, and a little before noon land was sighted, and what was thought to be a Brow Head was made out.

Meanwhile, between 11 A.M. and noon, the fog disappeared, the weather became clear, and the speed was increased to eighteen knots. The course of the vessel was nearly due east. At 11:25 A.M. Turner received the following message:

Submarines active in southern part of Irish Channel, last heard of twenty miles south of Coningbeg Light Vessel. Make certain *Lusitania* gets this.

At 12:40 P.M. the following additional wireless message from the Admiralty was received:

Submarine five miles south of Cape Clear, proceeding west when sighted at 10 A.M.

After picking up Brow Head and at about 12:40 P.M., the course was altered in shore by about thirty degrees, and land was sighted which the captain thought was Galley Head. He was not entirely sure.

The great liner knifed toward shore at eighteen knots. In the brilliant sunshine, passengers strolled on deck to watch the rapidly-materializing houses and trees of the shore. At 1:40 P.M. Turner recognized beyond question the familiar outjut, the Old Head of Kinsale.

He changed course to the east once more and ten minutes later ordered a four-point bearing. He estimated he was offshore about ten miles but he wished to be absolutely certain—methodical, one-time sailing ship skipper that he was.

The *Lusitania* was held steadily on course while the bearing was being taken—so steadily that, beneath the placid surface of the Atlantic, thirty-two-year-old Kapitanleutnant Walther Schwieger, had maneuvered his U-20 into perfect proximity for firing a torpedo. He had been waiting for the Cunarder ever since it appeared off Galley Head.

On the Marconi deck of the liner J. H. ("Jay") Brooks, Bridgeport, Connecticut, salesman, was strolling when he spied a glint in the water. He at once recognized a torpedo and watched it nearing the ship with detached fascination. Then he cupped his hands to his lips and shouted as loud as he could: "Torpedo!"

He next grasped the railing of the Marconi deck and leaned over, balancing himself with one foot off the planking and in the air. He stared as the torpedo was swallowed in the hull of the *Lusitania*.

It was exactly 2:10 P.M.

He waited in his terpsichorean stance, wondering why nothing happened.

In seconds, however, something did happen, as Schwieger himself, staring through his periscope, recorded:

"Shot hits starboard side right behind bridge. An unusually heavy detonation follows with a very strong explosion cloud (high in the air over first smokestack). Added to the explosion of the torpedo there must have been a second explosion (boiler, coal, or powder). The superstructure over point struck and the high bridge are rent asunder and fire breaks out and envelops the high bridge. The ship stops immediately and quickly heels to starboard, at the same time diving deeper at the bow."

On the bridge, Captain Turner reeled, recovered his balance, ordered the helm put over. It would not respond. When he heard a hissing from deep in the stricken liner's vitals like the "rattling of a Maxim gun" he knew the reason—her steam pipes, her electrical circuits, all her intricate nerve fibers, bronze and steel arteries had been ruptured beyond recall by the infinitely destructive blast.

He had hoped to beach the Lusitania. Now, he knew that was out of the question. With her rapidly increasing list, too, he feared it would be very difficult to launch the lifeboats.

The youthful submarine commander, curiously restrained from firing a second torpedo, noted the chaos he had produced:

"She has the appearance of being about to capsize. Great confusion on board, boats being cleared and some of them lowered to the water. They must have lost their heads. Many boats crowded come down bow first or stern first in the water and immediately fill and sink. Fewer lifeboats can be made clear owing to the slant of the boat [the Lusitania]. The ship blows off, in front appears the name Lusitania in gold letters."

There were, as in the Titanic disaster, acts of heroism, but, unlike the mortal panic which gripped the White Star liner in her last moments, there was little cowardice displayed on the *Lusitania.*

At 3:25 P.M., Schwieger recorded his quarry's death throes: "It seems as if the vessel will be afloat only a short time. Submerge to 24 meters and go to sea. I could not have fired a second torpedo into this throng of humanity attempting to save themselves."

The *Lusitania,* eleven miles offshore, almost due south of the glistening white lighthouse on the Old Head of Kinsale, where her agonies were being observed, was going. Sinking by the bow, the luxury ship was spectacular in her last moments. Because of her 790-foot length, her bow first touched the sandy bottom, only three hundred feet below the surface.

There, with her stern high in the air, she righted herself from the critical starboard list, which itself had caused so many casualties, then quivered for awesome seconds.

Next, like an immensely tired old person sitting down in a chair, she began to lower, lower her full length into the seas—settling now by the stern. Captain Turner himself was swept from the bridge.

At the end, there was an "explosion and rattling of all the loose material leaving her deck" and then her last stanchions visible on her stern vanished from sight.

George Kessler, New York wine merchant, who had left two million dollars in cash and securities in his cabin, stared incredulously from his collapsible boat and gasped: "My God—the *Lusitania's* gone!"

She took with her an inconsequential amount of war contraband—18 fuze cases, 125 shrapnel cases, containing empty shells, 4,200 cases of small-caliber ammunition, and almost a tramp ship's conglomeration of cargo: beef, Connecticut oysters, dental goods, leather sides, confectionary.

All of it taken together hardly outweighed the loss of 1,198 men, women, and children and especially, politically and emotionally speaking, of the 124 Americans who perished. Among the latter were Hubbard, Frohman, and Vanderbilt.

As the Kaiser, Admiral von Tirpitz, Chancellor von Bethmann-Hollweg, and other war lords of Germany were to admit, the torpedoing had been poor enough bargain, measured against its inestimable influence in hurrying America into the Great War. It happened on April 6, 1917, just less than two years after the *Lusitania* disappeared in the shimmering waters off the Old Head of Kinsale.

In the meantime, the personal backwash of the Cunarder's torpedoing continued. There was romance as well as tragedy wrought in its cauldron. And at least one *Lusitania* survivor had serious reason to question whether his survival actually was so providential.

"Lucky" Tower had lived to tell of the *Titanic, Empress of Ireland*, and now the *Lusitania* disasters. Undaunted, the stocky little oiler signed on another merchantman in Liverpool as soon as he had been paid off and provided with a new, dry suit of clothes.

By now, Lucky's fame had swept like a warning beacon before him. "We don't sail on no ship with Tower," the chief of the "black gang" informed the captain, who had to admit he was himself queasy at the prospect.

And that was the end of "Lucky" Tower's seagoing career. He vanished into the grubbing humdrum of Liverpool's waterfront employment.

By December of 1917, America's martial effort commenced to grind into higher gear. A steady stream of ships linked the east coast with Britain and France, far across the gray, wintry North Atlantic. They sailed with a rallying cry which had arisen on a sunny May day off the Irish coast: "Remember the *Lusitania!*"

Yet not all of the perils were war or even weather-wrought. There were, as always, accidents.

On a bleak Thursday, December 6th, off Cape Sambro, Nova Scotia—near the spot where the *Atlantic* had gone down forty-four years previously—the French freighter *Mont Blanc* picked up her pilot and headed for Halifax harbor. She steamed in past the towering headlands, through patches of cold fog.

In New York the 3,121-ton vessel had taken on a full cargo: TNT, picric acid, gun cotton, and, on deck, barrels of benzine. Altogether she was burdened with five thousand tons of high explosives and combustibles.

The *Mont Blanc* had sailed to the Canadian port to await convoy across the Atlantic. And even as she felt her way toward the inner harbor through patches of fog she passed *H.M.S. High Flyer*, the cruiser which would lead the convoy.

She continued ahead, sounding her horn at intervals, blending with the throaty symphony from many other ships in the busy port.

It was now about nine o'clock of a chill, lowering, winter morning. Business establishments had opened. Schools had been in session for the past hour. High on the hill overlooking the ancient city, the guns of the Citadel frowned harborward. Sentries paced their posts at the picturesque fort, built to withstand the weapons of two centuries ago.

The *Mont Blanc* was no more than half a mile off Pier 8, at an area where the harbor narrowed to a mile and the waterfront structures of neighboring Dartmouth confronted their counterparts of Halifax.

Now the pilot suddenly held down on the whistle lever for a long, continuing blast. It was answered even as the bow of another vessel appeared from out of the fog and swept unerringly toward the port side of the French freighter. It was the outbound *Imo*, a Belgian relief grain ship, which needed no armed escort.

Within seconds, the *Imo* bore into the *Mont Blanc's* side—a crunching, a shattering, followed by silence as both ships stopped their engines. The relief vessel had pierced deep into the side of the ammunition ship.

Then, the *Imo* reversed her propeller and backed off, once more absorbed by the same fog which had delivered her on a mission of involuntary execution.

The flames licked up from the wound in the *Mont Blanc's* side, as the order rang: "Abandon ship!"

Not lingering to fight the fire, the crew obeyed. They lowered lifeboats and started for shore, rowing like maniacs.

Through rifts in the fog, people on both shores observed what had happened. On Pier 8, a guard pulled the fire-alarm switch. At the American Sugar Refining plant, next to the pier, other watchmen debated whether to order the workers out.

At Richmond, a section of Halifax also bordering the harbor, Vincent Coleman, a telegraph operator, looked out of his window and tapped to Moncton and St. John: "A munition ship is on fire and is making for Pier 8. Good-by!"

A volunteer party from the cruiser *High Flayer* had put over the side and was making for the now fiercely burning *Mont Blanc*.

Halifax's only large motor-driven piece of fire-fighting apparatus—a monster of pumps, piping, and hose reels named *Patricia*—was responding to the alarm. She turned down Gottingen Street, then rumbled and rang her way toward Pier 8 as fast as her bulky gasoline engine permitted.

The *Mont Blanc's* crew now was heading in the opposite direction. All had landed on the pier and tumbled ashore without waiting to secure the boats.

"She's a munitioner!" they screamed. "She's going to explode!"

Their own panic was quickly translated to others in the dock area and in the city's streets which paralleled away from the area. People swarmed out of their homes and stores to join the accumulating throng stumbling up the steep hill to the Citadel. On the fringes, children shouted and dogs bounded along, barking.

Warped to a dock close to Pier 8, the British ammunition ship *Pictou* was abandoned.

The launch from the *High Flyer* drew alongside the blazing *Mont Blanc*. She was almost at the pier, and it seemed to witnesses that the British Navy men had won their gamble to board and sink her.

The fire engine Patricia was also at hand, rolling across the cobblestones at the entrance to Pier 8. In moments the tide should drift the burning freighter alongside the wharf.

The time was about 9:13 A.M.

Breathless, on the hill toward the Citadel, the macabre assemblage of people and dogs struggled upward. No more than fifteen minutes after the original collision, the ammunition could wait not a fraction of a second longer for the boarding party or for the lumbering, faithful fire truck.

Mont Blanc, Pier 8, the launch from the *High Flyer*, the engine Patricia were suddenly enveloped in a spreading mushroom of smoke, interlaced with tongues of flame.

William Barton, former telegraph editor for the *Montreal Gazette*, was breakfasting in the nearby Halifax Hotel when the French cargo vessel atomized herself.

"In ten seconds it was all over," he reported. "A low rumbling, a quake shock, with everything vibrating, then an indescribable noise followed by the fall of plaster and the smashing of glass. A cry went up: 'A German bomb!'

"A rush for the door, headlong down the hallway, a fall among pictures, glass and plaster, through the swinging doors of a few seconds before, now ripped from their hinges, through great projecting triangular pieces of glass to the street.

"Here I found myself with a burden. How she had come into my arms I do not know; yet here she was, hysterically shrieking: 'oh my poor sister, my poor sister!'

"Outside, overhead a giant smoke cloud was curling northward, and danger seemed over. I crossed the road, laying my feminine burden on a doorstep and returned to the hotel."

The Intercolonial Railway Station, a brick and stone structure in the heart of Halifax, collapsed under the impact of the explosion. People died on the platforms and inside the cars of waiting trains.

Esmond P. Barry, of St. John who was among the fortunate minority, asserted:

"It was terrible. People were dying in our car like flies. Some of them came to the place with noses shot off, eyes put out, faces slashed with flying glass, limbs torn and distorted. . . . Men, women, and children were lying on the streets."

Entire structures had vanished, with less visible rubble than remained even from the railway station: the sugar refinery, Pier 8—and with it the fire engine Patricia and its crew—and most other waterfront structures, including a cotton and clothing factory together with its hundred workers, a military gymnasium, and a skating rink.

The fiery cloud, with its incendiary gases, which Barton had observed, had left ruin wherever it dipped earthward, as devastating as the explosion itself.

At least one spontaneous act of unusual heroism had spared the city from even greater obliteration. J. W. Harrison, a marine superintendent, boarded the British ammunition ship Pictou, even as the wharf flamed, and opened her sea valves. He played a hose of water on the decks, then set the vessel adrift.

She settled in a few minutes on the harbor bottom.

The explosion followed even those who had deliberately fled its imminence. At least the chief gunner and wireless operator of the Mont Blanc perished under a fusillade of jagged steel as they raced and plowed their way to the Citadel. Others arrived at the gates of the lofty old fort with clothing torn off and bodies burned.

Schools had been among the principal sufferers. In the Richmond School, two hundred died—pupils beside their teachers. Not one soul survived in that medium-sized building. Also in Richmond, Coleman perished at his telegraph key after flashing the news.

On the outskirts of Halifax, the girls at St. Vincent's Academy knew that something "awful" had happened but were not certain what until a locomotive arrived, "hurrying up from the city rocking from side to side under its terrific speed.

"The engineer, the only man aboard, cried out: 'Give me anything you have! Blankets! Food! Bandages, or anything—the whole city is wrecked; and for the mercy of God be quick!'

"We girls immediately rushed to get anything that we could lay our hands on. Sweaters, coats, and other clothing were torn in strips for bandages. Everything was piled into the locomotive which then tore away at top speed for the scene of the disaster.

"No one at the convent was killed but some of the sisters were terribly cut by flying glass, which in our section of the city did most of the damage."

Barton returned briefly to his room at the Halifax Hotel, then started out for the core of the disaster area, hoping to be of assistance:

"Toward Citadel Hill we wended our way and the farther we went the more horrid the aftermath. The improvised stretchers met us on all sides, converging into the main thoroughfares from the highways and byways.

"The wounded were everywhere; but most of these unfortunates could hobble or walk. We kept on."

Nearly five thousand residents gathered, like bewildered sheep, in the city common. When the encircling flames died down and the unrelieved cold of a December morning returned, they slowly disbanded, to return to their stores or their homes—or what was left of these structures.

The city was snatched from greater punishment by the flooding of the naval ammunition depot, located near the Narrows. A military hospital at Rock Head, in the same area, withstood the onslaught, although every window was shattered and many patients cut by glass.

By early afternoon, it was over. The fires were mostly out, the dead were being counted, the extent of the destruction was the object of stock-taking.

It was evident that at least two thousand had died. Many times that number were injured. An uninterrupted 2½-square-mile area in the heart of the city was leveled, blackened.

Morgues were set up in garages and shops. Any dwelling with beds and clean sheets was commandeered for a hospital. Soon trains arrived from other cities. They bore doctors, nurses, medical supplies, blankets, and clothing.

Night came. Relief workers kept to their task in a dark, cold, and prostrate city. The electric plant had been thrown out for an indefinite period.

Snow began to fall, desultorily at first, thickening by midnight, swelling to a blizzard by dawn.

The ruins were cloaked thickly in white, and scores of the dead were hidden under this grotesque, cold cerement. Of the *Mont Blanc*, however, nothing, not even a broken mast or stanchion, protruded to meet the snow.

Only on Citadel Hill did small, jagged bits of the freighter's superstructure speck the earth like dragon's teeth—in dual testimony to her own last voyage and the city she almost obliterated.

One other ship disappeared in the strange, depleting war, but under circumstances far more perplexing than those attending the destruction of the *Mont Blanc*.

On April 15, 1918, as the fighting thundered seemingly in favor of the Kaiser and his allies, the *New York Herald* headlined: "Big War Supply Ship Vanishes Without Trace."

The story proved to be one of mingled mystery and tragedy. It reported, in its entirety:

The naval collier *Cyclops*, 19,000 tons, with 293 persons aboard, has been overdue at an Atlantic port since March 13th and has virtually been given up as lost by the Navy Department.

The disappearance of the vessel, which last reported at a West Indian port on March 4th, probably will prove to be not only one of the most serious naval disasters suffered by the United States during the present war but remain one of the unsolved mysteries of the sea.

On board the vessel, which was under the command of Lieutenant Commander G. W. Worley, United States Naval Reserve Force, were 15 officers and 231 men of the crew and 57 passengers. Among the latter was Alfred L. Morean Gottschalk, of New York, American Consul General at Rio de Janeiro, who was returning to the United States.

The Navy Department in announcing today the *Cyclops* had been overdue for upward of a month, said that the search for her was being continued. Wireless calls have been sent out from every possible point along the route she was to take, but no answering call has been received. Naval vessels have searched for her without finding a trace.

In its official statement the Navy Department says that extreme anxiety is felt for the safety of the vessel. Naval officers, who are unable to find any adequate explanation for her disappearance, are of the opinion that the collier has been sent to the bottom.

The mystery recalls the "spurlos versenkt" message of Count von Luxburg, formerly German charge d'Affaires in Argentina. It is regarded as possible that the *Cyclops* might have been "sunk without a trace" by a U-boat operating in West Indian waters. No attack, however, has been made on any other vessel in this region, so far as is known in Washington. The presence of a submarine has not been reported from any source.

The weather in the region which the *Cyclops* was to have traveled has not been unusually stormy. The theory that the collier was sunk by an internal explosion is also scouted by naval officers. The explosives carried in her magazines were not sufficient to sink her before wireless calls could be sent out, and it is improbable that sufficiently powerful bombs could not have been placed in her hold by enemy agents to destroy her without a trace.

One of the two engines of the *Cyclops* was damaged and she was running at reduced speed with the other engine compounded, but even if totally disabled the ship could have used storage batteries to send out radio calls for help.

Concerning the disappearance of the vessel the Navy Department today issued the following statement:

"The *U.S. Cyclops*, navy collier of 19,000 tons displacement, loaded with a cargo of manganese, and with a personnel on board of 15 officers and 231 men of the crew, and 57 passengers, is overdue at an Atlantic port since March 13th. She last reported at one of the West Indian islands, on March 4th, and since her departure from that port no trace of her nor any information concerning her has been obtained. Radio calls to the *Cyclops* from all possible points have been made and vessels sent to search for her along her probable route and areas in which she might be with no success.

"No well-founded reason can be given to explain the *Cyclop's* being overdue, as no radio communication with or trace of her has been had since leaving the West Indian port. The weather in the area in which the vessel must have passed has not been bad and could hardly have given the *Cyclops* trouble. While a raider or submarine could be responsible for her loss, there have been no reports that would indicate the presence of either in the locality in which the *Cyclops* was.

"It was known that one of the two engines of the *Cyclops* was injured and that she was proceeding at a reduced speed with one engine compounded. This fact would have no effect on her ability to communicate by radio, for even if her main engines were totally disabled, the ship would still be capable of using her radio plant.

"The search for the *Cyclops* still continues, but the Navy Department feels extremely anxious, as to her safety."

The *Cyclops* was built at the shipyard of William Cramp and Sons, Philadelphia. The keel was laid on June 2, 1909; she was launched May 7, 1910, and was commissioned November 7, 1910. She had a displacement of 19,000 tons. Her length over all was 542 feet, beam 65 feet, mean draft, loaded, 27 feet 8 inches, and cost $923,000.

For many days the naval authorities have clung to the hope that the ship would be found or that information would be picked up indicating how she met her fate, but to no avail. The sea has been swept by the wireless calls and naval vessels have searched carefully for traces of her but the mystery of her disappearance has remained unfathomed.

Naval officers admit that the collier might have been attacked by a submarine or a sea raider but the theory is all but disapproved by the fact that neither a submarine nor a raider has been seen in these waters. In either event the radio apparatus could have been used unless the ship were taken unawares and it had been disabled before calls could have been sent out. The same would have been true had the *Cyclops* struck a mine carried far from its moorings.

The route the *Cyclops* would have taken after leaving the West Indies was one of the ocean lanes of travel where steamships are frequently within sight and seldom more than 50 miles away at any point. It is quite improbable that any call the *Cyclops* might have sent out would not have been picked up by a passing vessel.

The theory of an internal explosion is also discredited. There were small magazines on the *Cyclops*, one forward and the other aft. In neither was there a large quantity of ammunition. Naval officers, some of whom hold that a magazine explosion offers the most reasonable explanation for the disappearance of the vessel, are mostly of the opinion that it would have remained afloat long enough to send out distress signals. It is also doubted that a sufficient quantity of explosives could have been placed in the cargo to sink the vessel at once.

On June 14th, Worley, the captain, and all navy personnel aboard were declared officially dead. Together with passengers, those who had presumably perished on the massive collier totaled 309.

Perhaps the last to communicate with her was the British ship *Vestris*. The captain of the Lamport and Holt liner revealed that radio messages were exchanged the day after the *Cyclops* sailed from Barbados. The latter, reporting "fair weather," did not indicate difficulties.

The disappearance of a major U.S. naval vessel was not without precedent. Since 1781, the Navy had reported seventeen missing. The most baffling up until the spring of 1918 had been that of the large United States sloop *Levant*, a name familiar as the ship to which "A Man Without a Country" had been banished.

Yet its sailing from Hawaii to nowhere in the fall of 1860 proved far stranger than the fiction Edward Everett Hale had penned about the *Levant's* passenger, Philip Nolan, who renounced his country. Its disappearance, with 210 aboard, troubled the Navy Department for so long afterward that in 1904 another vessel was actually sent to scout for an uncharted Pacific Island. There the *Levant's* crew were rumored to be leading a Pitcairn Island sort of existence.

When the search ship, the U.S.S. *Tacoma*, returned empty-

handed, the Navy had to face less romantically-minded taxpayers.

None, however, suggested a hunt for the *Cyclops*. There
seemed no place it could have gone in the West Indies where
its presence would not have become known.

The disappearance had its own further and unfortunate rami-
fications in the home of Mrs. Worley, in California. Her husband had been born in Germany, a fact that the unreasonable
seized upon as possible explanation for the loss of his collier.
The captain, in patriotic fervor to his original homeland, had
"scuttled" his command or sailed it to some forgotten island
for a rendezvous with the Imperial Navy.

So insistent was this minority that Mrs. Worley explained
her husband had sold property in Norfolk prior to his last voyage
with the intent of returning to California for a lengthy leave.
He was very tired, he had recently admitted.

"Do you think," she added, "my husband would prove a
traitor to his wife and little daughter? My husband was an
American through and through. He hated Germany. He came
here seeking freedom and would fight and die to maintain that
freedom. . . . I hope he lives to settle with his traducers."

For several months she clung desperately to the theory that
his vessel had been "disabled at sea" and that he and his crew
simply were "waiting to be picked up."

But the year, the war, and destiny moved on. Mrs. Worley
waited, but the sound of George's footsteps were not to be
heard on his front porch ever again.

After the Armistice, the German High Command searched
its records and swore that no U-boat had accounted for the
Cyclops. In a way, Washington was disappointed. The denial of
a recent enemy tended to eliminate the most logical answer to
a confounding question.

This having been done, theorists began to express themselves. A man who signed himself George Noble wrote to *The
National Marine:*

"About the only possible explanation incapable of contradic-
tion is that gargantuan squids—monster cuttlefish treated of in
fiction and in fact—may have reared themselves out of the sea
and instead of winding their tentacles around the hulls and
rigging and crushing the structure to matchwood before drag-
ging it to their lair at the bottom, may have helped themselves
to the ship's people as delicately and effectually as one plucks
gooseberries off a bush."

There were, however, the nautically-minded who found ex-
planations in this vein less than satisfactory. Lieutenant Commander Mahlon S. Tisdale, who had once served aboard the
Cyclops, wrote for the *U.S. Naval Institute Proceedings* his own
surmises.

During previous duty on a similar collier, the *Neptune,* he
had observed her distressing tendency to suddenly flop over on
one side "for no apparent reason." This "flop" or list could be
as acute as ten degrees, he had found. He attributed this in-
stability to the design of her water tanks, rigged in such a way
that hundreds of tons of water could slosh from one side of the
vessel to the other.

Relatively flat bottoms only accentuated the degree of roll,
as did a second, higher-level series of "topside tanks." Most of
those who had drawn duty upon the *Neptune* or *Cyclops* were
certain the naval architects had been Mephistophilean in their
intent.

In the autumn of 1916, a year and a half before her loss,
Lieutenant Commander Tisdale was ordered to the *Cyclops* as
communications officer, for "war games" off the New England
coast. He reported, four years later, in the *Proceedings:*

On the afternoon of the second day it began to blow. One by one the towlines parted. Captain Worley (Master U.S.N.A.S.) of the *Cyclops*, gave our tow—the *Conyngham*—all the line we had available and by so doing and by the *Conyngham* going ahead slow to ease the strain, we managed to hold our tow until all the other colliers had parted lines; but eventually ours snapped and as the sea was then too rough to attempt picking up another line, the destroyers were forced to come ahead on their own. The *Vestal* alone succeeded in holding her tow, and I believe that she had a towing engine.

The *Cyclops* had only one thousand tons of coal distributed among her various cargo holds and was riding high out of the water. The wind had worked itself into a gale and had beaten up a very rough sea. The destroyers were rolling so that it did not appear physically possible for them all to come through safely. During the afternoon of the third day conditions had grown steadily worse. The captain asked me to remain on the bridge while he went aft for supper. Upon his return—this was the evening of the third day out —I fought my way aft, wrapped myself around the particular stanchion that I had come to regard as mine, hurriedly ate a sandwich or two, filled my pockets with oranges for the long night ahead of me, and started back to the bridge.

On each side of these colliers, inboard against the cargo hatches run the steam lines for the winches and for the auxiliary machinery forward. These pipes are encased with light sheet metal and the cover is corrugated as are fire room floorplates. This forms a runway leading from the break of the forecastle aft to the break of the poop. The men call this the "bicycle track" for no better reason, I suppose, than that one could not ride a bicycle on it.

In going back to the bridge from the wardroom I started along the bicycle track as usual, but as I came abreast the manhole plate for the starboard after topside tank I was thrown off the track onto the main deck. We had lifelines rigged to assist in walking forward and aft, but the lurch of the ship broke my hold. I landed near the topside tank manhole and my attention was at once caught by the fact that the plate was *not* secured. I slid the plate into position as best I could with one hand—I was carrying a sigcode book—and set up the central screw finger-tight, thinking all the time I worked how fortunate it was that I had served on the *Neptune* and had there learned the value of keeping tank tops tight. On starting forward again I was astonished to find that the next plate was also cast off. Upon looking further, all plates were seen to be adrift. Deciding that securing all of them was too much of a job to do with one hand, I fought my way to the bridge and reported to the captain that some-one had opened all the topside tanks. He laughed at my earnestness and said they were *always left off* in accordance with instructions from the navy yard. . . . (I won't mention the yard, as I never saw the circular during my time in the colliers) as the air was "better for the bitumastic." The skipper was worrying not at all about the tanks. We were cavorting around the old ocean like a frisky colt, but, true enough, were taking no green seas over the main deck. As I have said, we were light and high out of the water. The captain was worrying about his cargo. With such a small amount of coal in the cargo holds and with no braces rigged to hold it in place, it was not improbable that the cargo might shift.

Standing at the clinometer that night I saw it register 48 degrees to port and 56 to starboard. So much for proof that these ships can roll when tempted. During this rolling she was dry so far as green seas were concerned, but this was due to her freeboard. I have seen the *Neptune* at full load ship seas on her well deck which carried away the side plating on the bicycle track to such an extent that we had to heave to for repairs.

It was "plausible," reasoned Tisdale, that the tremendous bulk of the *Cyclop's* cargo shifted, "perhaps only a little" but sufficient to increase its list and thereby allow water to slosh over the decks and into open manholes on the deck. The naval officer added:

This could all occur in a few seconds, and the ship would be bottom up before any one could abandon ship. Some few men from the bridge and poop might have been thrown clear of the ship. But with everything secured for sea there would be little wreckage. Remember that there would be nothing adrift except such gear as would be free to float off during the few seconds during the turn. There would be no debris such as always follows a sinking due to other marine casualty, as in the case of striking a mine or torpedo. There would have been no time for an "S.O.S." There would have been no time for anything. The few men in the water could not have lived long of their own accord. Such small gear as did float off would have been lost in the vastness of the ocean long before the rescue vessels started their search.

This seems to me a plausible solution of the loss of the *Cyclops*.

It was, at least, Tisdale's solution. There were other ones, sober as well as fanciful. T. H. Ferril put his thoughts in verse and transmitted them to the *Literary Digest*:

> Perhaps she plies through Arctic wastes,
> On some dim quest with Franklin's men,
> Or sees a new Pacific's blue,
> As those on Darien. . . .

This was one of seven stanzas.

Whatever happened, wherever she might be, the *Cyclops* had gone the way of the *Saratoga*, the *Insurgente*, the *Pickering*, the *Wasp*, and the rest of the ghostly band of seventeen.

The disappearance of the big collier was a continuing source of frustration to the exact-minded Navy, which liked everything properly explained. Such fate had never befallen a wireless-equipped vessel. Her complement could be declared legally dead but, none the less, the collier's own file could never be stamped "closed." It is not, to this day.

As Rear Admiral E. M. Eller, of the Chief of Naval Operations office, puts it by summation:

"On March 1918 the 19,000-ton collier *U.S.S. Cyclops* sailed from a West Indian port bound for Baltimore, Maryland, with a cargo of manganese ore. She was never heard from again. Radio

calls and vessels searching along her probable routes were unsuccessful. No trace of her or her more than three hundred passengers and crew members was ever found. Much has been said
and written through the years concerning the fate of this ship,
but no really satisfactory theory or evidence has as yet been
offered. The disappearance of the *Cyclops* is as baffling a
mystery today as it was in March 1918."

In March, 1921, exactly three years and three weeks after the
Cyclops sailed on her last voyage, the *U.S.S. Conestoga*, a 617-
ton ocean-going tug departed from Mare Island Navy Yard,
California, for Pearl Harbor and Samoa. Under the command
of Lieutenant Ernest L. Jones, she carried a complement of
three other officers and a crew of fifty-two men.

She had done yeoman service in the war, towing barges and
other vessels along the east coast, transporting guns and ammunition to Bermuda and the Azores, and escorting convoys.
With an overall length of 170-feet, she was as sturdy as some
small freighters and had weathered several near-hurricanes in
the Carribean.

There was no reason to suppose the *Conestoga* could not
endure any weather the Pacific could conjure.

Like the *Cyclops*, the *Conestoga* had indeed sailed into
oblivion. Of her disappearance, Eller notes:

"No further word was ever received from the vessel, and in
spite of an exhaustive search for the vessel, covering a period of
several months, in which all available naval and aircraft forces
were utilized, no trace of the vessel or any of the crew was discovered.

"The Department was, therefore, forced to declare the
U.S.S. Conestoga, together with her crew, as lost as of June 30,
1921.

"A lifeboat with the letter 'C' on the bow was located by the
Steamship *Senator* in latitude 18° 15′ N., longitude 115° 42′

W., on 17 May 1921. The letter 'C' was removed from the bow of the lifeboat by the crew of the merchant vessel in question and subsequently sent to the Department, the lifeboat being destroyed by the crew of the *Senator*.

"It is more than likely that this lifeboat belonged to the *Conestoga*, but such could not be definitely proven, as the lifeboat was destroyed. No survivors and no other wreckage was found, although all the islands in the vicinity in which the lifeboat was picked up were thoroughly searched, as well as the ocean thereabouts."

What happened to the *Cyclops* and the *Conestoga*, the last U.S. Navy ships to be lost without some easily deduced reason? Probably not even time will tell.

Off American Shores

THE TENTH ANNIVERSARY OF THE ARMISTICE WOULD BE OBSERVED
this November Sunday, though to most Americans the whole
war was now relegated to history, almost as improbable as the
War for the Union.

Life in America in 1928 was, to say the least, normal. Business
and pleasure were pursued with indomitable fervor. In commerce, trade with South America was soaring, and one of the
larger vessels plying to her sun-warmed ports was the 10,494-ton
Lamport and Holt liner, *Vestris*, which had been the last to
communicate with the missing *Cyclops*.

All week, winches rattled and cranes rasped, as a ponderous
cargo of automobiles, mail, canned goods, shoes, and patent
medicines were lifted aboard her from the Brooklyn pier. She
would call first at Barbados and then at many ports of the
United States' big Latin America neighbor.

A trim vessel with one funnel, the *Vestris* was fitted with
accommodations for several hundred passengers. This sailing
there were 129, including Thomas E. Mack, of Wyoming, a
construction engineer, and his friend Oliver L. Maxey, of Rich-
mond Virginia; Major Yoshio Inouye, military attache of the
Japanese Embassy in Buenos Aires, and Mrs. Inouye; Earl
Devore, automobile racing driver, of Los Angeles, and Mrs.
Devore, with their dog "Speedway Lady"; another racer,
Norman Batten, of Brooklyn, and Mrs. Batten, en route, as was
Devore to meets in South America; William W. Davies, U.S.

220

correspondent for *La Nacion*, in Buenos Aires; Mrs. Margaret Daugherty, a widow from Philadelphia, who had sold her boarding house in order to live with her daughter in Argentina. There were other women, traveling by themselves, and about a dozen children.

The crew outnumbered the passengers. Captain William J. Carey, fifty-nine years old, making his last voyage on the *Vestris* before being assigned to a sister ship, the *Voltaire*, headed a complement of two hundred. They included, as a few examples, Chief Officer Frank W. Johnson: Chief Marconi Operator Michael J. O'Laughlin: Alfred Duncan, a second steward; three Negro firemen, John Morris, Gerald Burton, and Joseph Boxill; and Quartermaster Lionel Licorish, Barbados-born.

When the last hatches were battened down and canvassed, it was past noon, on Saturday, November 10th. The weather was overcast and wind ruffled the Hudson River. The *Vestris* sailed at 3:45 P.M. Some who had come to wave *bon voyage* to friends thought she had a slight list to port. Her trim had been rendered more difficult by the fact she was still in ballast water, in spite of her burden of six thousand tons of cargo, which some considered about two hundred tons too much.

There was no cause for immediate concern, however. The *Vestris* had always been a "lucky ship." She had shown her heels during the Great War to the raider *Karlsruhe*, and carried thousands of doughboys and tens of thousands of tons of beef to France in safety.

By late evening the winds had freshened from the northeast as the *Vestris* steamed south one hundred miles off the coast. At dinner the passengers noticed a shift in the water-level of their glasses and an annoying sliding of plates and tableware. The ship's port list had switched to starboard. She stopped at approximately five degrees to the right of even keel and hung there, while occasionally rolling in response to the increasing seas.

The northeaster gathered velocity during the night. It was strong by 1 A.M., and was of gale force by dawn.

The few persons who appeared at breakfast heard ominous reports from the stewards. Water had mysteriously seeped into the coal bunkers, deep enough to wet the feet of the stokers. One of the "half-doors" on the starboard side, through which passengers or baggage came aboard, had sprung a leak, which the carpenter caulked.

There were no more people at divine services than at breakfast, this Sunday, Armistice Day.

By afternoon, the Vestris was experiencing more serious difficulties. The seas, still out of the northeast, were smashing her port hull and superstructure without letup. She was rolling markedly, and her starboard list had increased a degree or two—enough to register on the inclinometer.

Those on the bridge could not understand why a powerful twin-screw vessel such as the Vestris was having such trouble heading into the seas. Captain Carey gave up trying to hold her on course, as he instructed Chief Officer Johnson to keep her bow into the wind, without headway.

Johnson found he could not do that.

The carpenter, at 2:30 in the afternoon, reported that the half-door was spurting water again, and he would try to reseal the frame. Cold, salty water still sloshed over the feet of the stokers.

Mack, the construction engineer from Wyoming, had traveled considerably, but he did not like the looks or sound of things this grey, wet afternoon. In his estimation, "a hurricane" was roaring by four o'clock.

As a scientific and exact man, he did not believe the Vestris, wallowing as she was, would survive the fury of the storm. He told his friend Maxey so.

Other ships were within a 150-mile radius of the Lamport and Holt steamer. There was the massive Hamburg-America *Berlin*, driving toward New York from Europe, commanded by Captain H. von Thuelin, an old-timer who bore a remarkable resemblance to the Kaiser. The battleship *Wyoming* was hove to east of Hampton Roads, riding out the gale. Aboard was one of the ranking officers of the Navy, Vice Admiral N. M. Taylor, scouting fleet commander. There were also the *Ohio Maru*, the *American Shipper*, the *Creole*, the *Santa Barbara*, and the French tanker *Myriam* among a diverse ocean-going fleet being tossed about in the same segment of Atlantic coastal waters.

On shore, the progress of all the ships was plotted by the Naval Radio Compass Station at Bethany Beach. By listening to the commercial traffic dit-dahing from the vessels and taking cross-bearings, the station could determine relatively exact positions.

By Sunday evening, one Navy operator, Ray Myers, had come to a conclusion: something was wrong with the *Vestris*. Her bearings had changed but imperceptibly since noon. She should have been plowing ahead, unimpeded by the storm, as was the *Berlin*.

There were no requests for assistance from the South America-bound liner, not even a "stand by." Nonetheless, Myers wanted to place his concern on record.

"Guard her carefully," he told his night relief.

Mack, the construction engineer, was to record: "Sunday night the ship started to roll like a bottle and she began to list more and more on the starboard side as each hour passed. The passengers became nervous. All the paraphernalia on the port side was ripped from their fastenings."

Two giant waves, hitting at supper time, had caused the "paraphernalia" to be ripped off, and other more mortal damage. The few people on their feet or at tables were thrown to the deck. However, the Vestris righted back to an eight or ten degree starboard list. The officers came to the saloons to reassure the passengers that everything was all right and suggest they keep to their beds.

The gale abated at midnight. But the list increased, and the water continued to surge into the engine room and—presumably —the holds. Experienced voyagers, such as Mack, theorized that the cargo had shifted after the two staggering punches during supper.

Visibly, three deck crates, containing automobiles, had torn from their lashings and crashed half into the forecastle. The engine room was awash with loose bunker coal and dark, oily water. The fires were out on the starboard bank of boilers.

Shortly before 5 A.M., Monday, the master ordered three ballast tanks pumped put. Instead of bringing the Vestris back to even keel, the operation worsened her list. And yet, helpless and listing precariously, the Vestris wallowed in radio savoir faire. Carey would not call for assistance.

Her sister ship, the Voltaire, steaming for New York from South America, contacted the Vestris routinely at 5:30 A.M. She was nearly five hundred miles southward. The Vestris had "nothing" to communicate in reply.

"At 6 A.M.," wrote Mack, "when the sea became calmer and the gale died down, the starboard side continued to list more heavily. In fact it was dipping into the sea."

Her list now exceeded twenty degrees, which even the most landbound could not fail to recognize as a threat. It was difficult to maintain one's balance in any portion of the ship. Walking up the stairs, passengers found themselves treading more on the walls—or bulkheads, as the crew knew them—than the stairs.

At 8:30 A.M. Ray Myers, the Navy radio operator at Bethany Beach, returned to duty. He was so shocked to ascertain the Vestris was continuing in the same position that he contacted her and asked if she needed any help.

"Not now," tap-tapped the Morse reply.

Myers was not satisfied. He telephoned Cape May Coast Guard station and requested a cutter be sent to the Vestris.

Nearing the Vestris was a small freighter—the Montoso—bound from Porto Rico to Boston. But she was unaware of the Lamport and Holt vessel's difficulties, or, in fact, of any of the morning's wireless traffic. She carried no radio.

Within ten minutes of his denial of a need for assistance, Carey ordered Chief Operator O'Laughlin, twenty-nine years old, to flash a "stand by!" This was not an S.O.S., but a request that other ships guard their radios, in case assistance were needed.

The Coast Guard cutter was already casting off her lines and preparing to steam out from Cape May to the rescue. Yet, as the Coast Guard knew, the Vestris was well south of the Delaware Capes about 240 miles east of Norfolk and the same distance from New York. It was almost a day's run for the cutter, even at full speed and assuming the storm was over.

But the Coast Guard vessel was not the only potential source of aid. The Berlin, for one, was plotting the exact "collision" course which would arrow her to the crippled Vestris—if she received an S.O.S. The navigators on the Ohio Maru, the Myriam, and the American Shipper were doing the same thing. The battleship Wyoming, now that she had ridden out the blow, was pounding through the choppy Atlantic toward the Lamport and Holt liner, "just in case." Admiral Taylor himself had taken the bridge.

The Montoso was scarcely more than forty miles from the Vestris.

No one had eaten breakfast on the *Vestris*, where a cold fear, a telltale dryness of the throat was in possession of all. The passengers were assembled in the smoking lounge, then, as Mack reported, hurried on deck by Captain Carey who "ordered the life belts distributed."

Alfred Duncan, of Liverpool, second steward, was one of an emergency crew far below who had been bailing with buckets. It seemed "ridiculous" to him, but he obeyed anyhow.

He believed that the water was deep enough to have flooded the machinery as well as extinguish all fires. The fact that members of the "black gang" were quitting their duty posts in the vitals of the ship strengthened his impression.

At 10 A.M. Carey told O'Laughlin to send the S.O.S. It was recorded by shore stations at 10:05 A.M.: "*S.S. Vestris*, Lamport and Holt Line. Lat. 37–35 North, Longitude 71–08 West. Require immediate assistance." Her call letters, HWNK, followed.

It came almost a relief to the ships which had been waiting in silence. Von Thuelin, for one, ordered every ounce of steam from the *Berlin's* boilers as he altered course. Tuckerton, N.J., commercial maritime transmitting station, picked up the *Vestris'* call, magnified it with her electronic Sunday punch of tens of thousands of watts, and hurled it back onto the airways.

Ships plying the coastal waters of Europe could now hear the sea's frightening chant: S.O.S., S.O.S., S.O.S! "HWNK" was in dire trouble.

"The crew," recorded Mack, "began to lower lifeboats. It took two hours to lower four lifeboats, Numbers 4, 6, 8, and 10 —and while Number 8 was being lowered she crashed into the side of the ship, staving in the lifeboat.

"The passengers, most of whom were women and children, tumbled into the water. It was a horrible sight—confusion soon overwhelmed the passengers who had not yet got into the life-boats.

"From every side there came the screaming and howling of women and children. One woman in lifeboat Number 8 had two children with her. When the boat tumbled into the water her life preserver was torn from her and all three fell into the sea. They disappeared."

At 10:20 A.M. the *Santa Barbara* advised the *Vestris* she could be at her side within nine hours. She was a fast ship, but she was nearly two hundred miles distant.

Captain Carey now did not believe his command would stay afloat more than a few hours.

"Throughout all the panic," Mack continued, "Captain Carey appeared calm but he also appeared undecided as to what to do. Lifeboats Numbers 4 and 6 were lowered so late that they capsized."

At 10:45 A.M. O'Laughlin transmitted: "Rush at all speed to our aid immediately."

Three Negro firemen, Morris, Burton, and Boxill, calmly removed their shoes and coats and jumped overboard. While flailing the water to keep afloat, they tugged at a lifeboat which was partly in the water, half secured to its falls.

Passengers watched their efforts in mingled pity and fascination.

Along the coast the word had spread with the momentum and giddiness of a fever. At Lakehurst, N.J., the dirigible *Los Angeles* was ordered to "unbutton" from her mooring mast and fly through the winds and scudding clouds to the *Vestris'* assistance.

In New York, Lamport and Holt were among the last to hear of their vessel's predicament. The British owners, once informed in a roundabout fashion, prepared a dispatch asking to be advised "immediately" of their liner's "trouble."

At 10:52 A.M. the *Vestris* advised her office: "Hove to since noon yesterday. Last night developed 32-degree list. Starboard decks under water. Ship lying on beam ends. Impossible to proceed anywhere. Sea moderately rough."

The *Ohio Maru* revealed she was 135 miles from the *Vestris*. By "taking the wraps" off of her engines, she predicted she could be at the liner's side possibly by 5 P.M.

A few minutes later the Brooklyn Navy Yard informed the Lamport and Holt vessel that the destroyer *Davis* was proceeding from Norfolk as fast as she could. O'Laughlin replied: "Oh! Please come at once!"

Mack jumped into the water, unwilling to chance being trapped under the ship or in a poorly-launched boat. The *Vestris* appeared likely to capsize at any moment, since its list was almost forty-five degrees.

The three Negroes disengaged their lifeboat—Number 13— and were assisting women, who were already in the water, into it.

Ship after ship was telling the *Vestris* that she was proceeding to her side. Possibly the *American Shipper* was the nearest, although the *Berlin* was the largest and fastest.

The *Montoso* was now passing no more than twenty-five miles to westward. Without radio, she could not know even if she were but half that distance abeam.

Bos'n Mate Archibald Bannister took a look at Captain Carey, standing on the port side—the high side—of the liner, then dived into the churning water. He struck off in the direction of lifeboat Number 13, into which the Negroes had now assisted three women.

Admiral Taylor, on the *Wyoming*, made a new position check and tally of the rpm's of the battleship's engines. He radioed the *Vestris*:

"Will be there at 2 A.M."

At 11:04 the Vestris sent to the steamer Creole: "Please stand by us. We will have to take to lifeboats any moment now."

At 11:40 O'Laughlin was having a difficult time keeping his balance, sitting more on the bulkhead than his transmitter desk. He flashed: "It's the devil to work with this list—getting lifeboats out now." At 12:30 he added: "We will soon have to abandon ship."

The Vestris was going.

G. Gladianos, a pantryman clutching a small child in his arms, jumped into a lifeboat which was already being lowered. He was the last person to board it. There were a few other crewmen inside, as well as twenty women and babies.

As the boat touched the water a loosened boom crashed squarely across it. The baby was crushed and Gladianos' arm was broken, while most of the other occupants were hurled into the sea.

At 1:07 P.M. O'Laughlin received a message from Taylor. The Wyoming would be there at 9 P.M. He replied: "Can't wait any longer. Going to abandon!"

Earl Devore, the racer, leaped overboard, following his wife and pet dog, "Speedway Lady." His racing acquaintance, Norman Batten, had already gone over the side, as had Major Inouye, the Japanese military attache.

At 1:22 O'Laughlin advised: "Now going to lifeboats."

At 1:25 O'Laughlin transmitted his last message: "We are abandoning ship. We are taking to the lifeboats."

But Michael J. O'Laughlin, the youthful chief wireless operator, had stayed at his post too long.

The three Negro firemen had assisted five women into their lifeboat. Lionel Licorish, the quartermaster from Barbados, was directing the rowing of another lifeboat—Number 14—like some dark-skinned demon, here, there—wherever he saw a struggling form in the water. He did not pause until he had saved twenty-one lives.

Mack was swimming in wide circles, searching for his companion Maxey.

Alfred Duncan, the steward from Liverpool, encountered Captain Carey by the railing.

"All the lifeboats had gone. We were the last to jump," noted Duncan.

" 'Jump!' the master commanded.

" 'You better jump, sir,' I said.

" 'Hell no, you jump!' he barked. 'Get your lifebelt on. Pay no attention to me!'

"I jumped then, and I think he jumped after me. But I never saw him again.

"The ship flopped over on her side and lay there a minute, then slowly disappeared."

The firemen, Morris, Burton, and Boxill, were pulling Earl Devore into their boat. But it was too late. To Mrs. Devore, who happened to be in the lifeboat, it seemed that he still breathed when brought aboard, but then he "died in my arms."

By coincidence, Mrs. Inouye, in the same lifeboat, recognized her husband floating in the water. He, too, died in the lifeboat.

The afternoon passed, then the evening. The survivors were tossed about in open boats as the rescue fleet sought them in the dark, cold night. The air was filled with their wireless conversation.

At 3:15 A.M. the American Shipper believed she had the honor of being the first at the position of the sinking, as she tapped out: "3:15 A.M. Sighted red flares Latitude 37–19 North, Longitude 70–38 West."

At 4 A.M. she added: "One lifeboat."

The French tanker Myriam, in a few minutes was crisscrossing her searchlights with those of the American Shipper. At

4:55 A.M. she called out to any other vessels who might be near: "Come on. More boats to pick up. Am bound for New York myself. Have reached boat Number 5."

Among those aboard was Harry Fay, a boxer from Pittsburgh.

In a few minutes the *Myriam* had taken aboard sixty-three persons, including William Davies, the correspondent. They were all she could efficiently care for.

Now the bass horn of the *Berlin* was announcing her presence, her lights joining others. She fished out one man in his lifeboat, who reported that a woman with a child had drifted past him during the night.

At 6 A.M. the *Wyoming* had put a whaleboat over, as Admiral Taylor radioed Norfolk: "Five lifeboats and a raft accounted for."

But she had only a small number of the living: the three firemen, Mrs. Inouye and Mrs. Devore, three other women, and the dog, "Speedway Lady."

At 6:30 the *American Shipper* spoke again: "One boat, one raft missing."

She had hauled in a record number by breakfast time: thirty-three passengers and ninety crewmen. Among them was Thomas Mack and his friend Oliver Maxey. His rescue had come as a surprise to Mack, the engineer, who admitted: "We had been pals so long we decided to die like pals."

About 9 A.M. the *Berlin* pulled a figure from the water. When revived with brandy and coffee, Karl Schmidt, of Chicago, said he had been swimming and floating for twenty-two hours. The big Hamburg-America liner, with twenty-three survivors aboard, wirelessed at 11:10 A.M.: "Still searching for two lifeboats and makeshift raft said to have a number of women aboard."

But the rescue was over. One by one, the fleet turned away. The dirigible *Los Angeles* was recalled to Lakehurst.

Only minor wreckage—wood and empty life preservers, parts of food crates anything that would float—remained to mark the spot where a 10,494-ton liner had gone down, and 159 lives sacrificed. Not a child had survived.

Lost were the captain, the chief wireless operator, less-known members of the crew, less-known passengers—obscure people like Mrs. Daugherty, the widow from Philadelphia, who had closed her boarding house in order to commence a new life in South America.

The racing meets in South America would be held without the entries from the United States. Both Devore and Batten were dead.

Late Thursday, the *Montoso* docked in Boston—and learned of the tragedy which had taken place on Monday but a few miles away from her.

There remained only the funerals for those whose bodies were recovered, the memorial services for those claimed totally by the sea—and the official inquiries. In America, Navy Captain Jessup branded the loss "sheer stupidity, incompetence." U.S. Commissioner F. J. O'Neill declared: "The crew seems to have been competent if led, but they were not properly led."

It was, the *Literary Digest* observed, "the grimmest tragedy of the sea since the *Lusitania*."

There was agreement, with reference to the *Montoso*, that all ocean-going ships should be required to carry wireless and maintain an around-the-clock watch. As to the *Vestris*, the British Board of Trade, with primary jurisdiction over the disaster, noted that "overloading of the vessel beyond her loadline was one of the main contributory causes of the loss of the vessel and the loss of life."

Six years later, as the magnificent Ward Liner *Morro Castle* swept northward through the same east coast waters, there was no question of overloading or trim. Her 318 passengers, returning from a cruise to Havana, did not represent capacity. Cargo space of the four-year-old 11,520-ton vessel was limited by the pleasure-bent nature of her voyages.

About 2:45 A.M., September 8, 1934, Doris Wacker, of Roselle Park, New Jersey, was headed for bed. To pretty, twenty-three-year-old Doris and to fellow passengers, as well, the last night out had been somber. Amidst the horn-tooting and balloon-popping of the farewell banquet, Captain Robert Willmott had slumped in his chair as he was about to eat a melon.

Dr. De Witt Van Zile, senior ship's surgeon, pronounced the master dead. "Acute indigestion," was the verdict of the medical man, who was aware that the health of the fifty-five-year-old captain had been "indifferent."

Chief Officer William F. Warms, forty-seven, helped "lay out" the body of his long-time associate in the Ward Line, then assumed command of the fast turbo-electric ship. He prepared a wireless message to his office, announcing the death, and it was transmitted to the Ward Line in New York at 9:08 P.M.

He kept the cruise liner on course through rough seas whipped by a twenty-knot northeaster, until, shortly after midnight, lights of New Jersey shore resorts winked intermittently through squally skies.

Scotland Lightship and the New York channel, however, lay but a few more miles ahead. The passengers, if they so desired, could enjoy Saturday breakfast in Manhattan.

Doris Wacker, that early morning, paused at the library-writing room, where she observed a surprising as well as distressing sight—three men throwing buckets of water on a fire.

"There were no flames outside the room," she noted. "The room itself seemed to us all afire on the inside, though I couldn't see much except smoke." One man, a steward, told her he "could handle it," but even as he talked the smoke "got worse." She volunteered to run for assistance.

"He held up his hands," she continued, "and said not to say anything to anybody, that the fire was not bad."

Arthur J. Pender, a night watchman and one of the trio fighting the blaze, wasn't surprised. He had discovered a bit of tar paper aflame in the hold of the *Morro Castle* on a previous voyage. He had attributed this to an arson attempt by Cuban communists or even malcontents on the seething New York waterfront, and in this belief, Chief Officer Warms had concurred. His distrust, however, also extended to one or two of his own crew.

As the fire appeared to be crackling out of hand and as she had not noticed any attempt to close the fire doors around the writing room, Doris hurried toward her cabin to awaken her parents.

Within ten minutes, smoke began to seep through the passageways and into the cabins of the vessel, awakening a few of the travelers. Dr. Charles Cochrane, of Brooklyn, and chief urologist at King's County Hospital, was among the latter. Both the "pungent odor of smoke" and the rapping on his door by a steward impelled him to quit his bed and hastily dress.

When he looked into the passage the air was so heavy with smoke that he slammed the door again and decided to try the porthole, which was at deck level.

At the same time, George W. Rogers, corpulent thirty-seven-year-old chief radio operator, was awakened by his first assistant, George Alagna. Although there had apparently been no alarm or order from the bridge to rouse anyone, Alagna had taken it upon himself to notify his chief of the fire. He did this in spite of the fact the two were not the friendliest.

Rogers put on his earphones and sent Alagna to the bridge to ascertain if Chief Officer Warms wished to flash an S.O.S.

When Alagna did not return and the smoke billowed thicker into the radio room, Rogers told his second assistant, Charles Maki, to wrap a towel about his face and see what had happened to Alagna.

The *Morro Castle* continued to bash into the Atlantic storm at close to her maximum speed of twenty-one knots.

It was a few minutes after 3 A.M., approximately half an hour since the fire had been discovered. The flames had gained disastrous headway, and almost the entire liner, its saloons, cabins, and control rooms were boiling with smoke.

Nearly everyone was awake, although many passengers were trapped in their cabins. Some had, seemingly, heard the ringing of alarm bells. Others, who could recall no bells, had been aroused, as was Dr. Cochrane, by a knock on their doors or by coughing fits.

Dr. Cochrane by now had succeeded in attaining the deck through the porthole and encountered "much rushing about." Nevertheless he noticed "no apparent panic." The stocky, moustached physician, looking for a lifeboat, without warning was pushed headlong into one of them.

William Kitchen, an engineer officer, was asleep in his quarters just aft of the bridge when, as he believed, the ringing of the alarm awakened him.

"My cabin was filled with smoke," he noted, "and I could hear the crackle of flames outside. I was dazed and almost suffocated, but I fought my way down to my boat on A-deck.

"Most of the flames at that time were on B-deck, but they were licking up about us."

Martha Bradbury, a nurse at New York's Presbyterian Hospital, had been in the cabin she shared with Lillian Davidson.

The two girls dressed without becoming panicky, then walked on deck. It was crowded. To Martha, however, no one seemed excited, and that in itself struck her as remarkable.

"I heard one man singing 'Hail, Hail the Gang's All Here!' " she recalled. "Then someone else said; 'Don't sing that at a time like this. Say your prayers instead.'

"Everybody began praying. When we saw we could not get in a boat, Lillian and I decided to jump."

The minutes ticked on. The speed of the *Morro Castle* fanned the flames into a bonfire. Chief Officer Warms, a few speculated, must have been trying to beach the ship.

"Maki failed to return at all," Rogers reported. "At 3:13 A.M. Alagna returned and said to me, 'Come on, chief, get out of here. You'll die like a rat if you remain here.'

"I asked him what orders there were from the bridge. He replied: 'They're running around on the bridge and I can't get any cooperation there.'

"At that moment, I heard a message from the *Andrea Luckenbach* asking the shore station if they had any report of a ship afire at sea. I thought it advisable at that time to send a stand-by call.

"I sent the CQ [stand-by] three times. Around 3:18 I sent the same call again to keep the lanes open.

"The smoke in the radio room had become so thick it was almost impossible to see. The emergency lighting system should have started functioning automatically, but it did not.

"After the lights went out, I took out a large flashlight and by it managed to get the auxiliary transmitter started. I sent Alagna back again for instructions. I then became conscious my feet were burning and I put my hand on the floor and it was too hot for me to touch. Paint began to crack on the bulkhead. There was a shift in the wind and it sent the fire in the aft porthole and ignited a curtain.

"While waiting, the air was silent."

Alagna returned again from his shuttling between radio room and bridge, increasingly dismayed and provoked. He asserted

that he had seen Warms "in a daze, muttering over and over:
'Am I dreaming or is it true?' "

Then, as a postscript, he added: "They're a bunch of madmen
up there on the bridge."

Several ships, in addition to the nearby *Andrea Luckenbach*,
had picked up the stand-by. The *Monarch of Bermuda*, the
President Cleveland, homeward-bound from Manila, the *City
of Savannah*, the Coast Guard cutter *Tampa*, and a destroyer,
the *U.S.S. Chester*, were among others in the vicinity.

Still, there was no order for an S.O.S. On the bridge, Warms
reasoned: "I thought the crew could control the fire."

Now, at about three-twenty o'clock on Saturday morning,
and still within sight of the New Jersey coast, no one proved
able to control the leaping flames.

Martha Bradbury and her friend Lillian Davidson found it
difficult to reach the railing, once they had made the decision to
quit the ship. Passengers of a more indecisive turn of mind
thronged every available foot of deck space which was any distance from the spreading flames.

The two had to shoulder their way through.

"Finally," Martha continued, "we were able to jump. In a
moment I could see Lillian swimming beside me in the water. It
was a tragic thing. We swam as hard as we could but didn't seem
to get anywhere because the water was so cold and we didn't
have anything to hold onto.

"At first there were a lot of people swimming around us. They
had on nothing but their nightclothes."

Others, such as Dr. Cochrane, waited in lifeboats as the crew
struggled to launch them. It seemed to them an eternity.

Some firehoses were in operation. But it was like throwing
thimblefuls of water onto an open hearth. None—save perhaps
Warms—could fathom why the blazing ship was kept driving

into the storm, allowing the wind to fan the conflagration into incandescence.

About 3:20 A.M. Alagna returned to the radio shack from approximately his fifth trip to the bridge and said: "O.K. chief, send out the S.O.S."

Rogers tapped it on the key as fast as he could: "S.O.S.—S.O.S. *Morro Castle* afire twenty miles south of Scotland Light. Fire near wireless room."

When halfway through the message, Rogers watched "the corner of the table burst into flames."

There was an explosion. The air became filled with sulphuric gas from the batteries.

The heat melted the solder connecting his transmitter's wiring. The chief operator twisted two strands back together.

"I continued to send out the S.O.S. I couldn't see anything."

William O'Sullivan, a deck storekeeper, who thought the ship had been struck by lightning, first tried to fight the blaze with hoses. Realizing the futility, he plunged below decks to check whether any passengers were trapped in their cabins. The smoke was already too thick in most of them, and he returned topside.

He helped launch boats from the starboard, even though the ship was moving. On the windward port side the flames were sweeping the liner, making it impossible to launch those life boats.

"Black smoke poured down stairways and there was a rush of running feet," wrote Leroy C. Kelsey, a crewman from East Chatham, New York. "Flames cracked and roared and the black windows were shot with red and yellow gleams—were there people in these? We were trapped on the port side of the dying ship; three girls, too young to die, myself, and several men in the uniform of the steward's department.

"The flames swept down upon us from forward and closed

in from aft. She was no longer a ship. She was a flaming hell from which the consuming fire shot upward in angry, lurid iniquity.

"The world closed in about us, a world in which we had no place. It wasn't real. We could not possibly be there. Out there in the infinity beyond lay a black acuity and above us a boat and one chance at life."

Abraham Cohen, an ex-football star, from Hartford, Connecticut, and Mrs. Cohen slept a little past the time when most of the passengers were up and on deck. They could only throw their bathrobes about them and run from their cabin.

"We went out through the flames," recalled Mrs. Cohen, "and finally made our way to the B-deck. The decks were filled with screaming people. Everyone seemed excited.

"The smoke hung low. The fumes almost suffocated us. People were milling and jammed close together. There didn't seem to be anyone who could keep the people quiet. My husband and I made our way to the crowded railing and decided the best thing to do was to jump. We did—we were plenty scared all right, but there wasn't time to think about it."

Entire families, who had little faith in lifeboats, leapt into the water. Others, unable to leave by customary exits, were crawling through the portholes of their cabins and tumbling directly into the water without life jackets. Few could swim.

Dr. Cochrane's boat finally was lowered. Rowers bent to their oars, and he looked back at the *Morro Castle*, observing her "entire front part" now a "pillar of flame."

It wasn't much better inside. Chief Officer Warms, choked, rushed back to the cabin of the late Captain Willmott, his "pal." He stumbled down the short ladder leading to Willmott's quarters and broke the knuckles of his right hand, although he did not perceive the seriousness of his injury.

"The fire," he reported, "was following me all the time. I couldn't get any farther. I couldn't."

Warms turned back to the bridge.

Unknown to the acting captain, the liner had been stopped. Those on duty in the engine room, including an eighteen-year-old cadet, William Wesley Tripp, Massachusetts Institute of Technology student, had taken it upon themselves to throw the heavy gears into neutral. The engines pulsed, but the headlong speed had at last been bridled.

Once she was in the ocean, the first thought of Mrs. Cohen, a poor swimmer, was to get away from the ship.

"There were others struggling in the water around us. But after we got started and swam awhile we didn't see any more. We saw no lifeboats about us.

"We saw the lights of the shore and struck out. The water was warm. The waves seemed to help us along toward the shore. Best of all we kept side by side. We'd help each other keep afloat now and then, one of us taking it easy for awhile."

Two sisters, Ethel and Gladys Knight, of Shrewsbury, Massachusetts, were less fortunate. They were separated by the seas minutes after they jumped into the ocean. Ethel, twenty, three years older than Gladys, bumped into a young boy. He shrieked that he couldn't swim, and she hung onto him with one arm as she dog-paddled with the other.

Doris Wacker, who had first noticed the fire in the library, had succeeded in arousing her parents and hurrying them onto the deck.

"What about the lifeboats?" she asked her father.

"If we need them, somebody surely will call us," he replied confidently.

The flames suddenly appeared to shoot the full length of the deck even as the Wackers heard "Mr. Smith, the cruise director, trying to calm the passengers." He herded a group of them down to C-deck, momentarily a sanctuary from the flames.

A lifeboat seemed such a "frail thing" to crewman Kelsey.

"The fire lighted the scene with an unearthly glow," he continued, "and living men might have been lost souls waiting for Charon to come from the outer shades.

"The boat descended with a rush and a girl screamed in terror: 'Stop it! Stop it!'

"The lifeboat stopped at the edge of the deck. They clambered in—three young girls and a small handful of men fleeing a death inconceivably horrible. . . .

"Death loses its terror when it stares one straight in the face. . . . The raging flames roared at my back. . . . Only one fall had been released and now the lifeboat was a thing possessed. Men clung like leeches to a plunging, terrified cockleshell shaking to free itself from the flaming horror that had it in tow."

Kelsey grabbed a fire ax and smashed at the rope and chain holding the boat. The sparks flew from the head of the ax, to mingle with the flaming debris. Above the heads of those in the lifeboat, the giant ballroom windows surged outward, in again, finally gave under the molten heat. The plate glass exploded into fragments and showered the boat's occupants.

Nearby, Father Raymond Egan tried to calm the panicky with prayers. The assistant pastor of St. Mary's Church, the Bronx, who offered absolution to those so desiring, was a rallying point for men and women of all faiths.

George Rogers was desperate.

"Hurry, can't hold out much longer!" he transmitted, moments before the generator exploded. "I lay over the table, and thought if this is dying, it doesn't hurt very much.

"Then Alagna shook me. He told me the mate gave him orders to get me out of the radio room. He pulled me out the door and I saw only sheets of flame. I managed somehow to get to the bridge."

Leaning over the side, he was appalled at the sight of the people in the water. As he watched, he saw a woman, "naked,"

squeeze through a porthole, fall into the black, surging waters
—and vanish.

It was about 4 A.M. and Captain Henry Hill of the *Andrea
Luckenbach* had picked up the yellow glow mushrooming out
of the gloom. He could see the flaming silhouette of the *Morro
Castle* when about seven miles distant.

By now, the last of the eight boats to row clear of the burning
liner was gone. The occupants of Kelsey's boat, cut and bleeding
from the cascading glass splinters, rowed. The *Morro Castle*
"sailed on, crowned with flame, profaning God's sea and sky.
Women and children huddled on her after deck, awaiting destruction. A cry—'good-by!'—and then we were out of hearing."

Dr. Gouverneur Morris Phelps, prominent New York physician, Mrs. Phelps, and their twenty-five-year-old son, Morris,
Jr., a Harvard graduate, had jumped from the stern. The
younger Phelps slid down a rope into the sea.

Mrs. Cohen, beside her husband, kept watching the shore
lights as she struck out against the tumbling seas. The Wackers,
more fortunate, were in a boat.

About 4:30 A.M. the *Andrea Luckenbach* arrived within a
mile of the blazing hulk and lowered her boats. Her oarsmen at
once plucked eleven persons out of the water.

The *President Cleveland* and *Monarch of Bermuda* were
rapidly nearing the scene. Their officers could already discern
the fiery aurora on the horizon.

Rescue was in the air. Even three tiny New York City police
boats were butting toward the Lower Bay.

As dawn brightened through the overcast, Martha Bradbury
heard Lillian say: "I can't keep up very much longer."

The sea she found "very rough" and Martha many times was
tempted to give up, thinking in despair: "What's the use?" She
never considered herself much of a swimmer, but, since "there

was nothing else to be done," she kept stroking toward New Jersey.

"While there is life there is hope," she reminded herself. "So I said a prayer and kept on."

People thrashed in the choppy Atlantic. Some had already been carried so far away from the *Morro Castle* that the rescue fleet could not locate them. The Phelps family still stroked for shore, as did the Cohens and Ethel Knight. She held onto the boy—Benito Rueda, seven, of Brooklyn—as though her own life depended on saving him. Gladys, her sister, had somehow joined her again in the darkness.

Only fifteen living persons now remained on board the cruise liner. Among them were Warms and Rogers. Their continuing presence had been inspired by various motives, including a desperate hope of beaching the wreck, though burning, and a seaman's instinctive inclination to stick by his ship.

By 6 A.M., however, the group had been forced into the bow of the ship, next to the windlass machinery—the only spot which was not enveloped by fire and smoke. There they dropped an anchor and the *Morro Castle* at last hove to, with no headway.

Captain Robert E. Carey of the *President Cleveland* now surveyed the spectacle.

"Everything was on fire from the bridge clean aft," he reported. "The interior was entirely burned when we got there. All that was standing was the steel frames of the deck housing.

"We launched two lifeboats and both scouted for an hour and a half. Neither found a survivor or body."

The *City of Savannah* picked up a lone swimmer, Margaret Cotter, twenty-three, of Springfield, Massachusetts. She had been in the water for five hours. A Coast Guard surfboat from Avon, New Jersey, in the course of hunting in the troughs of the waves, saved nearly seventy persons. The Coast Guardsmen transferred them to the *Luckenbach* and went on the prowl for more survivors. The New York City police boats, however, were compelled to turn back.

Bishop Hiram Richard Hulse, sixty-six-year-old Episcopal Church prelate, and Mrs. Hulse were plucked from the water by crewmen of the *Monarch of Bermuda.*

Gasping, the Bishop admitted: "I don't know what we'd have done if you hadn't come along!"

Father Egan was rescued by the same ship. He brushed aside the plaudits of those who had seen him on deck in the last minutes, insisting he did "nothing more than any priest would do under the circumstances."

As for the *Morro Castle's* crew, he declared: "They were all heroes!"

About 9 A.M. Martha Bradbury was spotted by a plane and then picked up by the fishing boat *Paramount.* She had been in the water almost eight hours and was bruised and becoming ill with pneumonia. Contrary to her fears, Lillian Davidson, who had slipped away from her shortly after six o'clock, was also rescued.

At Sea Girt, the Cohens, of Hartford, floundered ashore. People on the beach waded out to help them in the final moments of their winning fight for survival.

In a hospital bed, Mrs. Cohen soon lit a cigarette and admitted she felt "pretty good." Her husband thought they would take a train home that night.

"After all," he said, "my vacation is over."

Saturday morning was well along, and a new era in sea rescues was born—aerial search. Small aircraft were converging over the stormy northern New Jersey coastal waters from all nearby cities. While most of the planes carried photographers—newspaper and newsreel—there were also National Guard and Army aircraft in the growing squadron, whose only mission was to hunt for survivors.

Governor A. Harry Moore, of New Jersey, happened to be flying in the Guard plane which spotted Dr. Phelps, his wife, and son, and dropped a smoke bomb to attract the surface fleet, also swarming to the scene.

The Knight sisters, from Shrewsbury, were rescued by small boats when nearly ashore. Separated from Ethel by the waves for the past few hours, Gladys, who was seventeen, was holding the Rueda child when she was taken aboard.

All in all, it looked like a newsman's bonanza. New York and Philadelphia papers were setting up offices in Asbury Park. The resort town was a likely headquarters, since most survivors were being carried into the Fitkin Memorial Hospital.

Radio broadcasters, arriving with their own cumbersome apparatus, could see far offshore the smoking liner. By noon, the newscasters had already filled the air with tens of thousands of words, to give America its first play-by-play account of a major sea disaster.

Since it was Saturday and many residents of New Jersey and nearby New York had the day off, there was a mass impulse to flock down to the ocean and look at the burning ship. By early afternoon the highways to Asbury Park and other shore communities were bumper-to-bumper with cars carrying the morbidly curious.

The seaside resorts themselves were taking the boards off refreshment booths and amusement centers which had been closed after Labor Day, now that the summer season was encored by an unanticipated bonus. Balloonmen and postcard sellers reappeared on the Asbury boardwalk.

The liners and freighters by this hour had saved all survivors in the vicinity of the burning *Morro Castle* and continued on their voyages. The Coast Guard cutter *Tampa*, however, was

standing by to secure a line on the vessel. First the anchor had to
be hacked off, since there was no power for hoisting it. Chief
Officer Warms, Rogers, and the small group with them labored
until one o'clock in the afternoon with hacksaws, to cut through
three-inch iron links of the chain.

Lieutenant Commander Earl G. Rose, commanding the
Tampa, labeled their efforts "heroic," especially since the sea
was mounting again, with a fresh storm sweeping in from the
south.

Rose, a few minutes after 1 p.m., when the cable finally
parted, exercised his prerogatives as senior Coast Guard officer
and ordered Warms and the others off the Morro Castle.

"Warms," he reported, "wanted to remain, but the storm was
increasing and I felt the men must come off. They got on the lee
side of the boat, forward, and came down ropes.

"The ship was still burning fiercely. They were exhausted,
and had been without food or water since the fire started."

Slowly, tied to a twelve-inch hemp hawser leading from the
cutter, the Morro Castle was under way once more, making
"slow progress," in the estimation of Rose. The vessels passed
within two miles of Sea Girt and set course for New York, after
being joined by the Sandy Hook pilot boat. With difficulty,
because flames were still licking aft, the smaller craft secured a
stern line, thus affording "drag rudder" control for the derelict.

Warms was clad in a blue uniform coat, turtle neck sweater,
old white trousers, and rubber boots, at once rain-drenched and
fire-scorched in a paradox of affliction. His right arm was bandaged, his feet were blistered, as he sat in Rose's cabin, semi-de-
lirious. Rogers was in not much sounder shape.

"We proceeded up the coast as far as Asbury Park," the Coast
Guard commander continued, "when the pilot boat line parted
—burned through. For a couple more hours we fought on up the
coast, trying to get the Morro Castle to calm water in New York

harbor and let the fire boats have a try at her. The storm and the weather became worse.

"We finally reached a point where we had the *Morro Castle's* bow pointed to sea, attempting to offset the inshore gale. We threw over sounding leads then, and found both ships were drifting toward the beach."

Rose, who had just assumed command of the *Tampa*, realized that he would either have to tow the almost molten wreck to sea or cut her loose to drift ashore. For the newsreel camermen, circling above, dipping under the low scudding clouds, it was a "once in a lifetime" action story. The stricken liner was plunging through her death agonies, like a nautical phoenix—and it would all be recorded for history.

The dead and the living were coming ashore during this Saturday afternoon, as Rose, though he knew not exactly why, fought to save a ship which was already lost. Dr. Cochrane's lifeboat landed at Spring Lake. Crewman Kelsey's boat grounded on a beach nearby.

Doris Wacker, the first passenger to spot the fire, and her parents were landed at Sea Girt, not too far from their home in Roselle Park. William Kitchen, engineering officer, arrived at Asbury Park in a lifeboat containing but thirteen others. Its capacity was rated at seventy. Another carried three people when it was lowered.

By supper time only eight lifeboats, with a total occupancy of eighty-five persons, had been accounted for. Other survivors had been pulled directly out of the sea, even as the morgues at Asbury Park and at Bellevue Hospital, Manhattan, where receiving the bodies of those who had perished.

As the evening wore on and light faded from the stormy skies, the *Morro Castle* and its shepherding *Tampa* both were wallowing closer to the beach.

"We stood it out an hour or two longer," said Rose, still unwilling to yield his burden. "We increased the revolutions of our engines and the towing hawser broke under the strain, the end snapping back and fouling our propeller.

"We were helpless, then, and dropped our anchor to keep from drifting down on the *Morro Castle* or going on the beach. Luckily, we held.

"Just a few minutes later, through the driving spray, we watched the *Morro Castle*, now a lumbering derelict, blot out her length of the lights at Asbury Park and come to rest on the beach. She was ashore."

It was nineteen hours since the fire was noticed smoldering in the library of a ship that had been beautiful and at once the "last word" in safety equipment. This late Saturday night she was hard aground off Convention Pier, burning without abatement.

People swarmed through the streets and sidewalks of Asbury Park and onto the pier, ignoring the rain. They darkened the sands with their very numbers as they came to gape and exclaim. They munched popcorn from boardwalk stands freshly reopened, and drank soft drinks.

In the background, the calliopes were cranked again, just as they had been in July and August, blaring a repetitive theme, "In The Good Old Summer Time, In The Good Old Summer Time. . . ."

In the foreground, there was another sound, equally intrusive —the sizzling of waves slapping against the liner's blistering plates.

The final death toll was established at 134 persons.

But what had caused the disaster? Oily rags or combustible cleaning fluids left in the writing room (by mistake or by design)? Overheating of the funnels where they passed within proximity of such materials as wood paneling? Lightning? An incendiary bomb?

Dickerson N. Hoover, assistant director of the Steamship Inspection Service, Department of Commerce, who conducted the *Morro Castle* inquiry, suggested spontaneous combustion as a possible cause. He cited, as contributing factors, "delays" in sounding an alarm, in awakening the passengers, and in transmitting an SOS. He added that "lack of training and discipline" in the crew were further elements which increased the "loss of life."

Hoover's principal conclusion was: "The human equation failed."

A federal court accused Chief Officer Warms, as well as his chief engineer, Eben S. Abbott, of "misconduct, negligence, and inattention to duties." The two were meted prison terms, but neither man commenced serving his sentence. An appellate court, reversing the harsh verdict, observed that Warms had "maintained the best traditions of the sea."

His master's license returned, Warms commented: "While patience is bitter it bears sweet fruit." He returned to sea as second officer of the freighter *Cauto*. But his nemesis continued to trail his wake: The *Cauto* grounded in the Gulf of Mexico and was a total loss.

The *Morro Castle*, meanwhile, guarded its secret with the impenetrability of a bank vault. In March, 1935, the blackened hulk was towed to Baltimore to be scrapped. Asbury Park city fathers, who had at first seriously considered it as a permanent tourist attraction, bade it good riddance, though the cruise liner which had been coffin to so many was to claim yet another victim. Harry Cole, forty-nine-year-old assistant wrecking master, was killed in a fall from B-deck to D-deck.

The *Morro Castle* persisted as a loathsome memory, and almost a curse. Ethel Knight, who with her sister, Gladys, had saved the seven-year-old Brooklyn boy, was seemingly about to erase a frightening past. She was wed to William Celatka, of Northampton.

Within four weeks, his bride was dead of a heart attack. The Massachusetts Humane Society, which too late had awarded her a silver medal, affixed the symbol of heroism to her tomb.

George W. Rogers, who received a medal from the mayor of Bayonne, shortly turned into something less than a hero. Leaving the sea and joining the police, he was convicted of planting a bomb "with intent to injure" the superior police officer, Vincent Doyle, whose job he allegedly sought. Rogers consistently maintained his innocence.

Released from prison, he was convicted of a yet more serious crime in 1954—the murder of an eighty-three-year-old retired printer and his fifty-eight-year-old daughter, whom he bludgeoned to death the day the old man drew twenty-four hundred dollars from the bank. He was convicted of "murder in the first degree" and sentenced to life imprisonment.

Rogers died four years later in the New Jersey State Prison of coronary occlusion. Leaning heavily on the dubiously admissible crutches of a criminal record in his youth and psychiatric theory, subsequent reconstruction has accused Rogers of setting the Morro Castle ablaze. The chief radio operator, being deceased, cannot be legally libelled. According to a Coast Guard spokesman, however, a person, on the basis of evidence—or lack of evidence—could just as well level an arson charge at any other one of the more than 500 passengers and crew aboard on that disastrous night.

Warms, a reserve lieutenant commander in the navy, was called to active duty in the war. The navy, however, proved less merciful than the U.S. Circuit Court of Appeals, as it banished him to a mosquito-ridden base of small boats in the sand flats of

Texas. There, at Corpus Christi, younger officers perpetuated the cruel joke that it was Warms' St. Helena.

(In 1942, this writer happened across him: a stooped, sad-eyed, hook-nosed man who seemed ever anticipating the inevitable question: "Are you the Warms of the *Morro Castle?*")

He retired from the sea in 1948 and went home to Pine Bush, New York, where he lived but five years longer. His daughter-in-law, Mrs. William Warms, Jr., is still conscious of what she considers injustice done the captain's memory. She and her mother-in-law feel that all retellings of the *Morro Castle* disaster "have had various endings concerning Dad's fate, all basically untrue."

Until now, she notes, no writer has ever troubled "to contact or consider the captain's family."

Others who lived through fire at sea that long-ago September morning have since found a peace that once must have seemed unattainable. William Wesley Tripp, eighteen-year-old M. I. T. engineering cadet, who helped stop the engines, has been dead "for several years," according to records in Cambridge.

Martha Bradbury, now Mrs. Donald Valentine of Ridgewood, New Jersey, is the mother of a fifteen-year-old boy. "I am not afraid of sea voyages but I am very fearful of fire," she says.

On the other hand, there are those, such as Dr. Cochrane, who continue life where they resumed it after they came ashore. He still pursues a busy practice in Brooklyn, while declining to reminisce.

"It's a dead issue," he commented.

A quarter of a century is a considerable span. Yet someday, someone on his deathbed may yet pronounce the final, revealing post-mortem on a "dead issue" which once horrified and captivated the nation in one paradox of emotion.

Lost At Sea

More than 850 Americans, most of them servicemen of the Army, Navy and Marine Corps, were lost early this month when enemy submarines sank 2 medium sized combination passenger-cargo vessels in the North Atlantic.

Both attacks occurred at night and both ships sank within 30 minutes. Loss of life was heavy.

More than 600 from the total complement of over 900 on the first vessel and more than half of the approximately 500 persons aboard the second ship are either known dead or missing.

Next of kin of the casualties have been notified.

U.S. Navy Communique, February, 1943

THE AGING DORCHESTER HAD NEVER BEEN DESIGNED FOR LARGE passenger lists or the rigors of the North Atlantic. The outbreak of World War II found her plodding the coastal waters of the eastern United States for the Merchants and Miners Line. She grossed 5,649 tons, could not exceed twelve knots, even under full steam, and her overall length of only 368 feet foreshortened her appearance.

When she sailed from New York on January 22, 1943, she carried 904 persons—troops and crew members—which was about three times the number of her original comfortable or safe capacity. Her destination was much the same as in the previous year: Newfoundland and Greenland—bleak regions in the summer, but cold, lonely and almost unbearable in the winter.

The Dorchester's convoy (SG-19), as customary on this

sparsely-traveled war route, was small: two other merchant ships beside herself, three Coast Guard cutters, as escort. The latter were slow, imperfectly armed, but about the best that could be supplied.

The North Atlantic was unusually stormy. Snow and gales lashed the sea into green fury and made the deck watches a freezing penance. For men enroute to the sub-Arctic wilderness, this was a source of further depression.

On the other hand, the Army was impartial in its selection for duty at the world's outposts. Four chaplains were also aboard. One, the Reverend George L. Fox, of Cambridge, Vermont, was an old hand at war. A medical corps assistant with the Marines in the First World War, he had won a Silver Star for rescuing a wounded soldier during a gas attack, though he himself wore no mask. Later, the *Croix de Guerre* was added, for bravery during an artillery barrage.

Short of stature, Fox, a Methodist, was known as "the little minister" in his Vermont parish. His physical condition was imperfect, since his last act of heroism in the preceding war had resulted in a spine injury.

Reverend Fox was accepted as an Army chaplain after he had pleaded: "I've got to go. I know from experience what our boys are about to face. They need me."

The last night in New York, "the little minister" wrote his daughter: "I want you to know how proud I am that your marks in school are so high—but always remember that kindness and charity are much more important."

Rabbi Alexander D. Goode, father of four children, was a native of Washington, where he had been an above-average athlete at Eastern High School. Too young to participate in World War I, he nonetheless was old enough to be present at the burial of the Unknown Soldier in Arlington National Cemetery. Later, after becoming a rabbi and obtaining a synagogue, he made clerical history by studying for and receiving a medical degree.

Before sailing for northern waters, Rabbi Goode wired his wife in Washington with reference to his unusual companionship with the fighting forces: "Having a wonderful experience."

John P. Washington's life had always been linked with the Roman Catholic Church. As a small boy, he sang in the choir. As a teen-ager, he turned to juvenile leadership, becoming director of the South Twelfth Street Boys, in Newark. He had been ordained a priest but a few years when the war came along and "Johnny" Washington, as his parishioners continued to know him, switched to a chaplain's uniform.

Clark V. Poling, younger than either Washington, Goode, or Fox, was the seventh in an unbroken succession of ministers of the gospel. His father, Dr. Daniel A. Poling, had been a chaplain in World War I and was presently editor of the *Christian Herald*.

Ordained in a Dutch Reformed Church, he won a pulpit and a bride, Betty, in Schenectady, N.Y. When he said good-by at the sooty old Schenectady railroad station, sailing orders in his pocket, the family had been augmented by a little boy, Corky— and a second child was due at Easter time.

. . . SG-19 was encountering severe icing. Even at the convoy's maximum speed of eleven and a half knots, the cutters could not keep up. At one time, they hove to and melted deck and superstructure ice by the use of steam hoses. Depth charges were frozen to their racks. The gun breeches were sealed as though welded. Underwater sound-detection equipment was ineffective because of the constant crash of waves against the battered little ships.

Except for the weather's reduced visibility, there was little protection against prowling U-boats.

The convoy, however, reached St. John's, Newfoundland, debarked some troops, unloaded cargo consignments, then put out in the wintry Atlantic once more, bound for Greenland. The ice, during port time, had been cleared away. Within hours of sailing it was back again on all of the ships—escort, *Dorchester*, and the other merchant vessels of SG-19.

On February 2nd, a Tuesday, the mother-hen of Allied shipping in the North Atlantic (the U.S. Navy Commander-in-Chief) sent a routine coded radio warning that a U-boat was patrolling waters between Newfoundland and southern Greenland—directly astride the route of SG-19.

The *Dorchester's* captain, who believed in keeping his passengers advised of conditions, propitious or ill, had the message read over the public address system.

The fastest of cutters, the *Tampa*, which once had towed the *Morro Castle*, pushed her throttles to maximum speed and pounded off on a lengthy search around the convoy. At fourteen and a half knots—barely exceeding the underwater speed of a submarine—the Coast Guard escort soon was lost in whitecaps and spray. This left the small convoy with two almost obsolete cutters, too slow to sweep the horizon for visual or sound contacts, barely able, in fact, even to keep up with a plodding, weary coaster like the *Dorchester*.

The four remaining vessels of the convoy, herded together, pitched their way on toward Greenland. But spirits were somewhat buoyed by the fact that journey's end was approaching. Cape Farewell, at the southern tip of the barren, mountainous continent, was less than 250 miles to the northeast.

In the afternoon, the gales moderated, leaving heavy swells rolling southward across green, ominous waters. Visibility improved—a fact which was as disturbing to the escort ships as it was heartening to the troops. The convoy adopted "evasive" action, though not formally zigzagging.

At dusk, there was a wink of recognition lights on the horizon

as the *Tampa* steamed back from her sweep. The results—
"negative!"

As night cloaked the North Atlantic, SG-19's speed throbbed
at a steady ten knots. At midnight, the convoy commodore
aboard the *Tampa* remained unconvinced that the submarine
had actually forsaken the waters off southern Greenland. He
ordered course altered thirty-six degrees southward.

The five vessels were now within two hundred miles of Cape
Farewell. On the other hand, the course change had unwittingly
aimed the convoy head-on for an enemy submarine assigned
to this sector of the Atlantic.

U-456 was "on station," somewhere between Cape Farewell
and a compass dot 150 miles westward in the open ocean. She
would remain until nearly out of fuel and torpedoes. Then she
would be relieved by another *Unterseeboot*.

At 3:30 A.M. all troops and those of the crew off watch were
sleeping. The improved weather provided a chance to catch up
on rest, just as evening chow had been well attended for the
first time in several days. At this dark hour, however, U-456
slipped past the *Tampa's* radar and past the imperfect, anti-
quated sound gear of the older, smaller escorts. The three vessels
had fanned out as dawn approached, hoping thereby to extend
their zone of watchfulness.

A few minutes before 4 A.M. the U-boat slammed one torpedo
into the *Dorchester's* starboard side.

The coastal steamer, never stressed for major damage and,
with four decks, slightly top-heavy, filled rapidly at the bow.
The alarm bells jangled throughout the mortally-hurt transport,
and the captain ordered "Abandon!"

Unhappily, other factors beside the weather had conspired
this cold night against the more than nine hundred souls aboard
the *Dorchester*. The torpedo blast had destroyed the electrical
system, making it impossible to transmit an S.O.S. Why the

radioman had not switched in emergency power, no one knew.

Perhaps because of the panic occasioned by sleepy men tumbling out on deck against the careening list, no one remembered to shoot up rockets. The escort thus was unaware that anything had happened, and the three cutters plowed on toward Cape Farewell, now 150 miles distant.

The War Department communique (issued twenty-two months later) reviewed what happened as it revolved around the lives of the four chaplains:

With complete disregard of their own safety, the chaplains made their way on deck and went among the confused, fear-stricken men, encouraging them, praying with them and assisting them into lifeboats and life jackets.

According to affidavits of *Dorchester* survivors, fear of the icy water had made many aboard almost helpless, convinced as they were that such a plunge could bring only death. The chaplains calmed their fears, and are given credit for saving many men by persuading them to go overboard where there was a chance of rescue.

Throughout the whole episode, the chaplains set a supreme example of courage and calmness.

Many of the survivors reported seeing the chaplains standing together on the *Dorchester's* forward deck, handing out life belts from a box. When the box was empty, each chaplain removed his own priceless life jacket and gave it to another man. They must have known, it was pointed out, that in doing so they were sacrificing their own lives.

The ship was sinking by the bow when men in the water and in lifeboats saw the chaplains link arms and raise their voices in prayer. They were still on the deck together, praying, when the stricken ship made her final plunge.

"The extraordinary heroism and devotion of these men of God," Chaplain (Brigadier General) William R. Arnold, Chief of Chaplains, said, "has been an unwavering beacon for the thousands of

Chaplains of the armed forces. Their example has inspired and strengthened men everywhere. The manner of their dying was one of the most noble deeds of the war."

The management of the war—and Convoy SG-19—at that juncture, however, could be considered something less than noble. Too late, it was realized that the *Dorchester* was not present. The *Tampa* continued on to Greenland with the other two merchant ships, while her sister escorts turned back to search.

It was a sobering scene that met the cutter's crew. Robert Weikart, twenty-year-old Cleveland signalman, counted "hundreds" of victims floating in the water, wrapped in their life belts.

Some, he observed, were in lifeboats, or in life rafts, frozen to death. A few, rigid as statues of ice, still clutched their oars.

Weikart thought a partially surfaced submarine moved off at the cutter's approach.

Those from the *Dorchester* who lived were so numbed that they could not grasp cargo nets. Volunteers from the escort craft plunged into the paralyzing waters to haul the men on board.

Less than three hundred of the 904 who had sailed survived.

Two years later, as the war, on land and at sea, thundered on, damp snow was falling on London. It lay lightly upon the streets and sidewalks in witness to the vehicles and footsteps which had passed. It cloaked the bomb ruins in white, incongruous grandeur.

Just off Grosvenor Square a four-story brick building, spared by bombings and rocketings, was used by the Navy as a dispensary. Next door stretched a jagged cavity where once had been another dwelling.

Diagonally across the street was one of numerous U.S.-British sponsored recreational halls. It was late, this winter night of

1945, late for wartime: almost 10 P.M. Soon the soldiers and the sailors would be filing out and on their way home.

Now the tinny music blared its vespers. It was the "Hokey Pokey," a formless, jungle-like dance which had swept the beleagured Island Kingdom. Through an opened window the strains undulated: "Oh, you stick your left leg out, you shake it all about . . . the hokey pokey, the hokey pokey, the hokey pokey. . . ."

The heavy oak door of the dispensary, which opened and closed again, shut out the music and the city hum of London. A warrant officer stood respectfully in the vestibule, which reeked its ageless whisperings of carbolic, and the pain and, sometimes, the relief from pain it symbolized.

"You've come to identify the Gunners Mate 3rd?" he asked, impersonally, but politely. He glanced at the clipboard he carried and then added, "Taylor, Graydon E., 203–63–89?"

The numbers swam. The room blurred. The disinfectant welled into a miasma. And the recent memory of the "Hokey Pokey" returned as a background discord to the jumble and the incredibility of night.

"Yes, Taylor, Graydon, E., 203–63–89."

. . . It was only last night that the men, and the boys to whom a war had assigned numbers were aboard a freighter moving along the English Channel toward the North Sea. They were the guncrewmen of the Liberty ship, *James Harrod*, loaded with ten thousand tons of gasoline in GI tins, consigned to Belgium and to the hard-pressed Allied defenders in the Ardennes.

The Atlantic crossing had been calm, considering the season of the year. One enemy submarine, with the new schnorkel, had been depth-charged astern of the convoy and its crew removed as prisoners.

Until this morning, the *James Harrod* had been at anchor in the Solent, just off the Isle of Wight, awaiting orders. First the *James Harrod* would go to Le Havre, then the destination was altered to Antwerp. The week in the Solent's sanctuary and the visits ashore to pastoral Wight were over.

With two other small coastal ships, and escorted by a gunboat, the Liberty ship crept along the Channel toward Dover. There were submarine alerts in the afternoon, depth-chargings and readiness at gun stations. But nothing happened.

By evening, mild and windless, attention turned from the sea to the skies. Planes, mostly without identification lights, swooped over the darkened convoy. Friend or foe? The young gunners itched to unleash the rapid-firing 20-mm. guns.

But no telltale white flares were dropped, which would have indicated an enemy plane about to start his bomb run.

Midnight arrived. Searchlights from Dover, which was hauling abeam, crisscrossed the black waters. To starboard, across the narrow twenty-mile neck of water was Calais.

Around the corner from Dover was "the Downs," an anchorage at the mouth of the Thames, where the *James Harrod* would join another convoy and continue across the North Sea to the Scheldt River, an area still bombed by aircraft, as well as V-1's and V-2's. A certain apprehension, thereby, became manifest among the crewmen, merchant marine as well as navy.

Yet, a new day, January 16th, was just commencing, and the morning orders had to be reviewed. Taylor, a gunner's mate, would have the petty officer's crew watch, Graydon E. Taylor, of Everett, Massachusetts—203–63–89.

Taylor, slight, blond, had had only a few days' time in which to make the sailing from Philadelphia. He was returning from leave, which he had consumed in wintry Vermont, honeymooning. At night he would write lengthy letters to his bride and talk of the future—of home and his aspirations to be an air conditioning engineer.

Other numbers resolved themselves from out of the dark to check on the night's duty. Walter T. Porter—802–42–51—a seaman, had the watch at the forward, port side bridge 20-mm. Porter, not quite twenty, came from South Natick, Massachusetts. He had his own focus of interest: motorcycles. His friends in the Boston suburb said Walt could do everything except make a 'cycle talk and they wouldn't be surprised if one day he'd do that, too.

Paul R. Thompson—969–48–31—had already gone to his early morning post at the stern 3-inch 50 gun. Thompson, from Greensboro, North Carolina, was slow-talking, deliberate. He had come aboard, recuperating from a hernia operation of a month ago. The doctors thought he was sufficiently recovered, but Thompson tired easily and could not lift the heavy shells without assistance.

Another southerner, whom, along with Thompson, they called "Rebel," was James F. Ricketts—644–93–56—of Homer, Louisiana. Big, raw-boned Jim Ricketts was the last of Mary Lou Ricketts' three sons. She had already lost two in the war. Her husband had died the previous year. Ricketts, in fact, was a member of the *James Harrod's* armed guard only by accident. He was replacement for a seaman who had deserted in Philadelphia.

As the Liberty ship transited the Dover Straits, Ricketts slept, in preparation for the 4 A.M. watch.

Few, however, were in their bunks. The Army cargo security officer, who normally slept like one under anesthesia, arrived on the bridge, fully uniformed even to sidearm and briefcase.

"I just woke up," he drawled, "and said to myself, 'Dautry, you've got to get out of this cabin and on deck.' "

The captain and third mate, who were also on the bridge, chuckled at his apprehension.

By 1 A.M. the *James Harrod* was entering the Southern Anchorage of the Downs. A slight mist had wisped in from the reaches of the North Sea, reducing visibility to about three miles. A strong southwesterly current was setting the low-lying freighter. She moved froglike, sideways as well as ahead.

Ahead, off the starboard bow, the anchor light of another ship blinked closer, closer.

Warnings came from those on the bridge to the mate to swing off, to reverse engines, since the heavily-laden *James Harrod* was obviously drifting into the bow of the ship at anchor, the silhouette of which indicated she was a sister Liberty.

It was too late—collision. The bow of the other vessel scraped half the length of the *James Harrod's* starboard side, shearing off life rafts and lifeboats, finally crunching with the sound of crumpling cardboard into an after cargo hold.

There the bow stuck momentarily. An alarm bell switch was thrown. Men turned from their guns to gape in disbelief—not an enemy torpedo but the historic nemesis of sea transportation, collision, had inflicted this wound in the Liberty's side.

In the next few seconds, an even worse enemy: fire. Small, yellow tongues of flame licked around the pinioned bow of the second freighter. The cargo of gasoline had been ignited.

Crewmen from the engine room, the galley, and other stations below deck began streaming upward. The weird yellow glow that was already mushrooming brighter and brighter over the ship told its own message: the *James Harrod* was doomed.

The second Liberty, in a demonstration of seamanship, hauled up anchor, while bow hoses were played on the fire, and backed clear. Her entire cargo was ammunition.

As she vanished into the night, exploding tins of gasoline arced into the water, soon starting an uninterrupted cauldron of fire to starboard. Any attempt to abandon ship on this side became out of the question.

The roar of the mounting pillar of fire combined with its saffron-hued light to distract the crew and impair judgment. It was an awesome spectacle, which made men use all the will power at their command even to come near to the inferno that was pouring from the hold.

Paul Thompson, from Greensboro, had already jumped overboard from his stern gun, not waiting for commands.

Others were piling into the water from the port side, some with life jackets, some without. Their reactions were identical—screaming in pain and terror as the forty-five-degree waters of the North Sea closed around them.

Those left on board tore off life rings, bits of lumber, anything floatable, and threw them into the water. One boat was lowered. Some of those struggling in the water hung onto its sides. Others scrambled down the cargo nets into the boat.

Another boat was lowered. Men still jumped. A few hammered at the life rafts forward and near the stern, but they were rusted to their skids.

A month before, the big tanker *Jacksonville* had been blown to bits in the Irish Sea. Only three survived. The fear had swept the seventy-some souls aboard the *James Harrod* that she, too, would be atomized at any moment in the eruption of her volatile cargo.

Graydon Taylor fought to unlimber the forward raft. He smashed at it with a crowbar.

Walter Porter jumped and struck out for the first boat, now loaded and pulling off.

An oiler appeared at the netting above the second boat. He had dressed, even to brown overcoat and hat. In his hand he carried a suitcase.

Soon that boat pulled away, but not so full as the first.

Ten, including the captain, were left aboard. The rest had jumped and were in the boats or trying to make them. But the boats were moving away fast into the night as the geyser of flame testified with insistence: "There isn't much more time."

None could approach near the stern now. The heat was its own repelling force.

One or two of the group of ten picked up the crowbar Taylor had left before he jumped, and continued pummeling the raft. The forward 3-inch gun was loaded and fired, in an effort to attract attention.

The ships which had been in the vicinity had poured on steam and streaked for safety. Their masters were not necessarily manifesting panic in thinking the burning Liberty was going to blow sky high in the next instant.

The minutes ticked on. The flames surged forward, yellow, hot, and emitting a disquieting, unceasing roar, now engulfing the 'midships structure, threatening the last foothold in the foredeck.

The doomed ship sank lower by the stern. The only uncertainty was whether the fire or the cold North Sea would claim the *James Harrod*.

Time went on, as a weary objectivity took possession of those left aboard. It was a waste, wasn't it? A waste of a ship, of a cargo, of expensively-trained personnel?

Yet, not all was waste, for a Dutch trawler, the *Tromp*, running the mails from Dover to Ostend, suddenly loomed out of the night, poked her bow through the flaming waters and picked off the survivors.

Salvation had come, but there was no elation—only the awareness of loss and defeat, and the question: who had made shore?

The trawler anchored the rest of the early morning within view of the blazing hulk, which stubbornly refused either to sink or be extinguished in spite of the efforts of a fireboat which later hove alongside. Then at dawn, the *Tromp* sailed past the gleaming white cliffs and on into Dover breakwater.

Later in the afternoon, at Ramsgate, the questions were answered. All were ashore except Taylor, Porter, Ricketts, and Thompson. Porter had come in with them, in a lifeboat—dead. They had pulled him out of the water minutes after he jumped in. In spite of night-long artificial respiration, his buddies could not start up his heart again.

It was odd, they thought, since one fellow had been fished out of the North Sea after swimming four hours.

Ricketts and Thompson had vanished into the night. Many had seen Taylor leap into the water and swim after the lifeboat, which he had never overtaken.

Tears welled into the eyes of the young men as they talked. Not even the "double-time" march from the muddy, snow-covered military cemetery at Cambridge could erase the memory and dry all the tears.

Taylor and Porter had been buried in the English earth, in a mass ceremony, along with some forty of their countrymen. The cold wind whined and overhead the B-17's roared noisily to and from a nearby U.S. Air Force base.

Then taps sounded, and it was all over, all over—only the bus ride to London remained, and transportation back to the States to pick up and reassemble this shattered wartime segment of people and material.

The weather cleared sufficiently to enable the "land armies" to till the fields, winter or not. A Red Cross lady, who sat beside the driver and who had come out for the services, talked as the bus coughed its way toward the sprawling metropolis of Empire.

She had been in London since early in the war and had survived bombings and rocketings. She had by now assumed an utter objectivity, having witnessed so much destruction.

"I began to realize that death," she said, "just came a little sooner for these people. Most had lived their lives and if the bomb hadn't gotten them, well what then? Why, the routine of their lives would have been protracted a few more years, or possibly months—the little butcher would have continued cutting meats, the old woman from East London way would have gone on struggling to keep her room warm, the tin pan vendor would have pushed his cart along his same route.

"What I've been trying to say is that people take themselves far too seriously. A bomb falls, it kills maybe a dozen persons—but what of it?

"The sun will rise in the morning as always, the people of London will return to work, the Underground will continue to run to Cockfosters, to Hounslow, to Tooting Broadway, and all the other places. I will probably be having my breakfast of porridge and tea and maybe some sweets, as they say.

"The war will end, as the Great War did. And what will it matter? What will it all mean? Who will remember?"

Who, indeed?

The American bands blared their trumpets that night in the Bottle Clubs, and drowned out the crash of V-2 bombs and the reverberation of their concussion over the vast, half-sleeping metropolis. The old people, too tired to endure any more of war's venom, scurried down into the air raid shelters, to live like moles until the danger, one day, would be past.

Soldiers and sailors and their officers reeled toward their barracks and their billets as dawn grayed London's eastern skies. There were ruins, some still smoking from the night's rockets, but most of them cold, and bedecked with a mantling of snow.

Tonight, even in this city, people had died, along with men who were much closer to the front lines. But, as the Red Cross woman had said, another day was coming and people would return to work. The Underground would be rattling through stations, deep below the pavements, the trams would shoulder politely from queue to queue, where people waited patiently, docilely, with perhaps the only complaint: "It was a bit rough last night, wasn't it?"

The war was as inscrutable as living and dying itself. Yet, would the people, the "little people" be forgotten, as the Red Cross woman had said?

What about Graydon Taylor and Walter Porter and Paul Thompson and James Ricketts? In the earth patches of Massachusetts, North Carolina, and Louisiana, where they had been born and had consumed their brief measure of life, would they be forgotten as yesterday's light flickerings?

Would no one remember the expressions upon their faces when they spoke, the sound of their footsteps . . . ?

Was their creation some accident, their endowment of human reason, compassion, vision, and hope no more than a cruel taunt? Were they, as their ship, destined only for oblivion?

The Impossible Collision

THE WAR WAS MORE OR LESS FORGOTTEN IN A SPAN OF TIME THAT was surprising and in some ways shocking to those who had been intimately concerned with it. Tourism to countries with which, short years before, America and Americans had been locked in mortal combat resumed robustly.

By the nineteen-fifties, onetime enemies were enjoying almost all the channels of economic health, including heavy industry. Italy, for one, was fast rebuilding her depleted merchant marine, with her "show" ship the 30,000-ton *Andrea Doria*—shiny, fast, a superliner in every respect, a favorite with those who were Mediterranean-bound and whose tastes in food, fashion, custom and the broader, less definable realms of decor were compatible.

On Wednesday, July 26, 1956, the *Andrea Doria*, New York-bound, was somewhere southeast of Nantucket Island, encountering increasingly thick fog as evening neared. None the less, she was loping toward Ambrose Channel at nearly twenty-two knots, within three knots of top speed.

With radar, it seemed to her captain, Piero Calamai, that "full speed ahead" was practicable in almost any weather. He was confident he would pick up the pilot boat on schedule, after dawn on Thursday.

Among the first class passengers were two westerners. One was Mrs. Ruby MacKenzie, wife of William A. MacKenzie, a Canon City, Colorado, cattle raiser, who was returning from a vacation with her fourteen-year-old daughter, Ann. The other was Mrs. Henrietta Freeman, of San Francisco, a widow.

"The fog was so dense," recalled Mrs. MacKenzie, "that we could only see the water if we stood at the rail and looked straight down. We had been to the movie in the afternoon and had scheduled a get-together party in the cocktail lounge, off the swimming pool deck, at 6:30, for disembarking fairly early in the morning.

"All of our baggage had been removed from our cabins, with the exception of a small bag to put our cosmetic kits and night-gowns in. All baggage had been placed on the starboard prome-nade deck. I remember we were talking at the "good-by party" about the density of the fog, but no one was worried much, be-cause as it was mentioned, all ships have radar, and, too, the *Andrea Doria* was unsinkable . . . and because of radar, a colli-sion could not happen.

"Some of us stayed in the lounge until it was time to go down to dinner. When we got on the elevator, at 8:15, to go to the dining room, Ann and I and our tour director, Miss Treat, and her mother, went down together. I said to Charlotte:

" 'I just read about the sinking of the *Titanic* shortly before coming on this trip. Wasn't that a fine story to read before going on an ocean voyage myself?'

"We had dinner and went to the main lounge to play bingo. However, the game was rather dull, so I suggested to the Peter-sons, from Florida, Olive Lynch, the fourth in our cabin, and Ruth that we play cards. Helen Peterson said she was tired and would go to bed, Ruth said she would write some letters and join us later. Ann had joined a group of teen-agers after dinner and I hadn't seen her.

"I went to the cabin to check on Ann before beginning the card game. Ann was in our cabin and said she believed she would undress and go to bed. I left the cabin and returned to the card room. Ann wasn't able to find her pajamas, so she went to bed in nothing except her panties.

"Olive, Bill Peterson, and I played cards for awhile and later Ruth joined us."

Mrs. Freeman, of California, thought she had heard "various fog horns" during the evening, but "I thought nothing of it since I lived in Berkeley several years and commuted across San Francisco Bay, where, at times, the fog was very heavy.

"About 9:30 P.M. my traveling companion and I decided it was time to go to bed. Our luggage was all packed and was on the starboard deck.

" 'Let's go and see all the luggage,' I said to my friend, as we glanced through an open door, leading to the baggage-covered deck. There seemed to be thousands of pieces of luggage. I remarked to my friends how lovely most of it was.

"One long bag, pure white leather with stock patent leather binding, was particularly lovely. 'That must belong to some young girl,' I laughed to one of the crew standing nearby.

" 'It was bought in Spain,' he answered.

"My friend and I went downstairs and prepared for bed."

It was now, according to Mrs. MacKenzie's wrist watch, 11:20 P.M. Mrs. Freeman, on the other hand, did not know or care what time it was. She was "dozing off."

The Canon City woman's first intimation of disaster was a loud "crunching, from the starboard side toward the bridge."

"I jumped up from the table and said, 'We've hit something!'

"I automatically picked up my purse as I got up from the table. My first thought was that I must get Ann at any cost. Our cabin was on the starboard side toward the stern. Before I could start for the stairs the ship listed at almost a twenty-degree angle.

"As I ran downstairs I became confused and thought that I was on the wrong side to reach our cabin. The *Cristoforo*

Colombo and the *Andrea Doria* are a maze of corridors and stairways. I finally found my way, but by that time Ruth had gone on ahead of me."

Mrs. Freeman was roused from her semi-sleep by a "terrific bump." The ship listed, but she felt confident it would shortly "right itself." Then she heard "men's loud voices in the corridor.

"I couldn't make out what they were saying. At first I thought the crewmen were having a fight. Then, on second thought, the listing of the ship could have nothing to do with a fight.

" 'We had better get out of here and see what the matter is,' I said to my friend. We jumped out of bed, grabbed our coats and purses, which we always kept on a chair near the door, and shoes.

" 'We'd better get our life preservers,' my friend said, rushing to the compartment over each closet, where they were kept. 'The door won't open!' she said as she pulled at the lock.

"I tried mine. It opened. Then I tried hers. I was a good deal taller and could reach it better. It opened.

" 'What if the lock to the outside door jammed when the ship listed,' I thought. 'We will be caught in here.' I kept my thoughts to myself until we reached the door. I turned the key. We were in the corridor."

Meanwhile, as passengers talked—and acted—there was a growing conversation of another and somewhat more objective breed. Ship-to-ship and ship-to-shore radio traffic was just commencing its own gossiping of the night's tragedy.

The Swedish-American liner *Stockholm*, about half the size of the *Andrea Doria*, which had plowed hard into the starboard side of the towering Italian vessel, was the first to flash the somber news into the night:

"11:22 P.M. Wednesday—we have collided with another ship. Please. Ship in collision."

In three minutes the Coast Guard, from its several stations

along the New England coast, had received the message of distress and flung it back, magnified, from its own high-voltage transmitters:

11:25 P.M.　*Andrea Doria* and *Stockholm* collided 11:22 local time. Lat. 40° 30′ N., Long. 69° 53′ W.

Stockholm to Andrea Doria

11:30 P.M.　If you can lower lifeboats we can pick you up.

Andrea Doria

11:35 P.M.　We are listing. Impossible. Put lifeboats at sea. Send immediate assistance—lifeboats.

Mrs. MacKenzie found Ann already awake in their cabin. She explained that the waves "pounding" against the porthole after the ship listed had aroused her.

Her mother said to "hurry" into her life jacket.

"It was with great difficulty that we made our way back upstairs to the main lounge, the place where we were told to assemble in case of emergency," the Colorado resident noted. "There was no one in charge there to tell us where to go, and we saw people out on the enclosed promenade deck on the portside, the high side, so we made our way through the lounge by pulling ourselves across, hanging on to the stools which were fastened to the floor.

"We reached the railing at the windows on the port side and held on there. The fog was still down. One announcement came over the loud speaker, I suppose it was from the captain but it was in Italian.

"Always during the trip, announcements would be made in Italian and then in English. However, this announcement came over the intercom only in Italian and it was the last one I heard. We waited and waited and there wasn't anything said by any member of the crew; in fact, during the time we were waiting I only saw two members and that was soon after we reached the railing."

Captain Calamai, however, was certain the announcement was "repeated . . . in English." He requested passengers and crew alike—some seventeen hundred all told—to "be calm" at the muster stations.

Lifeboat procedure was familiar to Mrs. Freeman, who had crossed on the sister ship, *Cristoforo Colombo*.

"One sentence one of the officers had spoken was to be with me during the hours I waited to either go down with the ship or be taken off her," she noted, recalling the drill on the other liner. "He had said, 'five short blasts and one long blast will be a signal to abandon ship.'

"We had been given instructions twice in case of disaster to put on our life perservers and go to the upper deck. But I never arrived there. In a corridor I lost my friend. I was just a short way ahead of her and a few minutes before she was right behind me in front of a small hallway leading into a huge lounge where a concert was held in the afternoon and a movie at night.

"I stood for a while, thinking she would come along. When she didn't, I went through a short hall in front of me, which was identical with the other one, and through a second door leading into the same lounge.

"The lights were blinking on and off and I thought I saw my friend far across the huge room sitting on a lounge with a group of people. Most of them seemed to be young women with young children, some of them frightened and crying.

"Hoping the lights would come on brightly so I could be certain as to my friend, I remained where I was, in a huge chair alone, and pretty far from anyone."

The radio messages continued as a newcomer, the freighter *Cape Ann* joined the urgent conversation.

Stockholm

12:08 A.M.   (Thursday)   Collided with another vessel in position 40° 34′ N., 69° 45′ W. But still undetermine our damage.

Stockholm

12:09 A.M.   Badly damaged. Full bow crushed. Our No. 1 hold filled with water. We have to stay in our position. Help if you can.

Andrea Doria

12:10 A.M.   S.O.S. Inspecting our damage.

Stockholm

12:21 A.M.   Badly damaged. The whole bow crushed. And No. 1 hold filled with water. Have to stay in our position. If you can lower your lifeboats we can pick them up.

Andrea Doria

12:21 A.M.   You have to row to us.

Stockholm

12:22 A.M.   Lower your lifeboats. We can pick you up.

Andrea Doria

12:35 A.M.   We are too listing. Impossible to put boats over side. Please send lifeboats immediately.

Cape Ann

12:36 A.M.   Now between the two ships and her boats are ready. Has two boats.

12:40 A.M.   Launched eight boats. Play your [*Andrea Doria's*] lights on them.

Coast Guard

12:45 A.M.   Ship 10 miles away. Have eighteen boats.

"There were three young Roman Catholic priests aboard the ship," Mrs. MacKenzie reported. "One of them came by, and

I asked him to say all the prayers he knew for us. He asked if we were Catholics and we said no. His reply then was: 'Say a prayer for me too, and ask that all your sins be forgiven.'

"As I hung on there at the railing the meaning of what the priest said came to me—that I could not ask that my life be spared, but if it was our time to go that we should die in as dignified a manner as we could and that we be really truly repentant of our sins. I did ask that Ann's life be spared."

Furniture in the lounge was now beginning to tear loose.

"Each time the ship listed," noted Mrs. Freeman, "something would go crashing down to the other end of the room. First all the musicians' instruments on the stage crashed. Their chairs began to crash, then a huge piece of glass broke into a hundred pieces as it crashed against the wall.

"I looked across the room to the far corner opposite me. A young priest and three nuns were there, praying together.

"There was another list and my chair started downhill but it was very heavy and I managed to stop it. I saw the young priest crawling toward me.

" 'Are you all right?' he asked.

"Assuring him that I was, he crawled downhill along toward where most of the people were congregated.

"Then the lights came on. The gray-haired lady I had seen in the dim light was not my friend. I would go out through the nearby door and up to the upper deck where we were supposed to be. But when I tried, one could no longer walk on it. It had listed too badly.

"I looked up and saw one of the nuns had fallen and was sliding downhill. It was dangerous to even try to stand on the floor now. Just then, the young man who had been in the lounge all the time, trying to catch the crashing articles and pacify the passengers, was coming toward me.

" 'I'll have to slide your chair down or you'll be the next to crash!' he told me.

"I found myself sitting next to a middle-aged woman clad in her nightgown and slippers. She couldn't speak any English (I think she was German). All she could say was 'water!' She kept repeating the word and taking my hand and have me feel the lower part of her nightgown. It was very wet.

"Then I realized she was trying to tell me the ship was full of water and she had had to wade through some of it. She was badly frightened.

"Suddenly, as fast as a rabbit, a little old sailor ran quickly (I guess he had been at sea all his life and had mastered the art of keeping topside up) across the huge room with a long thick rope. I was interested in what the young man to whom he gave it was going to do with it.

"He tried to tie it to posts leading to a door at the far side of the lounge. He would stand and fall, and fall again, until finally he succeeded. Then he called, 'We have two hours. Ships should be here. They are on the way!' "

Thursday, minute by minute, lengthened. The wireless monotone to which the voice of a large French liner was added, continued to crisscross the night.

Stockholm

12:50 A.M.   Andrea Doria has begun to abandon ship . . . Badly damaged . . . have to stay in own position.

Ile de France

1:05 A.M.   (to Cape Ann) Vessels near the scene; we shall be in area at 1:45 A.M. What can I do to help?

Cape Ann

1:10 A.M.   (to Ile de France) He says immediate need for lifeboats for about 1000 passengers and 500 crew.

Andrea Doria

1:12 A.M.   Need more lifeboats still.

Unidentified Ship

1:13 A.M.   We have 12 lifeboats.

Cape Ann

1:21 A.M.   How close do you want our ship to come to you?

1:24 A.M.   We have two boats for Andrea. Now proceeding to get close to her.

Andrea Doria

1:26 A.M.   Danger immediate. Need lifeboats, as many as possible. Can't use our lifeboats.

Stockholm

1:30 A.M.   Lat. 40° 34′ N. Long. 69° 45′ W.

Cape Ann

1:33 A.M.   (to Andrea Doria) Want Cape Ann to move in any closer than Cape Ann is now?

Ile de France

1:34 A.M.   We are nine miles from you. Will launch as many boats as possible.

Stockholm

1:35 A.M.   We are launching all available lifeboats.

Andrea Doria

1:43 A.M.   Danger immediate. Need lifeboats, as many as possible. Can't use our lifeboats.

"We had been holding on for a little over an hour," Mrs. MacKenzie continued, "when the fog lifted and off the stern and to the right, about two city blocks away, a ship was taking people from lifeboats, and I also saw one lifeboat filled with white-jacketed men rowing toward the ship, which I am sure now was the *Cape Ann,* a fruit freighter. I thought it was strange the one boat had all white-jacketed men in it, and I was sure they were crew members, but it went through my mind they were rowing toward the other ship to aid in some manner.

"It never occurred to me they were saving themselves first. . . . I'm sure that a greater number of officers and crew stayed aboard the *Andrea Doria.*"

Mrs. Freeman glanced around and realized the nuns had gone.

"They must have been taken out while I was looking elsewhere. I understand they were the first passengers taken off the ship.

"Finally, we were all told to line up, hold on to the rope, and one by one go through the door to a narrow deck. The deck was wet and slippery, the woman behind me knocked me down and I knocked the woman down in front of me.

" 'Take off your shoes!' a crewman called. I slipped mine off until I reached him and then slipped them on again.

"There was a long rope ladder hanging away from the ship although tied to the deck. I had a heavy over-shoulder purse with me and my nightgown was long. How would I get down the long ladder?"

Mrs. MacKenzie, of Colorado, was experiencing similar difficulties.

"The fog lifted," she wrote, "and the moon and the stars came out and we could hear the horns of other ships. After, it seemed, hours, we were motioned to come toward the stern, and we made our way down there, hanging on for dear life, for if we made one slip and let loose we would be thrown against the deck wall and possibly not be able to make it to the railing again.

"It was necessary to take off shoes, those of us who had dressed, for there were many who had on only night clothes.

Ann had on her panties and a short coat which Ruth had grabbed off a hook as she went by our cabin door, plus our life jackets.

"We worked our way through a doorway out onto the open deck, almost to the stern, when we were told we would have to go back and up some steps through a lounge off the deck, to get to the low side. Some ropes had been stretched up the steps, or we could never have made it. We went through the lounge down on to the open deck on the starboard side.

"The ship by this time had listed to a forty-five-degree angle and there were deck chairs thrown around, plus broken equipment which had been torn loose. We made it to the rope ladders and people started going down, a deck hand holding the ladder as tightly as he could against the side of the ship in order that we could get on.

"They told Ann to go ahead because she was young and could go faster. By this time there were only two men, a woman, and myself left at this station. When Ann went over the side, my thoughts were: 'Well at least she is over,' and I wasn't too worried then.

"After Ann went over the side they said the lifeboats were full and they could take no more. It was not long, though, that they told the four of us left they would take us in a motor lifeboat, which was being used to pull the other lifeboats back away from the suction of the ship.

"As I started to get on the ladder the boy who was holding it took my purse from off my arm and threw it toward the lifeboat. He missed and it fell into the ocean. Someone scooped it up and threw it into the lifeboat. I could never have made it down that ladder with that huge purse, for it was almost as wide as the ladder itself."

A gathering fleet of rescue craft by now was at or nearing the scene.

Unidentified Ship
1:46 A.M.   Two lifeboats on way over to you.

Cape Ann
1:50 A.M.   Andrea Doria says she doesn't know how long she can use her radio.

Manaqui
1:53 A.M.   Will arrive yours at 5 A.M. Have two lifeboats.

Andrea Doria
1:54 A.M.   O.K. Thanks.

Unidentified Norwegian Ship
1:56 A.M.   Will arrive yours 7 A.M.

Stockholm
1:59 A.M.   Relaying messages from the Andrea Doria. Need as many lifeboats as possible. Have 1000 passengers and 600 crew. Can't use our lifeboats as ship is bent [listing] too much.

Robert E. Hopkins
2:02 A.M.   About 18 or 19 miles east. Will arrive in about one hour. Have two lifeboats.

Laura Maersk
2:14 A.M.   We will be there in two hours.

Ile de France
2:17 A.M.   . . . yes, we are just in front of you.
2:20 A.M.   Now we have 10 boats in water.

Robert E. Hopkins
2:22 A.M.   Arriving with two lifeboats. Distress position 0300, 40 minutes from now.

Cape Ann
2:24 A.M.   First boat with survivors from Andrea Doria on board now.

Stockholm

2:25 A.M. *Andrea Doria* has begun to abandon ship.

Robert E. Hopkins

2:28 A.M. Is fog heavy?

Cape Ann

2:33 A.M. Lifeboat from *Andrea Doria* full of survivors alongside us now.

Robert E. Hopkins

2:38 A.M. Approaching, about five miles to go. Any instructions?

Stockholm

2:38 A.M. (relaying to *Andrea Doria*)

Robert E. Hopkins

2:40 A.M. Standing by to pick up survivors.

Ile de France

2:46 A.M. Will proceed New York full speed when all are rescued. Please ask another ship stop. My schedule is imperative.

Mrs. Freeman, of San Francisco, finally had an idea how to get down the ladder which seemed to stretch below her endlessly, to taunt and perplex her.

"I wrapped the long leather strap around my arm near my shoulder," she reported, "and it held. There was one crewman on either side of the ladder. One tied a rope around my waist; the other helped me over the side of the ship.

"The rope ladder was wet and slippery and at intervals were huge iron hooks and eyes which were difficult to hold to. When I had gone down about a third of the way to the boat beneath, I put one foot down to reach the next rung. Nothing was under me. I thought the ladder was separated and I was dangling in midair!

"I was really very badly frightened for the first time. Up to then I had rather resigned myself to what was to happen, if it happened. That would have been my late husband's philosophy and I had adopted it.

"But this was different. I was sure now I was to fall into the sea. Then I felt something move under me and I looked down. Two other women had been on the ladder and when the first one had stepped off, the ladder had swung back toward the ship. When the second left the ladder, I waited for it to take its trip, and when it swung back, went the rest of the way and into the lifeboat.

'My right hand was bleeding, but I found a handkerchief in my coat jacket and wrapped that around it. Was glad I had my shoes on, or my feet would have been cut, too.

"When the boat was full we took off. The fog had suddenly lifted and I saw the *Ile de France*, all lights on, looking beautiful in the moonlight. Then I realized there were other smaller ships around."

From larger and smaller ships the electronic interchange continued:

Cape Ann

2:48 A.M.   Medical assistance urgently required. Doctor.

2:52 A.M.   Require doctor for survivor.

Laura Maersk

2:54 A.M.   Will be alongside in one hour. Lifeboats ready.

Stockholm

3:20 A.M.   To all ships. . . . here Swedish *Stockholm*. Our foreship damaged and No. 1 hold flooded. Otherwise ship tight. Will try to proceed to New York with slow speed. As a precaution we want a ship to keep us company to New York. Please indicate.

3:05 A.M.   (to *Ile de France*) Our foreship damaged. Our No. 1

hold flooded. Otherwise ship all right. Will try to proceed to New York at slow speed. If you are going to New York with passengers from *Andrea Doria* can we keep company?

3:07 A.M.   (to a British vessel) Here heavy damage but no SOS yet.

Ile de France

3:07 A.M.   Will proceed to New York full speed when all rescued. Please ask another ship. My schedule imperative.

Robert E. Hopkins

3:11 A.M.   Are they going to use flares to indicate which ships *Andrea?*

Stockholm

3:12 A.M.   Will tell him.

3:14 A.M.   Ships asking if you are able to send flares for indication which ship in distress.

Robert E. Hopkins

3:15 A.M.   When do you wish to go to New York?

Stockholm

3:22 A.M.   SLFC [call letters of another ship] is now proceeding toward you and 75 miles away.

3:24 A.M.   *Robert E. Hopkins* wants you to send up flares.

3:26 A.M.   *Andrea Doria* is in great need of all possible assistance.

Unidentified Ship

3:27 A.M.   Did you get company for trip?

Stockholm

3:28 A.M.   Not yet, but now think we will proceed New York as soon as we get our lifeboats aboard. Please stand by.

Ile de France

3:30 A.M.   (to *Cape Ann*) How many rescued people have you on board?

Coast Guard Cutter Evergreen

3:32 A.M.   Cape Ann is picking up Andrea Doria survivors. Andrea Doria says require medical assistance urgently. . . . Stockholm is damaged but appears seaworthy.

Undentified ship

3:32 A.M.   Our boats going over. We are going pick up from Andrea.

Cape Ann

3:38. A.M.   We have about 200 survivors aboard with more coming.

Stockholm

3:47 A.M.   Coast Guard ships proceeding, arrival 11 A.M.

Unidentified British Ship

3:48 A.M.   Now on position. Lowering boats as soon as possible.

Stockholm

3:50 A.M.   Urgent message to nearest Coast Guard station. Have three serious casualties aboard our ship from Andrea who need immediate attention. Please investigate, if possible send helicopter to position.

Mrs. Freeman was taken to the transport Thomas.

"As I looked back en route and saw the Andrea Doria almost on its side, with the torrent of water pouring from her, I realized how wonderful the crew had been. They kept us ignorant of the tragedies that were going on, stayed at their posts, and worked hard to keep her afloat until they could get the passengers off. . . .

"We were taken by motor boat to the S.S. Thomas. The last boat was pulled up to the deck of the Thomas and we climbed right out on the deck."

Mrs. MacKenzie "never" saw Ann after she went down the

ladder. "But I felt sure she was in one of the other lifeboats. The last four of us were taken to the *Ile de France* a luxury liner on her way out of New York. . . . The motor lifeboat I was in was commanded by a young French officer.

"On the way over I looked at my watch by the light in the enclosure over the motor and it was 3:15 then. We reached the side of the *Ile de France* very soon and we stepped from one empty lifeboat to another to get to the ladder which had been lowered from the hole in the side of the ship.

"I was motioned to wait because in the bottom of one of the boats was a woman who was clad only in a thin nightdress of some sort, and was injured, covered with blood and unconscious. They brought a stretcher from the ship, and she was put on it, but not lashed on. I thought that she was going to slip off before they managed to pull her up."

The surrounding ships, meanwhile, were noting the completion of the rescue operations.

Manaqui

3:52 A.M.   Arriving at distress position now.

Ile de France

3:54 A.M.   I intend to return full speed to New York as soon as you will release me. Are you abandoning ship or do you stay on board with party? How many persons have you still got on board to evacuate, more or less?

3:56 A.M.   This is a U.S. Navy vessel and we have a doctor and hospital staff aboard.

Evergreen

3:59 A.M.   Cape Ann has picked up 200 survivors. Require medical assistance urgently.

Pvt. William H. Thomas (military transport)

4:05 A.M.   Have picked up 50 survivors.

Stockholm

4:10 A.M.   Foreship damaged. No. 1 hold flooded . . . otherwise tight. . . . Will try to proceed to New York . . . slow speed . . . want ship to keep us company.

Evergreen

4:10 A.M.   Will be in position 8 A.M.

Stockholm

4:12 A.M.   Still in contact *Andrea Doria,* which has switched to emergency radio power.

Robert E. Hopkins

4:18 A.M.   We close to you now. Our lifeboats have not returned yet.

Andrea Doria

4:19 A.M.   . . . put 10 boats in water.

Stockholm

4:25 A.M.   Have approximately 425 survivors aboard *Stockholm.*

Kelley (Coast Guard ship)

4:33 A.M.   Have one doctor aboard and be in your position about one hour.

Stockholm

4:34 A.M.   (to Coast Guard) It is desired to give *Andrea Doria* your medical assistance. We have helicopter on way for our injured.

4:40 A.M.   Please tell our lifeboat to return to us immediately please look after its number, please.

Tamaroa (Coast Guard ship)

4:44 A.M.   U.S. Coast Guard vessel *Tamaroa* arriving at position 10 A.M.

Coast Guard radio

4:55 A.M.   . . . 875 survivors picked up. A helicopter is standing by to take off from Salem, Mass. *Stockholm* ready to proceed to New York but not yet under way.

Ile de France

4:58 A.M.   All passengers rescued. Proceeding to New York full speed. Coast Guard vessel standing by *Andrea*. No more help needed.

Cape Ann

5:04 A.M.   Have 175 passengers aboard. Requesting permission to proceed to New York.

Manaqui

5:10 A.M.   We are ready to launch boats in case of need.

Stockholm

5:11 A.M.   Not needed now but ask *Ile de France*.

5:13 A.M.   Is there any navy ship that can be ready to escort us to New York as a precaution as soon as we pick up our lifeboats in about one hour?

Ile de France

5:15 A.M.   No more help needed.

Robert E. Hopkins

5:34 A.M.   We have two lifeboats in water, whereabouts unknown. We waiting for them.

Stockholm

5:36 A.M.   Still need the copter.

Robert E. Hopkins

5:48 A.M.   Lifeboat returned. We have only one survivor.

Laura Maersk

6:07 A.M.   Bound New York. Can we help?

Coast Guard

6:08 A.M.   No further assistance needed.

Unidentified Ship

6:10 A.M.   *Andrea Doria* listing heavily. The main deckline is at the water.

Free State

6:12 A.M.   Is more help needed? . . . 15 miles away.

Coast Guard, New York

6:19 A.M.   (to *Stockholm*) The USCG *Tamaroa* and the USCG *Owasco* will arrive your position approximately 10 A.M. They will escort you to New York.

6:25 A.M.   (to CG ships on scene) Request advice latest on *Andrea Doria*. Has crew been taken off and any information on her seaworthiness?

Stockholm

6:35 A.M.   We have now five critical casualties aboard who need immediate attention.

Robert E. Hopkins

6:38 A.M.   Picked up one survivor, Robert Hudson. 606 Iberville, New Orleans. Request be released to proceed New York.

Coast Guard

6:45 A.M.   (to *Stockholm*) Concur. Please give present position and course so can intercept.

Stockholm

6:47 A.M.   No radio contact with *Andrea Doria*. Apparently unable to use radio further.

6:53 A.M.   Going proceed slowly direction New York.

Navy to Coast Guard

7 A.M.   The *Andrea Doria* is listing badly to starboard and apparently is abandoned.

Coast Guard

7:07 A.M.   (to *Hopkins*) request further details on your survivor. Was man in water? Are there any indications of anyone in water?

Ile de France

7:10 A.M.   Picked up 1,000 survivors.

As night turned into dawn, then day, the majority of the rescued passengers watched the *Andrea Doria* from the vantage points of their new-found security.

"The *Ile de France*," wrote Mrs. MacKenzie, "stayed at the scene of the crash until after daybreak, and we could see the *Doria* listing more and more. About an hour after daybreak, the *France* started back to New York with around seven hundred *Andrea Doria* passengers. The passengers and crew on the French ship did everything they could for us.

"A woman gave me a pair of sandals, and a Dr. Lowery from Wooster, Ohio, let me use his cabin to clean up in and rest in for awhile. As soon as I could I sent Bill a radiogram that we were safe. That was all that I could say then."

The morning continued. The ships, their mission accomplished, began to leave, one by one.

Cape Ann

7:18 A.M.   They are all off and count is difficult. Two seriously injured. Bruises and shock plentiful but two doctors in attendance. Used all lifeboats. Very proud of conduct of officers and crew. ETA Ambrose 5 P.M. Count 168 survivors . . . count is difficult . . . two seriously injured . . . am making best possible speed.

Unidentified Ship

7:24 A.M.   One of our boats just came back and said the master and 11 men were still aboard *Doria*.

Cape Ann

7:30 A.M.   Our count is 168 survivors. They are all over and it is difficult. . . .

Transport *Thomas*

7:40 A.M.   No communication with *Andrea Doria*. Has 45° starboard list. Large gash below starboard bridge wing. List increasing. Seaworthiness nil. Last report captain and 11 crew still on board. No passengers.

Robert E. Hopkins

7:45 A.M.   Have on board Robert L. Hudson, survivor of *Andrea Doria*. Found hanging on debarkation net. Man is all right but shaky.

Coast Guard plane escorting helicopter.

7:47 A.M.   Landing on *Stockholm* by helicopters not feasible. Will try rescue by basket.

Ile de France

7:48 A.M.   Number of rescued persons aboard the *Ile de France* about 730 or a little more.

Stockholm

8 A.M.   Copter arrived.

Coast Guard plane

8 A.M.   Injured child rescued in basket.

Transport *Thomas*

8:09 A.M.   Latest info. received from deck officer of the *Andrea Doria* still on board captain, staff captain, chief engineer, 17 assorted ratings. Ramps going. List has stopped.

Coast Guard

8:30 A.M.   20 men including the master, executive officer and chief engineer remain aboard *Andrea Doria*. . . . five injured removed from *Stockholm* by helicopter.

Mrs. Freeman believed the *Thomas* was the last ship bearing survivors to leave. The time, she thought, was 9:10 A.M.

"As we pulled away, I said to the handsome young Italian

who had served us tea in our deck chairs each afternoon on the *Andrea Doria*: 'Can't anything be done to save her?'

"He squeezed my arm, the tears came into his eyes and mine, as we took a last look at the beautiful ship lying over on her side, her bow starting to go under the water."

Now checking herself over, Mrs. Freeman found "I was terribly tired, my body was black and blue, my shoulder hurt some; but I was alive, after a narrow escape, no limbs broken and no internal injuries."

The radio messages dwindled, finally ceased altogether after the Coast Guard's own requiem:

12:31 P.M. *S.S. Andrea Doria* sank 10:09 A.M. position 40° 29′ N., 69° 50′ W. Survivors picked up *S.S. Stockholm, Ile de France*. Many lives saved by outstanding rescue of vessels on scene . . . QUM (international signal for end of distress traffic).

The ship believed to be virtually unsinkable was gone—victim of a collision believed to have been impossible.

That Thursday evening Mrs. MacKenzie was landed in New York. Not until the following morning did she receive a radiogram from Ann, announcing she was on the *Stockholm*. Later the same day the Swedish vessel, her bow virtually sheared off, limped into New York harbor. No whistles greeted her arrival as they had that of the *Ile de France*.

Ann MacKenzie now wore a bit more than her panties, but not much more. A boy on the *Stockholm* had given her a pair of shorts, a woman had contributed sandals and a shirt. Thus was the teen-ager clad as she walked down the gangplank. She also clutched her life jacket, which no persuasion could make her relinquish.

Altogether, she was a photographer's and telecaster's dream.

They Sailed Into Oblivion

ON JANUARY 7, 1959, THE 2,875-TON HANS HEDTOFT SAILED FROM Copenhagen on her maiden voyage to Greenland.

While her winter-time route was one of the world's worst—through stormy seas and fields of ice—the new vessel, with a sturdy double bottom, seven watertight compartments, and a high, reinforced bow, was believed more than a match for whatever the elements could hurl at her. Her skipper, Captain P. L. Rasmussen, fifty-eight-year-old mentor on northerly navigation, predicted his Diesel-powered command would "revolutionize" Arctic voyaging.

The *Hedtoft*, named after a Danish hero, somewhat resembled a tanker, with living quarters and bridge aft, cargo holds forward. Radar and other electronic gear jutted from her superstructure designed to afford her nautical clairvoyance against all dangers.

However, her inception had been attended with debate in Denmark's parliament, since her purpose was primarily to maintain year-around service with the big Danish possession in the North Atlantic. The Ministry of Greenland, which would own her, had been challenged by various parliament members, among whom Augo Lynge was one of the most vocal.

Lynge, himself a Greenlander, pointed out that the ship must necessarily sail several hundred miles north of waters guarded by the International Ice Patrol, that—with all modern safety gear and excellence of design—it was simply too perilous to travel to Greenland by ship in the winter months. After all, the total population of the territory was but seventeen thousand, and those mostly Eskimos.

He had warned, ominously, that, in the event of an accident, "there is no rescue to expect." On the other hand, he forecast an ultimate change in the atmosphere of abandonment for winter voyagers in the north; "but it will take an accident."

None the less, construction commenced in 1957.

Her maiden voyage was successful. She discharged passengers and cargo at Godthaab, Greenland's capital, located on the west coast of the icy, mountainous land. Late Thursday, January 29th, the *Hedtoft* cast off her moorings and sailed from wintry Godthaab on her return voyage. Aboard, in addition to a crew of forty, were fifty-five passengers, among them nineteen women, six children and—Augo Lynge, the parliament member who had expressed such concern at the winter schedules to Greenland.

Down the austere, rocky coast the *Hedtoft* sailed that night, past Frederikshaab, past aptly named Cape Desolation, probing her way through the ice-choked Davis Strait into the North Atlantic. The barometer fell, hour by hour, the winds picked up.

By 4 A.M. Friday, as she turned to round Cape Farewell and set course for home, gales were blowing at fifty miles an hour. At this time, the little vessel was passing a few miles east of the spot where the *Dorchester* was torpedoed and about six hundred miles north of the *Titanic's* final position.

During a howling, murky dawn, she was butting her way ahead about ten miles off of Greenland's southernmost tip, where massive, snow-covered mountains rose steep and severe from the sea. She picked her way eastward, at speeds of approximately twelve knots, through fields of many types of ice, including bergs towering to two hundred feet and the yet more menacing "growlers," small above the surface but with their greatest bulk—displacing a quarter of a million tons or more—underwater.

The sea continued to swell in green fury, as the winds picked up to sixty miles an hour.

By 1:54 P.M., nearly 120 miles east of Cape Farewell, she was a dot lost in a shifting wilderness of sea and ice. At exactly this moment, the U.S. Coast Guard Cutter *Campbell*, on navigational patrol, received a radio message from the *Hedtoft*:

"Collision with iceberg. Position 59.5 North, 43.0 West."

At once the *Campbell* relayed the message to the Coast Guard Rescue Coordination Center in New York, which ordered the cutter off its station and to the *Hedtoft's* position —which was almost three hundred miles north of her. Because of the weather and the ice, it would require twenty-four hours or more for the cutter to reach the stricken vessel's side.

At 2:42 P.M. the *Hedtoft* radioed: "Filling with water in the engine room."

Meanwhile, the Coast Guard had established contact with the small German trawler *Johannes Kruess*, within a few miles of the *Hedtoft's* wirelessed position. She, too, hurried with all possible speed to the rescue.

At 3:22 P.M. the Danish ship messaged: "Taking a lot of water in the engine room."

About two hours later, the *Hedtoft* sent one more plea: "Slowly sinking and need immediate assistance."

After that—silence.

About an hour later, the *Johannes Kruess* advised she was on the scene, that she had an "object on radar," and was "searching." The *Campbell* fought her way toward Cape Farewell.

That evening, the *Kruess*, imperiled, nearly gave up the hunt as she flashed:

"Nothing found or seen. No lights or lifeboats or ship.

Plenty ice from northwest. Cannot remain this area. Bound Newfoundland for fishing. We must go. We are becoming ice-bound. There is too much ice from the northwest. It is danger-ous for the ship and we can do no more."

None the less, the plucky little trawler kept on the quest through the violent night. Her decks were heavy with ice. It was even difficult to manipulate her searchlight and keep the lens clear of ice.

At dawn, Saturday, U.S. Navy and Air Force planes arrived at the scene. Light rain and snow was falling, obscuring visibility, but the seas, at last, had moderated. The battered *Johannes Kruess* was able to search more effectively.

At noon, the *Campbell*, having made a remarkably fast run against obstacles—even as the *Carpathia* had once done to reach the *Titanic*—arrived at the *Hedtoft's* last reported position. Her findings corroborated those already relayed to her by the air-craft which had been crisscrossing the empty seas:

"No sign of distressed vessel. Numerous icebergs and sea conditions prevented adequate radar search. Weather generally good with exception of showers. Encountering scattered heavy ice consisting of bergs, bergy bits, growlers and brash [small broken pieces of ice] plus occasional floe bergs."

With dusk, Captain Fred J. Scheiber, veteran Coast Guard officer, steered his *Campbell* southward to avoid the same pos-sible fate which had overtaken the *Hedtoft*. Her sideplates were far thinner than those of the vanished Danish motorship.

The *Johanna Kruess* moved out, as well, having reported that she had combed 744 square miles of sea without once turning up "evidence of Hans Hedtoft."

An Air Force C-54 transport, however, landed at the large base at Goose Bay, Labrador, that night, as its pilot reported seeing a "double-ended object with black stripe lengthwise, pos-sible overturned lifeboat."

The Royal Greenland Trading Company, operators of the
Hedtoft, at once denied this object could have come from their
ship, which was equipped with aluminum and wood lifeboats,
aluminum life rafts, and rubber dinghies, none of which were
painted with a stripe or otherwise answered the description of
what was sighted.

Sunday, February 1st, arrived. The winds picked up again,
roaring in from the south at sixty knots. Air and surface search
continued. Then, late Sunday night, the *Campbell's* radio
watch received "unidentified signals, intermittent dots and
dashes with no meaning, then steady, signals moderate to strong
duration several minutes." The signalmen, however, were "unable to obtain bearing."

Simultaneously, Prince Christian Sound—Radio Greenland,
which had rebroadcast the *Hedtoft's* original SOS, picked up
"weak signals."

Hope for survivors again rose. It was theorized that passengers, unacquainted with code or transmitting technique, were
using the hand-operated wireless sets with which the lifeboats of
the *Hedtoft* were equipped.

However, the signals were not heard again.

On Monday evening, the crew of a Navy Neptune patrol
bomber believed there were "dim flickering lights on the
water," and the bow lookout of the *Campbell* thought he saw a
flare shoot up in the distance. Yet, as the Coast Guard cutter
narrowed down this new sighting area with radar, discourage-
ment was, once more, the only result. Nothing but the cold,
frothing seas—and ice—surrounded the *Campbell*.

The week wore on. Various flotsam was observed in the
water, by aircraft and by ships which had joined the hunt: "part
of a wooden boat," oil drums which could have come from the
Hedtoft's deck cargo, a "yellow grey log or spar."

By Saturday it was apparent that further hope—or search op-

erations—would be self-deception, on the one hand, and dangerous folly of the worst sort, on the other. The Coast Guard
ordered the *Campbell* back to its normal station, wirelessing
Captain Scheiber and his crew a "well done!" At the same time,
the Danish government, through its Greenland command, expressed its appreciation for a "magnificent effort."

The search was over. Denmark, as well as its vast, wilderness
territory beginning in the North Atlantic and extending far into
the Arctic Ocean, was in mourning. Churches which had
prayed the past Sunday for the safety of the ninety-five aboard
the *Hedtoft*, now offered supplication for the repose of their
souls.

The Ministry for Greenland wondered, belatedly, if it should
have heeded Augo Lynge's entreaties. Even as he had predicted,
it had required an accident in order that "this will be changed."

What Lynge, the member of parliament from Greenland, apparently had not foreseen was that he himself would add further
eloquence to the sacrificial "accident."

The *Hans Hedtoft* was gone without any proven trace. Her
name would join many others whose epitaph was but a question
mark: the *City of Glasgow*, the *Erebus* and *Terror*, the *Atalanta*,
the *Portland*, the *Cyclops*—as well as those equally doomed but
whose fate was no mystery; the *Ocean Monarch*, the *Sultana*,
the *Atlantic*, the *Ville-du-Havre*, the *City of Columbus*, the *La
Bourgogne*, the *Norge*, the *Titanic*, the *Volturno* the *Empress
of Ireland*, the *Cap Trafalgar*, the *Lusitania*, the *Mont Blanc*,
the *Vestris*, the *Morro Castle*, the *Dorchester*, the *James Harrod*, and the *Andrea Doria*.

Governmental and maritime officials would join with the
clergy and the bereaved in pondering the meaning and many
implications of the *Hans Hedtoft*'s especially confounding loss,
even as their predecessors had done whenever a large ship went
down. And their conclusions, even as before, would be as varied

and as quantitative as those who sought an answer. It would conceivably be "an act of God," "negligence of captain or crew," "faulty construction," although the far more comprehensible "a victim of war," could not apply this time.

One fact and one fact alone was certain and undeniable. Every person aboard the *Hans Hedtoft*, along with their wonderful new ship, had sailed into oblivion.

Bibliography
and Acknowledgments

Expedition to Nowhere
   Beesley, A. H. *Sir John Franklin*. New York: G. P. Putnam and Son, 1881.
   Hall, Charles F. *Sir John Franklin, 1786–1847*. New York: Harper and Brothers, 1865.
   Markham, Albert Hastings. *Life of Sir John Franklin and the Northwest Passage*. New York: Dodd, Mead and Company,
   Files of the *London Times* and *Illustrated London News*.

The Immigrants
   Files of the *London Times*; the memoirs of Captain Murdoch as noted in the text.

Death on the Mississippi
   Berry, Chester D. *Loss of the Sultana*. Lansing, Mich.: D. D. Thorp Company, 1892.
   "The Sultana Disaster," comprising the accounts of Joseph Taylor Elliott and others, *The Indiana Historical Society Magazine*, vol. 5, 1913.
   "The Burning of the Sultana," *The Wisconsin Magazine of History*, April, 1927.
   Official Records, War of the Rebellion, Government Printing Office.
   Magazine and Book Branch, Office of Information, Department

of the Army, including the personal efforts of Lt. Col. James A. Chesnutt.

Suggestions from Frederick Way, Jr., steamboat historian.

Disaster in '73

Shaw, Frank H. *Full Fathom Five.* New York: The Macmillan Company, 1936.

Weiss, Nathaniel. *Personal Recollections of the Wreck of the Ville-du-Havre.* New York: Anson Randolph Company, 1875.

Files of the *Eastern Argus* (Portland), *New York Herald, Boston Transcript, London Times, Illustrated London News,* and *The New York Times.*

Letter from Mrs. Mary Adams Bulkley of Rye, New York, to her mother, Mrs. Adams of Augusta, Georgia, privately printed.

The "Cranky" Atalanta

Files of the *London Times* and *Illustrated London News.*

Trouble in Vineyard Sound

Report of Board of Inspectors of Steam Vessels for the District of Charlestown and Boston, 1884.

Files of the principal Boston newspapers.

As the Century Ended

In addition to eastern United States newspapers and periodicals of the time (especially the *Portland Evening Express*), source material was obtained from people related to those who perished on the *Portland* or, in a few instances, those who watched the luckless steamer sail from Boston. Thanks are due Mrs. George Bushway, Clyde Doyle, Flora M. Durfee, Henry T. Hooper, Mrs. Nora Metcalfe, Mrs. E. O. Pollard, Roy Randall, Beatrice Scannell, Frederick Small, William M. Varrell, Ralph Whalen, and Ida May Whitcomb, among others. Mrs. John Liscomb, of Portland, whose late husband was a grandson of the old steamship line's manager, made available a valuable clipping and photographic file. Of great help also were the Peabody Museum, Essex Institute, and Mariners Museum, all of which contributed to the textual and photographic recreation of other ship disasters included in this volume.

Great credit is due Ralph E. Cropley of the Marine Museum, Seamen's Church Institute, New York, one of the veteran and eminent authorities on maritime matters. While the loss of the *La Bourgogne* was one of the shocking tragedies of its day, the disaster is all but forgotten save in the memories of such men as Cropley. The author also expresses thanks to him for his recollection of several other disasters of similar vintage.

Documentation for this chapter comes from the files of the *Literary Digest*, *The New York Times*, and *Boston Herald*.

The Lonely Men

Baldwin, Hanson. *Sea Fights and Shipwrecks*. New York: Hastings House, 1955.

Beesley, Lawrence. *The Loss of the SS Titanic*. Boston: Houghton, Mifflin Company, 1912.

Lord, Walter. *A Night to Remember*. New York: Henry Holt and Company, 1955.

Hearings conducted by Lord Mersey, wreck commissioner of Great Britain, as published by 62nd U.S. Congress.

Files of *The New York Times*, *London Times*, and *Boston Herald*.

Articles in the *Illustrated London News*, *Harper's*, *Literary Digest*, and *Scribner's*.

Special thanks are owed Walter Lord for recalling anecdotal material not in his own authoritative and absorbing study. Washington Dodge, who was a passenger aboard the *Titanic* when he was five years old, has also been most kind in his assistance.

Fire on the Atlantic

Baarslag, Karl. *S.O.S. to the Rescue*. New York: Oxford University Press, 1935.

Files of *The New York Times*, *Literary Digest*, *Illustrated London News* and *London Times*.

Till We Meet Again

Logan, Marshall. *The Tragic Story of the Empress of Ireland*. 1914.

Files of the *Literary Digest, London Times,* and *Illustrated London News;* individual sources such as the Salvation Army and the Canadian Pacific Railway.

Flotsam of the Great War
Corbett, Sir Julian S. *Naval Operations.* London: Longmans, Green and Company, 1920.
Hoehling, A. A. and Mary. *The Last Voyage of the Lusitania.* New York, Henry Holt and Company, 1956
Seymour, Charles. *The Intimate Papers of Colonel House.* Boston: Houghton, Mifflin Company, 1926.
Tisdale, Lt. Cdr. Mahlon, "Did the Cyclops Turn Turtle?" *U.S. Naval Institute Proceedings,* January, 1920. Used by special permission.
Files of *The New York Times, Illustrated London News, Literary Digest,* and *London Times.*
Special research from the office of Rear Adm. E. M. Eller, Chief of Naval History; also from maritime historical societies as previously noted.

Off American Shores
Snow, Edward Rowe. *Great Gales and Dire Disasters.* New York: Dodd, Mead and Company, 1952.
Department of Commerce hearings.
Schribner's, March, 1935 (Kelsey's report).
Files of *The New York Times, Literary Digest, Illustrated London News,* and *London Times.*
Special thanks are due Mrs. Grace Warms and Mrs. Martha Bradbury Valentine, as well as Rear Adm. Earl G. Rose, U.S.C.G. (ret.) and Capt. R. L. Mellen, U.S.C.G.

Lost at Sea
Morison, Samuel Eliot. *The Battle of the Atlantic.* Vol. I. Boston: Little, Brown and Company, 1947.
Magazine and Book Branch, Office of Information, Department of the Army.
Office of Naval History.

The Rev. Dr. Daniel A. Poling, Editor, *Christian Herald*; the Rev. Walter H. White, Chaplain, Chapel of the Four Chaplains. Files of the *New York Herald Tribune* and *Boston Herald*.

The account of the loss of the *James Harrod* is the author's personal reminiscence.

The Impossible Collision
Radio log from *The New York Times*, as compiled by the newspaper's radio facilities and the Associated Press and United Press.

The reports of Mrs. MacKenzie and Mrs. Freeman are printed in this volume for the first time.

General thanks are owed the public libraries of Portland (Maine), Boston, and New York, and the Widener Memorial Library of Harvard University.

Index of Ships

This is a listing of the principal ships referred to in this volume, as well as others of more than incidental involvement.